Contemporary South Asia

Footloose labour

Contemporary South Asia 2

Editorial board
JAN BREMAN, G. P. HAWTHORN, AYESHA JALAL, PATRICIA
JEFFERY, ATUL KOHLI, DHARMA KUMAR

Contemporary South Asia has been established to publish books on
the politics, society and culture of South Asia since 1947. In accessible
and comprehensive studies, authors who are already engaged in
researching specific aspects of South Asian society explore a wide
variety of broad-ranging and topical themes. The series will be of
interest to anyone who is concerned with the study of South Asia and
with the legacy of its colonial past.

1 Ayesha Jalal *Democracy and authoritarianism in South Asia: a
comparative and historical perspective*

Footloose labour

Working in India's informal economy

Jan Breman

University of Amsterdam

CAMBRIDGE
UNIVERSITY PRESS

Published by the Press Syndicate of the University of Cambridge
The Pitt Building, Trumpington Street, Cambridge CB2 1RP
40 West 20th Street, New York, NY 10011-4211, USA
10 Stamford Road, Oakleigh, Melbourne 3166, Australia

First published 1996

A catalogue record for this book is available from the British Library

Library of Congress cataloguing in publication data

Breman, Jan.
  Footloose labour : working in India's internal economy / Jan
Breman.
      p.   cm.
  Includes bibliographical references.
  ISBN 0 521 56083 7 (hc.) – ISBN 0 521 56824 2 (pb)
    1. Agricultural laborers – India – Gujarat – Case studies.
  2. Migrant agricultural laborers – India – Gujarat – Case studies.
  3. Rural poor – India – Gujarat – Case studies.   I. Title.
  HD1537.I4B73   1996
  331.5′44′095475–dc20   95-49938   CIP

ISBN 0 521 56083 7 hardback
ISBN 0 521 56824 2 paperback

Transferred to digital printing 2003

SE

Contents

Tables

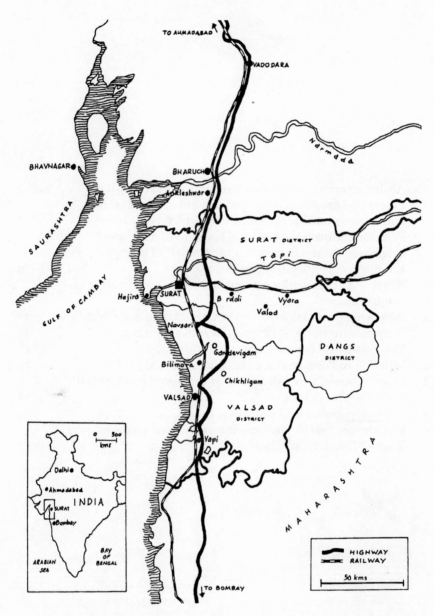

Map of south Gujarat identifying rural and urban fieldwork sites in
Surat and Valsad districts

1 Introduction

Micro-research within a macro-framework

This book is about wage labour in the lower echelons of the non-agrarian economy of south Gujarat towards the end of the twentieth century.[1] I have been privileged to make a local level study of the process of economic diversification in this part of west India over a period of more than thirty years. The village research which I started in the early 1960s was dominated by changes that were taking place in the relationship between high caste landowners and low caste agricultural workers (Breman 1974). In my account of this fieldwork carried out more than thirty years ago I already mentioned the growing significance of the non-agrarian economy for employment of the local proletariat. Several visits thereafter showed that this trend accelerated during subsequent years. What was the destination of those workers who left or who were pushed out of agriculture?

Debates on the social transformation process that India has experienced since Independence in 1947 were at first dominated by the concept of an economic dualism between village and town which coincided with the distinction between agriculture and industry. While cultivation of the land had traditionally been the principal source of livelihood in rural areas, and even the sole source for most of the population, the economic dualism concept considered the urban environment to be the natural location for the country's new industries. The gradual conversion from an agrarian to an industrial society which was about to occur meant, in terms of labour, a transition from field to factory, a sectoral shift that could have no other result than a massive displacement of people.

The male factory hand was marked out as prototype of the modern

---

[1] The research reported has been sponsored by the Indo-Dutch Programme on Alternatives in Development (IDPAD). The fieldwork was carried out between 1987 and 1994 during short spells of leave granted by the University of Amsterdam and extended by academic holidays.

worker. He exemplified the social progress that had been achieved and was expressed in the improvement of both the quality and dignity of labour.

He is no longer the unskilled coolie of the days gone by, engaged in an unending struggle to eke out his existence, neglected by society except for his labour, and with very limited aspirations. He has now a personality of his own. He shares the benefits, albeit meagre, which a welfare state with a vast population and inadequate resources can offer, and some more. He enjoys a measure of social security; he is secure in his employment once he enters it; he cannot be dismissed unjustly and has been given statutory protection against retrenchment and lay-off. (Report NCL 1969: 31–2)

Nevertheless, the transition from agrarian to industrial production was not as streamlined as this optimistic scenario suggests. This can be deduced from the fact that a sizeable category apparently became bogged down in the transitional process. These were the unorganized and unprotected workers regarding whom little was known, according to the Commission's report quoted above, and for whom even less was done to alleviate their miserable working conditions (434).

This was the predominant type of labour that I encountered during my urban research in south Gujarat a decade after completing my initial fieldwork in the region. It was in that period that the dualism discussion focused on the urban economy which became divided into a formal and an informal sector. It was frequently stated that the latter would act as an absorptive reservoir and a clearing house for the raw labour, undisciplined and untrained, coming from the countryside. After a period of adjustment, these migrant masses would qualify for employment in the gradually expanding formal sector of the economy. My scepticism regarding the analytical usefulness and predictive value of such opinions is voiced in the report on my findings in 1971–72 in the town of Valsad, the headquarters in the similarly-named district of south Gujarat (Breman 1977).

What has been the impact on the rural proletariat of the decreasing significance of agricultural employment such as has occurred during the last quarter-century in Gujarat? Since 1986–87 I have regularly returned to Chikhligam and Gandevigam with this question in mind. In these villages, the site of my initial fieldwork, my attention has again been mainly concentrated on the landless, the majority of whom belong to the tribal Halpati caste. The results of the survey that I held in their hamlets confirmed that agricultural labour is no longer the principal source of income for the majority of households. The changes that have taken place during the last two or three decades in local relations between landowners and landless are discussed in detail in a recent publication which I have devoted to continuity and change since my first visit to the two villages (Breman 1993b). The consequences of those changes for the pattern of employment, particularly the increased significance for people belonging to this rural underclass of work away from agriculture and the village, are not discussed in that book. The subject forms the basis of another and more comprehensive study, undertaken between 1986 and early 1994, on the circulation of the labour proletariat in the rural and urban economy of south Gujarat. Between 1978 and 1990 I devoted a number of pre-studies to the theme; these have been compiled into another recent publication (Breman 1994).

The informal sector reconsidered

In the early 1970s researchers and policy-makers gave an enthusiastic reception to the 'informal sector' concept which has since then lost little of its popularity. A sizeable literature continues to draw attention to the disparate, irregular and fluid labour system functioning in the lower ranks of the economy. Among the criticisms I expressed in earlier publications, three have been of significance for the planning and execution of the empirical research reported upon in the following chapters. Those reservations concern firstly the suggestion that the informal sector, also called the unorganized sector, is part of the urban economy; secondly, the lack of clarity concerning its size and dynamics; and finally, the assumption that self-employment is the principal mode of employment.

The direct and on-going emphasis in the debate on the urban milieu appears to stem from an earlier conceptualization of dualism, namely, the contrast made between countryside and town or city, and the identification of the rural economy with agriculture. In this line of thought, urban agglomerations are seen as the location of all other economic activities which are then divided into formal and informal sector employment. This type of interpretation has a number of drawbacks. For a start, why should the formal-informal distinction be restricted to urban labour? The concept loses some of its practical and policy relevance when it is not simultaneously applied to the rural economy, including agricultural employment (see e.g. Jaganathan 1987). An analysis which takes the totality of economic activities as its point of departure shows, as we shall see later, how small the portion of the working population it is that has gained a place in the formalized labour order. In the second place, it is not correct to assume that non-agrarian activities are principally or even entirely tied to urban locations. In the countryside, non-agricultural work has always occupied an important place in the employment pattern, and the percentage of the population

[handwritten annotations in top margin: "informal unclude agri ↓ decreasing + diversifying"]

Table 1.1. *All-India sectorial distribution of main workers, 1991*

	Organized Sector		Unorganized Sector		Total	
	Persons (in lakhs)	Percentage share	Persons (in lakhs)	Percentage share	Persons (in lakhs)	Percentage Share
Occupation:						
Agriculture and allied activities	15	5.6	1847	73.3	1862	68.8
Mining and manufacturing	98	36.5	257	10.2	355	13.5
Services	155	57.9	417	16.5	572	17.7
Total	268	100.0	2521	100.0	2789	100.0

Source: Centre for Monitoring Indian Economy, August 1993; see also Kulkarni 1993: 659.

who are thus involved, whether entirely or partially, has increased strongly in most parts of the country during the last few decades. Data concerning all rural households in India show that at the end of the 1980s, non-agrarian work of varying kinds had become the principal activity for one out of every four male workers and for one out of six female workers (Chadha 1993: 324–5). The rising trend which can be seen at the national level has grown even more rapidly in Gujarat. In 1987–88 a survey of the incomes of the inhabitants of thirty villages dispersed over ten sub-districts of Gujarat showed that 'agrarian' as an occupational classification nowadays applies to less than half of all households (45.7 per cent) (Basant 1993: 365–6). A similar shift in the pattern of employment during the last twenty years in the countryside of south Gujarat has formed the basis of the research whose results are reported upon in this study.

The earlier but now strongly increased diversification of the rural economy makes it impossible to ignore the occupational pattern inherent to it in considering the informal sector concept. The totality of activities covered by this label are found both in and outside the urban milieu. This brings me to emphasize that there is no logical reason why agriculture should be excluded when enumerating all the diverse occupations grouped under the 'informal sector' heading. Integration into a more comprehensive analytical framework of all economic activity provides a sector division which, insofar as the distinction between formal and informal is concerned, is shown in Table 1.1.

Not more than 10 per cent of all workers in India appear to form part of the formal sector. This greatly distorted distribution is caused above all by the almost complete lack of formal working arrangements in agriculture. But even in industry and in the service sector, the other aggregated components of the economy, employment is predominantly on an informal basis.

In such calculations the problem immediately arises that formal and informal employment are not immediately comparable. The first type of employment is characterized by late entrance, partly due to formal education, and early retirement. Closely linked to this is the larger share of non-working dependants at the household level. The lower income usually earned from informal sector jobs makes it far more difficult for both very young and old-age members of rural households to ignore the need to contribute as much and as often as possible to family income. Such pressure does not alter the fact, however, that their involvement in the labour process is subjected to greater discontinuity. That lack of constancy is due primarily to considerable seasonal fluctuations, not so much in the supply as in the demand for labour power in the informal sector. Measured in other ways than terms of availability, that is to say the degree of potential rather than actual work performance, the comparison cannot but result in under-exposure of the significance of informal sector employment.

The point I am trying to make is that more than the persistence of the informal sector economy, the emergence of formal sector employment needs explanation. The latter process dates back to the late-colonial era mainly as the result of the introduction of a legal framework imposed on the labour regime in enclaves of modern industrial production and government administration. This trend continued, although slowly and partially, and was articulated by post-Independence state policies aimed at bringing the social organization of capital under control. The dualism in the labour market which arose should certainly not be interpreted as the schism between more and less modern or advanced economic segments. As Gordon already noticed at the very beginning of the debate 'the distinction between the two sectors is not so much technologically but historically determined' (Gordon 1972: 47).

Since the very beginning, available statistics have provided only a very weak basis for discussions over the informal sector concept. Initial calculations, which were concerned exclusively with the significance of informal sector employment in major urban agglomerations in Third World countries, ran from almost 30 to approximately 70 per cent of the total labour force. Such a wide variation says a great deal about the lack of analytical refinement. The higher percentages undoubtedly indicate a more realistic picture of social reality. In Surat, the largest city of south

Table 1.2. *Percentage growth in organized and unorganized sector employment outside agriculture, all-India, 1973–1987*

	Organized Sector	Unorganized Sector
	%	%
Mining and quarrying	2.78	11.81
Manufacturing	1.44	4.57
Construction	0.37	9.73
Transport, storage and communication	1.70	10.34
Services incl. trade	2.77	4.13

Source: Naidu 1993: 26–7.

Gujarat with one-and-a-half million inhabitants in 1991, I estimate that roughly two-thirds of the working population belong to the informal sector. In the rural hinterland, where my fieldwork has been concentrated, employment in the formal sector is of almost negligible significance. As a result, I calculate that in the towns and countryside together of south Gujarat the ratio of informal to formal employment in the non-agrarian economy is almost 8:2, a division that accords with the situation reported for the country as a whole.

No shifts of any magnitude appear to have occurred in the recent past in the ratio between formal and informal sector labour. This is remarkable in view of the repeatedly expressed opinion that the informal sector is meant to function as waiting room for unskilled rural workers who manage to migrate to urban destinations. After a period of adjustment and skill formation, this first generation of workers would then somehow find their way upwards to the formal sector. The assumption that this superior sector of the labour system would gradually expand as an indicator of modernization has been proven much too optimistic. Between 1980 and 1989, the volume of industrial labour occupied in manufacturing, which is generally seen as spearheading the economic transformation process in India, increased little if at all in proportion to the growth of the working population in that period. Naidu has calculated that, between 1973 and 1987 in the country as a whole, employment in various non-agrarian branches of economy showed far greater growth in the informal sector. The figures given in Table 1.2 are derived from his comparative survey.

The stagnation of employment in the formal sector in general and in that of an industrial character in particular is not in doubt. On the basis of data compiled by government agencies, Papola has concluded:

It is, indeed, a fact that employment growth in the organised manufacturing sector has been low; in fact, it was negative during 1980–81 to 1988–89 in the private organised sector of manufacturing industry. Overall growth of employment decelerated in all the sectors. It was only 1.77 per cent during 1983–88, as against over 2 per cent in the previous quinquennium (Planning Commission, 1990). But the deceleration was particularly sharp in the organised manufacturing; it was -0.09 per cent per annum during 1983–88 as against 2.07 per cent during 1978–1983. (Papola 1994: 11)

The large-scale capital-intensive industry to which this statement refers is still tied largely to urban locations. Nevertheless, industries operating at an advanced technological level and based on modern management practices have been set up in the countryside during the last dozen years or so. In south Gujarat these include agro-industries that process the yield of peasant production in surrounding villages. In this study, following up on earlier publications, I shall pay attention to the enormous labour input in modern agribusiness. One of its pertinent features is that the massive army of harvesters, hired each year by co-operative sugar factories for the duration of the campaign, remains strongly characterized by informal sector work conditions. The incipient introduction of formalized labour relations in the countryside, both in and out of agriculture, ricocheted on sabotage by employers and, subsequently, on the still half-hearted, reluctant willingness on the part of government to take a strong stand against such opposition. This lack of reasonable equilibrium in social power relations is a major reason why formal sector employment still retains a definitely urban accent. But even this statement needs to be amended in view of the stagnation or even destruction of formal labour arrangements in urban private enterprise. Naidu draws attention to the fact that, influenced by this trend, formal sector employment coincides more and more with employment in the public sector (Naidu 1993: 16).

The conclusion that up to four-fifths of all non-agrarian employment is carried out under conditions that are strongly determined by informal sector arrangements necessitates further breakdown and qualification of this concept. With such a preponderance it has become impossible to handle it as a homogeneous category. Far too many elements, which really require separate attention, have been brought together under one label. This differentiation demands further specification of this mode of employment.

Occupational censuses that record the working population in other economic sectors than agriculture also include categories which, without entering into a relationship of employment, live on the proceeds of the capital that they own or manage. This social class, which restricts itself to

Definitions

leasing-out land, houses or money, for example, is not covered by the distinction made between formal and informal labour regimes. This also applies to the far greater category of those who exist by having others work for them. As a consequence, those who provide employment, together with their agents, e.g. labour brokers, supervisors and foremen, are also excluded from the comparison. If these occupational categories, which I estimate to include 15 per cent of the total working population of south Gujarat, are left out of consideration, we then arrive at that part of the labour force which can be divided according to the nature of employment.

There is a tendency to define informal sector employment primarily in terms of self-employment. Hart considered this to be the most striking feature of the concept which he introduced. 'The distinction between formal and informal income opportunities is based essentially on that between wage-earning and self-employment' (Hart 1973: 86). This emphasis, which was made when the concept was introduced, continues unabated in the literature. To give but one example: in a recent analysis of informal sector politics Sanyal states, without further qualification or presenting empirical evidence, that the large majority of urban informal sector labour is self-employed (Sanyal 1991: 41). In the following chapters it will become obvious that an analysis in these terms is highly questionable. Correction does not alter the fact, however, that work for one's own account and at one's own risk is indeed a very common phenomenon in the urban and rural economy of south Gujarat. According to my fieldwork-based estimates, roughly one-fifth to one-sixth of all self-employment pertains to work carried out in a formal sector sphere. This applies, for example, to professionals in diverse independent occupations that demand a high level of training and/or the possession of a considerable amount of capital. In the bottom ranks of the privileged category I would include those intermediaries who, operating on the interface between formal and informal sector employment, bring employers and workers into contact with one another. At the other end of the self-employment spectrum is the far greater multitude, representing 25 to 30 per cent of south Gujarat's total working population, of street vendors, independent artisans and Jacks-of-all-trades who have to exist on their earnings from casual labour. Nevertheless, it is my opinion that what at first sight seems like self-employment and which also presents itself as such, often conceals sundry forms of wage labour. This impression, derived from my own research experience, is supported by various recent publications which draw attention to the rapid increase of casual wage labour accompanied by a simultaneous drop in the percentage of independent workers. Naidu

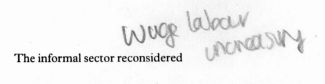

Table 1.3. *Percentage distribution of rural households and persons in agricultural and non-agricultural activities by state and mode of employment, 1987–1988*

| | Percentage of households engaged in | | | | Percentage of persons engaged in | | | |
| | Agriculture | | Non-agriculture | | Agriculture | | Non-agriculture | |
	SE	WL	SE	WL	SE	WL	SE	WL
Andhra Pradesh	27.7	39.5	13.7	19.0	32.1	37.3	14.1	16.5
Assam	47.2	19.7	11.5	21.5	53.6	16.8	11.3	18.3
Bihar	34.7	36.1	12.1	16.5	39.8	32.0	12.9	15.3
Gujarat	30.0	34.3	7.9	27.8	34.8	32.3	8.1	24.8
Haryana	41.6	19.7	15.2	23.5	48.5	17.8	14.3	19.4
Himachal	64.9	4.8	8.7	21.6	68.1	4.4	8.8	18.7
Jammu-Kashmir	52.3	5.6	12.4	29.7	54.6	5.3	13.4	26.7
Karnataka	34.7	39.3	10.5	15.5	40.6	35.7	11.1	12.6
Kerala	23.8	30.1	15.5	30.6	23.9	30.3	16.4	29.4
Madhya Pradesh	49.4	31.4	8.6	10.6	54.8	28.0	8.5	8.7
Maharashtra	35.5	38.6	8.6	19.3	38.0	36.5	9.1	16.4
Orissa	32.4	35.2	14.1	18.3	38.0	31.9	14.5	15.6
Punjab	34.3	28.1	16.5	21.1	37.7	24.2	17.8	19.0
Rajasthan	45.2	12.7	12.9	29.2	48.9	11.3	13.8	26.0
Tamil Nadu	22.4	40.2	13.5	23.9	25.0	38.7	14.4	21.9
Uttar Pradesh	53.8	20.1	12.7	13.4	58.5	17.6	12.9	11.0
West Bengal	29.3	35.9	15.9	18.9	34.3	33.0	17.0	15.7
INDIA	37.7	30.0	12.3	19.3	42.0	27.8	12.8	16.6

SE=Self-employment, WL=Wage-labour

Source: Chadha 1993: 325.

summarizes this trend, which is apparent in both town and countryside, as follows:

> NSS data clearly reveal the increase in the number of rural landless labour during the last one and half decades which means a fall in the proportion of self-employed, leading to an increase in the casualness of labour (due to lack of opportunities in organised employment). In urban areas also, the decline in traditional industries led to similar situation. (Naidu 1993: 16)

Table 1.3 shows that Gujarat is one of the states leading the way in this shift at the rural household level from self-employment to wage labour, both in and out of agriculture.

The fall in self-employment and the stagnation or even relative decline in formal working arrangements indicate the great and growing significance of wage dependency in informal sector employment. The excessive

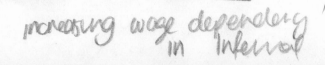

Vulnerabely/ Margin of women

Table 1.4. *Rural and urban working population
outside agriculture in south Gujarat, based on the
distinction formal–informal sector employment*

Occupational Distribution in	%
Formal and informal sector employers and non-employing capital owners	15
Formal sector self-employment	5
Formal sector employees	10
Informal sector self-employment	15–30
Informal sector labourers	40–45

Source: author's estimate based on fieldwork data and
secondary sources.

Casualisation + increaledmobily

vulnerability of this category in general and the progressive marginalization of women in particular is not adequately expressed in government
statistics and other official censuses. The report on my empirical fieldwork
in south Gujarat deals with this labour at the bottom of the urban and
rural economies, which I estimate to amount to 40–45 per cent, i.e. the
largest segment of the working population. A breakdown into occupations
shows that the qualification 'informal sector employment' covers two-
thirds to three-quarters of the working population outside agriculture.
Within this voluminous sector is an equally skewed division between self-
employed and wage labour, as Table 1.4 illustrates.

Casualization of the mass of workers at the bottom of the economy, to
which various authors draw attention, is accompanied by increasing
labour mobility. In ever growing numbers working-class people leave
their homes in search of jobs elsewhere for a shorter or longer period.
This time-bound exodus is by no means a new phenomenon. Migration
to seasonal or semi-permanent worksites became a necessity for many
small landholders and landless workers in the late-colonial period, i.e.
during the first half of the twentieth century. The annual trek to the brick-
kilns and saltpans at the outskirts of Bombay had already started then in
the villages of my fieldwork in south Gujarat. After Independence,
however, this type of mobility accelerated due to the huge expansion of
the building trade in towns and cities all along India's west coast. A large
proportion of this mobile labour army makes for nearby towns or more
distant cities in the expectation that jobs are more easily accessible there,
that employment is characterized by fewer fluctuations than in their own
locale and, finally, that it is better paid. Gujarat is second to Maharashtra

in its degree of urbanization, namely 34.4 per cent of all inhabitants in 1991. Still understated though certainly no less significant in numbers, is the mass movement of people within the rural milieu. Facilitated by the modernization of transport and communications, labour migration shows a strongly rhythmic, circulatory character. The periodic drift of workers in an uneven rhythm of inclusion–exclusion ranges from short to long distances, extending far beyond the borders of their own state. In an employment arena that is more fluid and much wider in scale than ever before, the rural hinterland functions as an almost inexhaustible reservoir of informal sector workers who leave their homes and, after some period of time, mostly return again to their place of origin. In the region of my fieldwork, this type of nomadism has become a striking characteristic of the pattern of work and life for major segments of the population.

Global setting

Workers in an Integrating World is the title of the World Development Report (1995) in which the World Bank analyses the global state of labour towards the end of the twentieth century. The formal–informal sector dichotomy is one of the major features that are discussed in various chapters of this policy document. The formal sector of the non-agrarian economy is defined as including all enterprises, whether private or public, that hire workers under contract as wage-earning employees. In low-income countries (having a GNP per capita of $695 or less in 1993) such as India not more than 15 per cent of the total workforce outside agriculture holds a formal sector job, according to the World Bank's estimate. With rising income per capita and industrialization, informal work arrangements and small-scale production tend to diminish. Consequently, formal sector employment increases to 45 per cent in middle-income countries (having a GNP per capita of between $695 and $8,626 in 1993).

Adhering to a rather conventional view of the labour dynamics that pertain once the growth process starts, the report maintains that, as employment in agriculture declines, job opportunities simultaneously expand in services and industry. Economic diversification causes rural workers to move to urban areas and from the informal to the formal sector. For the majority of working mankind, however, this success story is far from complete. A good measure of the domination of informal labour in today's world is that wage employees in the formal sector of low- and middle-income countries together make up only 20 per cent of the global labour force. The report acknowledges that workers prefer the switch to a formal contract because of the security of a regular wage and

WB ▷ move up

various forms of protection, backed up by legal regulations, that go together with it. The World Bank seems to approve of the trend towards formalization, arguing that a shift to a less distorted and more formalized labour market can function as an equalizing mechanism. This can be read as a fair appraisal of the outcome of the industrialization process that has been going on in different parts of the world. One might, therefore, expect concern to be expressed about stagnation in the growth of modern sector employment in many poor countries since the 1980s. The World Bank document, however, proves to be in favour of a shift in the opposite direction, i.e. towards informalization:

> In many Latin American, South Asian and Middle Eastern countries, labour laws establish *onerous* [my emphasis] job security regulations, rendering hiring decisions practically irreversible; and the system of worker representation and dispute resolution is subject to often unpredictable government decision making, adding uncertainty to firms' estimates of future labor cost. (*World Development Report 1995*: 34)

The policy–makers of the World Bank show themselves to be opposed to formal labour markets which, in their considered opinion, are inherently distorted and biased against the working poor. The basic argument is that, by dismantling the entrenched position of a small but privileged segment of the workforce, more jobs can be created. Labour market dualism, resulting from a faulty policy towards formalization of work arrangements at the wrong time and place, will have to go for the sake of a better future for all.

> Policies that favor the formation of small groups of workers in high-productivity activities lead to dualism (segmentation of the labor force into privileged and underprivileged groups) and tend to close the formal sector off from broader influences from the labor market, at the cost of job growth. (*World Development Report 1995*: 34)

In agreement with received wisdom, the World Bank claims that, on leaving the countryside, self-employed peasants first tend to become waged labourers in the urban informal sector, earn some money and learn skills during their halt at the bottom of the urban economy, save, and ultimately set up an independent business. During my research in the milieu of the working poor, I have seldom encountered this trajectory to a happy life. In the Bank's presentation, flexibility is a winner's and not a loser's game. The myth helps to explain why the report so fulsomely praises maximal adaptability as the principal talent required for successfully making one's way up the labour hierarchy. The self-employed, which is also the Bank's favoured category in its portrait of informal sector workers, have no real need for the security and protection which comfort the life of the labour aristocracy in the formal sector economy.

In rejecting labour market dualism as harmful, the Bank's panel of neo-classical economists has wilfully ignored another policy option, i.e. the gradual extension of security and protection to the huge workforce at drift in the rural and urban informal sector economy. The verdict goes the other way round. Minimum wages are said to be both dysfunctional and inoperative, and most other labour regulations which aim to stifle the free flow of market forces are equally ill-advised. Has not painful experience taught that capital, forced by the need for continuous versatility in the process of economic globalization, is only interested in flexible work contracts? This implies that labour should be willing to go where it is needed and to work as long or as short as there is a demand for it. Under these conditions it is in the enlightened self-interest of workers not to insist on secondary labour rights or even to expect the early enforcement of health and safety standards. The free-for-all climate that should reign, according to the recommended scenario, is first and foremost the freedom for capital not to accept binding restrictions on how to deal with labour. Capital is footloose, and that is how it operates most successfully; on the other hand, labour has to obey capital's whimsical commands and to submit unconditionally to its erratic flows around the global economy.

The World Bank report strongly suggests that informal sector workers are not really so vulnerable that they may rightfully claim all kinds of benefits and provisions in order to survive.

Studies of rural labor markets in developing countries find that subtle social and economic forces often influence wages. In poor villages wages may be set at a level that ensures that workers have enough to eat to work effectively. More commonly, wages will be set for a given task for a season, and considerations of what is fair may apply. Studies in India find that daily wage rates in particular rural areas are strikingly uniform for workers of the same sex, despite differences in individual productivity. (*World Development Report 1995*: 26)

The World Bank's authors refer here to arguments derived from the moral economy school of thought which, if they were ever practised so widely and generously in the past, are certainly now out of date. In the course of my own recurrent research for a period over more than three decades into the plight of agricultural labour in India past and present, I have had occasion to check and reject such notions of 'fairness' imposed by employers.

The report wants us to believe that employer–worker relations in the informal economy continue to be governed by a wide range of social customs and traditions that mitigate the insecurity of the working poor. Employers are said to extend loans to workers who face unexpected expenses, to support older workers or those unable to work on health grounds, and to continue wage payments during the slack season. In the following passage, with its strong taste of wishful thinking, the reader is told that, although never formally agreed upon in advance, informal commitments by employers are an important element of socially sanctioned codes of conduct, especially in rural areas. We further learn, that in addition to these forms of institutionalized patronage, more horizontal ties of solidarity along familial lines diminish the urge to lighten the burden of the working poor and to ease their lack of security by setting up a public safety net:

Financial help from relatives remains the principal form of income support and distribution in developing countries. The extended family system is an important way of providing extra income and security to individual workers and their immediate households . . . Private transfers play an important insurance function in addition to reducing income inequality: they provide old age support and ameliorate the effect of disability, illness and unemployment. In most developing countries, especially in rural areas, older generations rely on the young to supplement their income. (87)

The Bank considers such community support to be the hallmark of traditional societies. One wonders, however, which societies are still worthy of the label 'traditional' in view of the earlier statement that by the year 2000 fewer than 10 per cent of all workers will not be incorporated in the global economy.

In my critique of the *World Development Report* (1995) I conclude that the outcome of my micro-level study in rural and urban south Gujarat published in the present book, does not corroborate the World Bank's analysis and dynamics of the informal sector economy (Breman 1995b). Neither do I agree, on the basis of my findings, with the policy recommendations put forward in the report. At the same time I am aware that the views and proposals made by the Bank as a powerful actor in the business of globalization, are readily endorsed by the government of Gujarat in the current climate of economic liberalization. This rapidly growing state on India's west coast is trying to emulate South-East Asian countries in industrial advancement. According to an official source, the new industrial policy to be announced shortly will be 'user-friendly'. In this context, 'users' have to be defined in terms of capital rather than of labour. A senior Gujarat official has gone on record saying that 'we are benchmarking ourselves not so much against other States but to achieve growth rates comparable to South-East Asian countries' (*Indian Express*, Delhi edition, 30 July 1995). This telling remark is illustrative of the ambitions of Gujarat's economic, political and bureaucratic elite who, to realize this objective, need to keep intact the state of informality that conditions the work and life of the major part of the population.

Account of research and fieldwork

This study examines the growing significance of non-agricultural work and income in the countryside of south Gujarat. Over a thirty year period I have closely monitored the process of economic diversification that has occurred in this region of west India. The village study that I started at the beginning of the 1960s was marked by changes in relationships between the local landowning elite and the landless. In reporting on the results of that research I drew attention to the increasing significance that non-agricultural sectors of the economy had for the pattern of employment (Breman 1974). Numerous subsequent visits have shown that this trend has continued undiminished. Gradually I came to feel the need to test those impressions with the help of new research in the villages of my initial fieldwork, i.e. Chikhligam and Gandevigam.

I was particularly interested in the consequences that economic changes had for the underclass of landless labourers in rural areas. Putting the problem in this way explains why it is that members of the Halpati caste continue to play a central role in my work. In 1986–87 I again surveyed the hamlets where they lived in order to gain some idea of the size and composition of the male working population in the lowest echelons of the labour hierarchy. The result of this census confirmed the decreasing importance of agricultural work. I have discussed this important trend in a recent publication (Breman 1993b) devoted to the change that has come about during the last few decades in relations between landowners and landless in my fieldwork villages. In my presentation of those data compiled for this purpose I have mentioned that a growing percentage of male Halpatis depend for their livelihood on non-agricultural income earned away from the village.

I started by investigating how the local landless managed to gain access to non-agricultural employment. In the years before and after carrying out the survey mentioned above, I frequently visited the localities in which the landless lived in order to gain more understanding of the economic life of these working households. For a start, this brought me into contact with various categories of workers who continued to live in the village but went outside, either in permanent employ or as day labourers. The increasing ease with which distances can be covered has greatly stimulated the mobility of rural labour. In my fieldwork I therefore gave much attention to the extension of scale that has come about in linking the supply and demand side. Secondly, in addition to a pattern of commuting in which workers continue to live at home, my fieldwork extended to employment locations more distant from the village. From enquiries made among relatives who had stayed back I managed to find a number of workers in their new abode or else spoke to them when they visited their home in the village. Under-represented in my inventory are individuals or households who have left permanently or at least indefinitely, breaking all ties with their village of origin. Based on my familiarity with the two fieldwork locations, gained over a period of more than thirty years, I have concluded that permanent shifting for reasons other than marriage is a rare occurrence. On the other hand, short-term labour migration which takes the form of seasonal circulation, is increasing. This phenomenon forms the principal part of my research into the blurring outlines of the rural labour market. Even during my first visit to south Gujarat in the beginning of the 1960s I sought out Halpatis from Chikhligam in the neighbourhood of Bombay, where they spent many months of the year employed in the brickworks. Such labour migration still continues, and on numerous occasions I have accompanied groups of Halpatis who travelled to such destinations after the end of the rainy season.

My research into the dynamics of non-agrarian employment in the countryside of south Gujarat has been expanded in two directions. Firstly, I concluded that it would not be possible to restrict myself to merely compiling data concerning Halpati households, by and large landless, in the two villages of my initial fieldwork. To some extent my investigations in Chikhligam and Gandevigam had to be extended to the small landowners. Not all members of these castes, Dhodhiyas and Kolis respectively, managed to maintain themselves as agriculturalists by supplementing the yield from their small plot of land with work in other economic sectors away from the village. Increasing numbers of these low-caste households have even slid down into a landless existence. Their entry into the rural proletariat raises the question of whether and how their situation differs from that of the traditionally landless Halpatis.

Secondly, I soon reached the conclusion that the complicated configuration of the market for unskilled labour in south Gujarat could not be understood if my study remained confined only to the two villages. It was not sufficient to try to compensate that shortcoming merely by tracing lines of employment from Chikhligam and Gandevigam to other places. To avoid that limitation, my research was extended in two respects: on the one hand, by including the labour mobility of Halpati households from other villages whom I encountered in non-agricultural employment locations in the fieldwork region and, on the other hand, by examining the labour force of both transient and semi-permanent workers who flowed into the plain and coastal tracks of south Gujarat. The massiveness of that influx immediately set restrictions on that part of the study. I therefore concentrated principally on labour migrants from elsewhere who come to Chikhligam or Gandevigam or their immediate vicinity in search of short-term or long-term employment. Finally, this was complemented with information gathered in Surat, the largest city and the most important industrial growth pole in south Gujarat, in an attempt to understand why it is that rural labour from the nearby rural hinterland experiences such difficulty in gaining access to this work arena. Exclusion of local labour, in fact, is linked to the presence in these rapidly growing urban enclaves of employment of large numbers of migrants who have been brought in from much further away.

Taking my initial fieldwork villages as point of departure, therefore, I entered into a far greater arena whose boundaries are difficult to fix in research terms. That wider area is denoted here as south Gujarat. Administratively, it includes three districts: Valsad, Surat and Dangs. The locations of employment discussed here are all situated in the first two of these. Valsad and Surat districts, with a total population of 5,561,194 in 1991, belong to the coastal and plain area of south Gujarat in which also all major urban centres are concentrated. The Dangs to the east, a hilly region and thinly populated by tribals, does not fall within the scope of this research. However, its inhabitants do appear as seasonal migrants who, a few decades ago, started to travel in increasing numbers westwards to Chikhligam and Gandevigam and other places in the central plain. In mapping my route in this extensive territory I was able to use contacts made during earlier visits. In the following chapters, I shall refer to the results of that earlier fieldwork in so far as they are relevant to the present work. This applies, for example, to the vast army of cane cutters who migrate to the plain each year, an influx discussed in depth in my other publications. The research reported in the subsequent chapters has been rather comprehensive, not only analytically but also in terms of actual fieldwork. The task was facilitated by my familiarity with local conditions and changes therein studied at close range for over thirty years. It took several years to compile the material. However, a major part of the data was collected between 1986 and 1994 during frequent visits to south Gujarat; these ranged from multiple annual visits lasting a few weeks to stays of some months.

My academic work schedule in the Netherlands does not allow for long spells of absence. This meant that fieldwork had to be spread out in a way that would ensure adequate coverage over different seasons and locations. Only thus could I conform to the anthropological maxim that the people under study should be examined from close proximity for as long as possible. Such fragmented research over a fairly long period, rather than a coherent one-off survey, obviously has its disadvantages, but these were countered by the fact that, during the course of my study, social dynamics more or less forced themselves upon me. My findings constantly needed adjustment in the light of events and processes that occurred before my eyes. The following analysis is also based on the results of empirical researches in the region which I started as a young student early in 1962. The present publication can therefore be seen as a report on longitudinal study into the process of social transformation which, within thirty years, has ended the agrarian proletariat's firm embeddedness in the local economy. In addition to my own data, I have utilized a large variety of secondary sources. These included in the first place numerous studies written by fellow researchers, the majority being reports and other publications based on surveys of conditions in a particular branch of industry or case-studies of non-agrarian labour segments in south Gujarat. The strongly quantitative nature of such analyses formed a welcome supplement to my own more qualitative database. Within the context of themes that will be discussed in the following chapters I shall refer repeatedly to these secondary sources.

To a lesser degree, this also applies to official statistics and other documentation produced by state organs. Government agencies have a limited insight into operations of the informal sector which forms such a large segment of the total economy. Accumulation and investment of capital in a great range of activities, together with circulation of labour to which it gives rise, are registered imperfectly, if at all, for reasons that will be examined hereafter. For example, it would be fruitless to search for so-called hard evidence that at least 60 per cent of all financial transactions in Surat are in 'black' money. Moreover, the defective coverage of social reality is not rectified by the decadal censuses which update the existing stock of knowledge regarding population composition and dynamics. The strong increase in labour mobility is one of the phenomena that remain grossly under-exposed in this reporting, which is often praised for its 'reliability'. For example, the enormous extent of intra-rural labour migration in various parts of India largely seems to have escaped the attention of official enumerators. With regard to south Gujarat, my conclusion on the basis of earlier fieldwork is confirmed in the recent report by the National Commission for Rural Labour:

it appears that circular migration is much higher than what can be discerned from the NSS [National Sample Survey] and Census data. Moreover, both the NSS and Census data is dated; the developments since the mid-seventies, such as the Green Revolution, are not reflected. For instance, the presence of migrant workers from Maharashtra who speak Khandeshi seems to have been ignored by the 1981 Census in three taluks of Surat district - Kamrej, Bardoli and Palsana - where according to micro in-depth studies, around 60,000–70,000 migrant workers during that period worked in sugarcane farms. But the Census only reports 11,373 Marathi and only 6 Khandeshi speaking persons. And the Marathi speaking persons reported by the Census seem to have been non-farm employees. It seems the enumerators might not have collected information from those who were living on farms or outside villages. (Report NCRL, vol. 11, 1991: K–17)

The problem of under-enumeration is not restricted to rural labour. The 1991 Census was carried out during 9–28 February of that year. Homeless people and travellers were registered on the latter date from 10.30p.m. in the evening until dawn the following day. The time allocated to this residual category was too short to register the army of transients who customarily stayed in or on the outskirts of the cities. I myself made a night-time tour of a number of sites in Surat where tens of thousands of men, women and children bivouacked in the open air. Although directives given to enumerators anticipated the presence of such irregular and disorderly concentrations, I am convinced that the large majority of these labour nomads should be considered as 'missing in action'.

Composition of the study

Chapter 2 discusses effects of the falling significance of agricultural employment for landless labourers in the research villages. During the past thirty years the Halpatis seem to have lost their status as a caste of agricultural labourers pure and simple. Males in particular increasingly leave the village to earn a livelihood outside agriculture. Caring and reproductive tasks in the household prevent the women from forming part of this non-agrarian labour process to the same degree. Casual labour of varying nature is the predominant type of employment. Spatial mobility causes the men to remain away from home for shorter or longer periods. But people at the bottom of the village economy find it difficult to get access to outside jobs on a more permanent basis.

In Chapter 3 the massive inflow of labour into urban and rural south Gujarat is described and analysed. After a period ranging from a few weeks or months to an entire season or even some years, most of these labour migrants leave the area again. Employers show a definite preference for these alien workers, with the result that men and women who belong to the region are denied access to branches of industry that have shown rapid growth during the last decade or two.

Chapter 4 focuses on who takes part in labour circulation and how contact is made with employment opportunities located far from the home village. Those who seek work may leave singly or in groups. Seasonal fluctuations in various branches of industry cause large-scale movements of labour, both into and out of south Gujarat. An important role in this coming and going is played by labour brokers who recruit workers in the villages and accompany them to the worksite, where they then act as gang bosses. Debt bondage is the way in which these labour nomads are usually mobilized.

Chapter 5 starts by establishing that the majority of workers are trained principally through practical experience. Those who manage to learn technical skills of a particular trade do so under the eye of more seasoned workers. Most of them remain poorly skilled and develop the capacity of being quickly able to change to quite different types of work which invariably require heavy and prolonged physical effort. The labouring landscape is heterogeneous with little vertical differentiation. A regular feature, however, is the gender inequality, i.e. a superior–inferior relationship between males and females. The majority of workers do not own tools, and have little or no experience with handling more complicated technical equipment. Those branches of economic activity that have been investigated are all distinguished by great labour intensity. Working hours are usually long and also extremely irregular. Wastage in the labour process is accelerated through a combination of overwork and the insalubrious conditions in which people are compelled to work.

Chapter 6 discusses payments made to unskilled labour. Wage levels and modes of payment vary widely, not only between various economic sectors, but even among workers employed by the same boss. Piece rates and job work rather than time rates form the basis on which labour is remunerated, accompanied by various contracting and subcontracting arrangements that extend into the working household itself. The binding of labour by means of cash advances has as counterpart delayed payment, which means that the total wage earned is accumulated over a long period and only settled at the time of dismissal. Secondary conditions of employment include a code of good behaviour to which all unskilled workers must adhere on pain of non-engagement or instant dismissal. Chapter 7 starts by defining 'formal sector' employment and by observing that, in the fieldwork villages, access to that sector is to a large extent restricted to members of the higher castes. The widely held impression that proper regulation is lacking in the much bigger unorganized and irregular sector of the economy, proved to be incorrect. Even at the beginning of the 1960s the government of Gujarat took the initiative of announcing a minimum wage and other protective measures especially designed for the lower ranks of labour. I discuss the background to this legislation and the manner in which the newly formed labour inspectorate has discharged its funding. Separate attention is given to attempts by politicians and bureaucrats to put an end to forms of bonded labour.

The eighth and final chapter nullifies the impression that the proletarian mass at the base of the economy passively accepts the work regime laid upon it. The focus of this study is the very heterogeneous collection of casual workers who are characterized by a high degree of both sectoral and spatial mobility. The fate of those who are even weaker than they, i.e. the old, unfit and underemployed men and women, remains in the shade. The footloose proletariat is detached from its place of origin, but does not strike roots in the workplaces to which it temporarily finds its way. Mobility of labour cannot be understood properly by limiting the research to the two villages of my fieldwork. Widening 'the field' to the greater region of south Gujarat brought the realization that the distinction conventionally made between urban and rural labour markets is only of limited value. Employers make use of primordial ties with which to exercise control over labour for shorter or longer time periods. Conversely, such parochial attachments are equally important for the mass of workers to optimize its resistance and manoeuvrability. Although this is not necessarily expressed in a generalized horizontal solidarity, i.e. manifest in class organization and action, nomadic workers nevertheless show signs of social consciousness which is essentially proletarian in nature. In my opinion, their mental make-up and lifestyle are indicative of the capitalist basis of the economy, in both its urban and rural manifestations.

My study has the character of a monograph, based on fieldwork and placed within the context of similar researches by other scholars with respect to south Gujarat. To what extent can the results be generalized for other parts of India? During the last ten years the economy of Gujarat state has experienced particularly rapid growth, coupled with a strong increase in non-agricultural employment. It would be incorrect to conclude without more ado that these dynamics can be found in all parts of the country. Still, what is happening in south Gujarat seems indeed to have more general validity. Not least because there are policy-makers, in both national and international agencies, who would like to see in south Gujarat's pattern of industrialization a model for economic growth under the new liberalized regime.

I strongly disagree with the authoritative view that the economy of Village India continues to operate as a closed arena and that in this enclave labour is firmly institutionalized in a comprehensive system of patronage. To quote a prominent proponent of this school of thought:

Life in the village may be harsh, but there is an element of security provided by the family and the community. This is sustained by norms of behaviour by which people abide. You can't simply pack up and leave for better prospects in a neighbouring village. For one thing you may not be welcome; for another, your departure would be seen as an unsocial act, and this could inflict costs on your kin through a reduction in the support system your village community provides for them. (Dasgupta 1993: 234)

Even as a reconstruction of peasant society as it is supposed to have functioned in the past this observation is formulated in sociologically rather naive terms. To conclude that the average present-day rural locality in India has to be analysed as a moral community based on persistent patron–client relationships, comes close to a caricature. The village is not and never was an enclave nor has the market for agricultural labour remained closed within the boundaries of this small-scale territory, as I have argued elsewhere (Breman 1985b; 1993b). The assumed localized nature of production and the perceived immobility of labour as another distinct feature can be questioned by specifically considering, instead of neglecting, the rapid expansion of the non-agrarian economy in many rural areas throughout the country. As a matter of fact, that process of sectoral diversification and its repercussions for the pattern of employment were the point of departure for this study.

My appraisal is guided primarily by the report on rural labour published by a national committee in 1991. This conglomerate of working classes in India's countryside, estimated in 1987–88 at 150 million, includes small and marginal peasant farmers and poor artisans who depend for their existence wholly or partially on wage labour in or out of agriculture, in addition to landless labourers (Report NCRL, vol.1, 1991: 6–8). The authors of that report also inferred a shift from employment in agriculture to other sectors. Running parallel with this trend is a shift towards casual work to the detriment of regular employment, while labour's spatial mobility also evinces a considerable increase. Has the rural proletariat benefited from the trend towards economic diversification? Notwithstanding an increase in real wages in the 1980s in particular, the sombre conclusion must be that there is little sign of any substantial improvement in living standards at the bottom of village society:

Though the increases in money terms [i.e. between 1977 and 1983] are quite impressive, i.e. above 69 per cent, in real terms the total consumption expenditure of rural labour households increased by only 2.8 per cent and that of food expenditure by even less than 2 per cent in 1983 over 1977–8. In fact, there has been a decline in per capita consumption of cereals from 480 grams to 437 grams, mainly due to decline in coarse cereals, though the proportion of expenditure on food items remained static at 68.6 per cent.' (Report NCRL, vol.1, 1991: 11)

With regard to conditions in south Gujarat the situation seems to be a bit less dismal. 'Persistent poverty' is how I have described conditions suffered by a large majority of landless households in this region marked

by a high rate of economic growth. My own fieldwork data show that
those who live here at the bottom of rural society are forced to spend not
less than 70–80 per cent of their meagre income on food (Breman 1993b:
330). Survey-based research has recently brought to light that nearly half
of all agricultural labour households in Valsad district reported non-
availability of two square meals a day throughout the year (Basant 1993:
384). In other words, members of this rural underclass in the area of my
fieldwork, as also in other parts of Gujarat, are driven out of agriculture
and the village by sheer hunger.

Finally, I would draw the more general conclusion that expansion of
the non-agrarian economy has not brought a commensurate increase in
formal sector labour in towns and cities, while informal sector
employment in the countryside has not formalized, even when there was
good reason for it. Mobilization of casual labour, hired and fired
according to the needs of the moment, and transported for the duration
of the job to destinations far distant from the home village, is
characteristic of the capitalist regime presently dominating in South Asia.

The skilled and protected industrial worker who, a quarter-century
ago, was seen as the prototype modern worker, is still a fairly rare
phenomenon on the non-agrarian labour scene. As in the days of yore, the
dominant figure on that scene, whether in the village or town, is still that
of the *coolie*. To be sure, government has removed him from official
terminology in view of the denigratory implications,[2] but it has not found
it possible to remove him and her (the female coolie was never
mentioned) from social reality. In addition to unorganized labour, the
National Commission's 1969 report distinguished yet another
'unprotected' category. Policy-makers have become aware of the latter's
existence rather late in the day. That at least is suggested by the following
statement: 'Very little is known about it and much less has been done to
ameliorate its conditions of work' (Report NCL 1969: 434). The *coolies*
may have been spirited away on paper but in practice they are very much
around, both in the rural and urban landscape of work.

Our knowledge of the appalling living and working conditions of this
massive army of workers is more comprehensive than it was a quarter of a
century ago, but efforts to introduce improvements have so far met with
little success.

[2] 'The term "coolie" is now banned for official use', according to the Report of the NCL
1969: 31, n. 2.

2 Changing profile of rural labour

Non-agrarian work identities in Chikhligam and Gandevigam

Work away from agriculture is no new phenomenon in the village economy, and in the past landless households had also to depend on work in the non-agrarian sphere for at least part of the year. Nevertheless, work on the land was by far the principal mode of employment for the landless masses. This applied to the tribal Halpatis even more than for most other rural castes in the region. Just a few decades ago, according to the 1961 Census, 78 per cent of Halpatis depended for their living on agricultural labour, a situation that has been irreversibly changed by the progressive diversification of the rural economy. The structural shift that has taken place can be illustrated on the basis of male employment censuses which I conducted in 1962–63 and again in 1986–87 in the Halpati quarters of my fieldwork locations (Table 2.1). Against the background of an increasing workforce over a twenty-five-year period, the number of agricultural labourers has remained more or less constant in the two villages, while other sectors of employment show considerable growth. Elsewhere I have given extensive consideration to the stagnating absorption of the local landless in agriculture (Breman 1993b: 286–96).

The expansion of non-agrarian employment occurred earlier and more vigorously in Chikhligam. Even during my first visit in the early 1960s only a minority of Halpatis worked on land all the year round. The end of the monsoon saw the start of seasonal migration of men, women and children to brickworks and the population of Halpati hamlets decreased substantially. The majority of Halpatis in Gandevigam still work in the primary sector of the economy. However, the percentage is clearly declining and also indicative of the trend away from agriculture is the reduction in the number of farm-hands as compared to that of day workers (Table 2.2).

Farm-hands are steadily employed by substantial landowners, and agricultural work is for them more of a permanent job than it is for day

Table 2.1. *Employment of Halpati males in
Gandevigam and Chikhligam*

| | Agrarian | | Non-agrarian | |
	1962–63	1986–87	1962–63	1986–87
Chikhligam	38	32	57	132
Gandevigam	62	72	23	52
Total	100	104	80	184

Source: fieldwork censuses.

Table 2.2. *Employment status of Halpati males in agriculture*

| | 1962–63 | | 1986–87 | |
	Farm-hands	Day workers	Farm-hands	Day workers
Chikhligam	21	17	13	19
Gandevigam	50	12	30	42
Total	71	29	43	61

Source: fieldwork censuses.

workers who, when convenient, will seek other work away from agriculture. As we shall see, occupational multiplicity is an important characteristic in the lifestyle of casual workers. In fact, the pattern of their activities strikingly illustrates the declining significance of local labour in agriculture. These dynamics, and the manner in which landowners continue to assure themselves of the necessary workers, are analysed in a separate publication (Breman 1993b). The remainder of this chapter will survey employment away from agriculture to which almost two-thirds of all Halpati males in the fieldwork villages, i.e. 184 of the total of 288, have managed to gain access (Table 2.3).

The first distinction to be made is that between the small minority of Halpatis who work independently and the large majority who depend on wage labour. The first category includes artisans who are self-employed: bricklayers, carpenters, blacksmiths, house painters and tailors, fourteen in total. In addition, the households belonging to this segment also own a small plot of land (highly exceptional among the Halpatis) on which, like other marginal peasants, they grow food grains for their own consumption. Their modest agrarian property helps them to become and

Table 2.3. *Work status of Halpati males, 1986–1987*

Primary occupation	Chikhligam	Gandevigam	Total
(a) *In agriculture*			
Farm-hand	13	30	43
Day worker	19	42	61
Subtotal	32	72	104
(b) *Outside agriculture*			
1 Self-employed			
• Artisan	9	5	14
• Shopkeeper	1	3	4
• Other	—	5	5
2 Permanent employment			
• Government employee	7	1	8
• Bus driver GSTC	—	2	2
• Road worker PWD	4	—	4
3 Casual employment			
Regular work			
• Diamond cutter	7	2	9
• Lorry driver	7	1	8
• Shop assistant/hotel boy	5	6	11
• Factory/workshop labourer	9	15	24
Casual work			
• Building labourer	6	3	9
• Truck-loader	5	6	11
• Navvy	5	3	8
4 Seasonal migrant	67	—	67
Subtotal	132	52	184
Total working Halpati males	164	124	288

Source: fieldwork census.

remain micro-entrepreneurs who are accustomed to work for their own account and at their own risk. The males among these Halpatis have picked up the tricks of their trade in day-to-day practice, usually by accompanying more skilled relatives as helpers from a young age. They possess only elementary and commonly used tools. More specialized work is beyond their capability. Demand for the services of these rather crude craftsmen has increased in rural areas due to a rise in living standards among the social middle classes, as seen in the construction of new houses or rebuilding old ones with durable material. Halpati carpenters, masons and house painters who live in Gandevigam and Chikhligam are involved in such work, and cater for clients mostly belonging to the small peasant castes in the close vicinity.

Shopkeepers are included in the same category. These are Halpatis who have set up shop in their hamlet to sell basic commodities. They stock modest assortments of daily necessities supplied by a big shop in the village or obtained directly from traders in the town. Also independent in providing their services are, finally, a buyer of windfall fruit, a peddler who visits neighbouring villages with a hand-cart, a bicycle repairer and two full-time distiller-sellers of country liquor. This handful completes my summary of Halpati men who earn their living with some form of own-account work: 23 of the 184 who work outside agriculture, i.e. 12.5 per cent.

The large majority dependent on wage labour can further be divided into permanent and casual workers. Those Halpatis, fourteen in all, who can claim protected working conditions as offered by government agencies, are in an enviable position. These fortunate few include four postmen, two peons (porters-errand boys), a *talati* (village clerk) and a primary school teacher. The last two are among the rare cases in their generation who had some schooling when young. The clerk and two porters owe their appointments to the intercession of a local-level politician. The four postmen all belong to the same family in which the grandfather was the first to be accepted for this work at a time when it required little if any education. He managed to place two sons and a grandson in the same office in the *taluka* town. Finally, formal sector protection is extended to the two bus drivers employed by the Gujarat State Transport Corporation (GSTC). The four roadworkers are employed by the Public Works Department of the *taluka panchayat* in Chikhli. After having been engaged for many years on a casual basis, and to their own surprise, these workers were recently given permanent jobs. This could not have happened without some political patronage. They belong to the exceptional cases of unskilled labourers who receive a regular monthly wage and enjoy all fringe benefits associated with permanent employment.

Casual workers do not form a homogeneous category but are split into various segments. They include, firstly, those who usually go to the same employer each day but nevertheless have no work security. The employer reserves the right to end the relationship arbitrarily or to change the terms of employment unilaterally. These workers are in principle free to stay or to leave without notice, but this applies only if they have not accepted an advance payment which has to be repaid through the provision of labour at the required time.

Those who work regularly on a semi-permanent basis include nine diamond cutters-polishers engaged by owners of small workshops in the main town of the *taluka* or in a large village not far away. The city of Surat enjoys considerable fame as a stronghold of the diamond industry in West India. That central function continues, but in the late 1960s the progressive electrification of the surrounding countryside caused ateliers to be opened in the rural hinterland. In most cases, the initiative was taken by sons of peasants who themselves had formerly worked as diamond cutters in the city (Breman 1985b: 45–6). In the 1970s in particular, the rapid growth of this industry provided access to members of lower rural castes who had no formal education or industrial experience. It was even possible at that time for a few Halpati youths to be given an apprenticeship at the ateliers that sprang up like mushrooms in their neighbourhood.

Secondly, the category of people in more or less regular work but without permanency includes eight lorry drivers and eleven shop assistants or 'hotel boys'. The last are helpers to owners of tea-stalls or eating places along the highway. Finally, there are twenty-four industrial labourers who work in factories or other establishments. Even those who have worked for several years continuously for the same employer have not managed to become one of the happy few with a work contract, as is customary in the formal economic sector. In the modality of their non-agricultural employment, these Halpatis, fifty-two in all, differ little from regular farm-hands in the service of landowners. These agricultural labourers are used more or less continuously by their masters who, however, accept no binding obligation to guarantee steady work and income.

The next segment in the labour hierarchy consists of casual and unskilled workers; in my Halpati census these total twenty-eight males who frequently change their work and workplace. They include nine building workers, eleven truck loaders, and eight navvies. It is rather dubious to list such occupations in their case since they also do various sorts of irregular jobs: for example, taking sand and gravel from the river-bed, digging wells, hewing trees and, not to be ignored, working in the fields during harvest time and other peak periods in the agrarian cycle. On the other hand, it is equally arbitrary to consider the sixty-one day workers whom I have qualified primarily as agricultural labourers as working exclusively in agriculture. If opportunity arises, they are equally ready to work in other sectors of the economy. An analysis of this category's pattern of employment through various seasons of the year shows that in their case the divide between agricultural and non-agricultural is most problematic. If this ambiguous classification is rejected, there remains a

Table 2.4. *Working and non-working Halpatis, 1986–1987*

Population	Chikhligam	Gandevigam	Total
Total households	86	79	165
Total members	493	396	889
Average membership	5.7	5.0	5.4
Economically non-active	2.5	2.2	2.3
Economically active	3.2	2.8	3.1
• of which men	1.9	1.6	1.8
• of which women & children	1.3	1.2	1.3

Source: fieldwork census.

body of casual workers inside and outside agriculture which, with eighty-nine males, represents the predominant labour profile in my census.

The remainder of the male working population in Halpati hamlets, sixty-seven in all, are noted in my classification as seasonal migrants. They leave home as soon as the rainy season ends and do not return until shortly before the start of the next monsoon. This category of annual circulants is only found in Chikhligam and consists entirely of brick-makers. It is a type of labour mobility that was not encountered among the landless of Gandevigam, even at the time of my initial fieldwork. The difference reflects the diverse nature of agrarian economy in the fieldwork villages and its consequences for the pattern of local and non-local employment. This subject, i.e. the spatial mobility of labour, will be examined further in the next chapter.

The above survey covers only Halpati males of 16 years and above. To restrict the work to this gender and age group would naturally signify an inexcusable detraction from the economically active in labouring households. All members of the family who are employable in a major or minor way must help to earn the income needed to ensure their survival and reproduction. Why, then, have I ignored women and children in my census? Because their work away from home is periodical and not continual. Their contribution to wage labour is so spasmodic in intensity and frequency that a one-off census would give a biased picture of the workforce composition in the Halpati neighbourhoods. In Table 2.4 I have made an attempt to adjust the image of male dominance in a way that helps to present a more balanced picture of social reality.

Children are gradually inducted into the labour process. At a very young age they are assigned tasks at home either to release older people so that they can earn money, or to help save money. These tasks include collecting wood and dung for fuel, grass for domestic animals, fetching water, caring for siblings and doing shopping. Girls seem to be called for such activities earlier than boys and also far more often. At 8–10 years of age, sometimes even earlier, children start to work away from home, first under the care of older people and as unpaid help. A few years later they are young labourers not yet doing a full day's work and earning at most 50 per cent of a day's wage for adults. From the age of 15 or 16 they are considered adults; boys do the same work as men while girls follow the example given by women. School attendance has not yet made any fundamental encroachment on the various phases through which a working child must pass. From numerous conversations on this issue it became quite clear that most parents are fully aware of the importance of education as a precondition of a better life for their offspring. However, that acknowledgement is difficult to combine with the necessity to contribute even at a very tender age to the rapidly fluctuating household income. This overriding economic pressure is a major explanation why many Halpati children drop out from school after the first few standards, even though this does not mean that from then on they go to work each and every day.

Halpati women, like those of other castes, are responsible for running the household: preparing meals, making and repairing clothes, looking after children and, in some cases, taking care of a cow or a goat. A few women are maid servants in the employ of big landowners. The majority do some kind of wage labour but on an irregular basis. Formerly, farmers often called on them for numerous jobs on the land. That has been reduced due to the inflow of migrants, including women, who stay in the village as transients or for a longer time as seasonal labourers, thus replacing the local workers. The landless women of Chikhligam and Gandevigam suffer a reduction in employment even more than the men. Given the almost total lack of non-agricultural work in the villages, the result is underemployment for many days of the year. Women with small children are less mobile, and are unable to follow the men in seeking casual or semi-permanent employment within a 15–20 km radius from the village. Older women and young women without encumbrance are able to do so and may be found, accompanied by male relatives, working in the building trade or loading and unloading lorries. Women who do not leave the village as migrant labour, either singly or together with other household members, thus earn a wage for only a limited part of the year, whether in or out of agriculture: I estimate this to be 30–60 days in Chikhligam and 90–120 days in Gandevigam. These levels are considerably higher for the men: at least 150 days, increasing to 240 days per year. For women in particular these figures are significantly lower than reported in a survey on workforce participation of agricultural labour households. According to these figures, collected for all parts of Gujarat, the number of days worked is for men only 10 to 15 per cent higher than for women. The rates for Surat and Valsad districts are respectively 179 and 155 days for males, 155 and 135 days for females (Parikh 1985: 134). My fieldwork data show a much wider gender gap in workforce participation of 40 per cent or even more on an annual basis. It was easy to come into contact with Halpati women, many of them present in their hamlets at all times of the day and almost throughout the year – not because they prefer to remain unemployed: free riders are not tolerated in the milieu of the landpoor and the landless. Actually women who refuse to go for wage work whenever opportunity arises are blamed of imperilling their household. Not only are they morally and socially obliged to contribute to the family income, the return on their labour also strengthens their bargaining position *vis-à-vis* men of the household. Still, for most of them there is not much to do for most of the time. 'We have to sit and wait until we are called for' was the recurrent answer to my query as to how they obtained occasional work.

An exceptional case is that of two young women in Gandevigam who have gained access to the formal sector, thanks to having persevered in school attendance. As primary school teacher and nurse in a public hospital, they are both in government service. Factory work does not fall within the horizons of Halpati women in my fieldwork villages since the industrial estates located at the periphery of the *taluka* towns are too distant to be reached on foot. Moreover, the social convention that women employed away from home should whenever possible be under the care of male relatives or at least of older women, limits the ability of younger women to work independently. Widows or divorced women are in no position to respect such a code of conduct, and are only able to care for their children by leaving even the youngest alone for much of the day. A few Halpati girls are in domestic service in Bombay or Surat, thanks to mediation by members of higher castes. With these exceptions, landless women who work outside the village belong to Chikhligam's category of seasonal labourers. Together with husbands and children, they are recruited to work in far distant brickworks in a manner that leaves them little if any say over their own labour power.

My conclusion is that local demand for the labour power of women in the fieldwork villages is far smaller than the available supply. This disproportion was a major reason to restrict my quantified registration of the working population in Halpati neighbourhoods to the male gender. However, survival for the landless is only feasible if all available household members are mobilized, irrespective of age or sex, when the occasion arises. Early entry into and late exit from the labour process characterize the life of the proletariat in the countryside of south Gujarat.

Out-migration for work

Casual labour, paid on a daily basis, is the predominant type of work at the disposal of Halpatis in Chikhligam and Gandevigam. Very few of the landless castes are able to work for themselves and at their own risk. In the eyes of suppliers of credit, the total absence of resources deprives people of creditworthiness. Another handicap to independent work is the lack of experience in building up and maintaining a clientele. Life at the bottom of the village economy thus depends on wage labour.

As we observed, the desirable status of permanent worker under protected employment conditions is available to few Halpatis. A fixed weekly or monthly wage paid without fail, is a resource that goes a long way in improving one's chances of a reasonable life. To that extent the value attributed to *pagar* (regular salary) is reminiscent of that given to land in the agrarian way of life. From the viewpoint of Halpatis, hard work alone does not ensure access to either form of property. It is above all a question of good fortune, although opposition or support by people high up in society can exert a decisive influence in efforts to control fate.

The work done by most Halpatis shows a noticeable lack of specificity and regularity. They are expected first and foremost to be able to endure heavy physical strain and to work long and irregular hours. From childhood onwards labour gets broken in on the job by those who came earlier. The dexterity and ability necessary for adequate work performance are not acquired in preliminary training but on the job. The experience thus gained is one that tolerates great work diversity. The flexible input of the casual worker, both as regards place and time, is perhaps the most remarkable feature of this occupational profile. Within the space of a few days, weeks or months, many of my informants in Chikhligam might work as harvester, navvy, lorry loader-unloader, building worker or brick-maker. They rotate among different economic sectors and workplaces without experiencing the transition as a drastic change. To their mind, all such cases are concerned with *majuri kam*, i.e. unspecified, unskilled and occasional labour that demands physical effort. Of the total of 288 Halpati males included in my occupational classification, 156 or 54 per cent earn their living in this way. When women and children who do wage-work away from home are included, the proportion of casual workers rises to over three-quarters of the working population in the hamlets of the rural landless.

The predominance of this mode of multiple employment is

accentuated because even those Halpatis who are accustomed to work for only one employer do not shun casual labour if it suits them. However, they must obtain prior permission from their boss. The employer has little objection to some flexibility on the part of his regular workers, because he accepts no obligation to pay a wage on days without work. Rather than making a cash advance which is unlikely to be repaid, he prefers to allow his employee to work temporarily for another on such occasions. This explains, for example, why farm-hands sometimes search for casual work in or out of agriculture. Such erratic employment can even be found in industrial enterprises. Among seasonal workers in the brickworks I encountered some Halpatis who had been sent away by a textile factory owner in Bilimora during a temporary fall in production, with the message that they should return in six months' time.

Horizontal movements by unskilled labour are manifold and cut across all economic sectors. The great manoeuvrability practised out of necessity in the lowest echelons of the labour system compares noticeably with scarce vertical mobility. Very few Halpatis manage to work themselves up the occupational ladder and to rise substantially above the subsistence level. To the extent there is any evidence of upward mobility among members of this landless caste, it invariably entails leaving not only agriculture but also the village. This spatial movement of labour will be discussed in the next chapter. It can be stated here, however, that the stronger attachment of women to the home environment means that they are even less able than Halpati men to find their way to skilled and better paid work. Apart from the trend towards marginalization of female labour in agriculture already noted, this also means progressive fixation of women workers in the most inferior and least hopeful domains of labour.

To the landless class in the south Gujarat countryside, separation between home and work is not a new phenomenon. To suggest that in the past labour was restricted to the place of birth would be to miscalculate the long existing patterns of work migration. Nevertheless, it is quite clear that the economic dynamics in the post-colonial era have strongly increased the mobility of the working population of Chikhligam and Gandevigam, both as regards extent and scale of operations. Measured in distance and over time, employment away from the village shows great diversity. It is hardly surprising that duration of absence increases proportionately as distance to the destination increases. Three types of labour migration are distinguished here: (a) daily commuting, (b) seasonal circulation and (c) semi-permanent or permanent settlement elsewhere. Let me make clear immediately that the predominant pattern of labour mobility is not migration but circulation. The enlargement in scale of economic activity is illustrated by the growing number of Halpatis who leave the village in which they live early in the morning but return before dusk. Increase in this daily commuting has been made possible by a substantial improvement in the physical infrastructure over time. The country roads that led to Chikhligam in the beginning of the 1960s were almost impassable during the monsoon, and when the streams that criss-cross the landscape could not be forded due to floods, the village was cut off from the outside world for days or even weeks at a time. Though relatively backward, road surfacing and construction of bridges have made this location of my earlier fieldwork more accessible throughout the year. Motorized transport was unknown thirty years ago, but in the summer of 1991 villagers were able to make use of twenty-one buses halting at the village daily and going in opposite directions. Gandevigam's situation on a through-road connecting the main towns of two *talukas* meant that it had a head start when the development of modern communication started to accelerate. Shortly after my first stay in Gandevigam in 1961–62, the link-up with the electricity network and the simultaneous arrival of the first telephone line emphasized the greater orientation to the outside world which characterizes the central plain of south Gujarat.

The category of work commuters includes all Halpatis who are in permanent employment. These are firstly the few members of landless households whose job in the formal sector demands their daily presence, mostly in the main town of the sub-district. The same journey is made by regular workers who do not have the protection of tenured employment: shop assistants, hotel boys, tailors, diamond cutters-cum-polishers and others engaged in urban workplaces. Further away but still within reach of the two fieldwork villages is Bilimora, a rising industrial town situated on the Bombay-Surat railway line. During the last decade or so, more and more Halpatis have found their way to the factories set up along the roads leading to Bilimora. Their assimilation seems to be more than a mere consequence of increased recruitment due to expansion of existing industry. Manufacturers give the impression that they are increasingly willing to seek factory-hands in social milieux in the hinterland formerly not considered for employment. Until recently, factory labour in Gandevigam was regarded as confined to Kolis in particular. However, the younger members of this lower-middle caste show less and less interest in industrial work that is unskilled and low paid, and which offers little prospect for upward mobility. Conversely, factory owners complain about the exigency and unreliability of the Kolis, members of small peasant households who refuse to turn up during peaks of the agricultural cycle. Consequently, employers have started to place more trust in the landless Halpatis and other castes who, in daily parlance, are known as 'b.c.' (backward community). The term is intended to remove any misunderstanding as to their social inferiority in general and their sloppy work performance in particular. Despite this stigmatization, employers regard these tribals as being easy to discipline for industrial labour that does not demand any skill, and as submissive and reasonably regular in their daily attendance. At first, the status of *badli* is all that these newcomers can hope for. That is to say that they must report daily and are only given work if a regular employee is absent or if the employer temporarily increases his regular workforce due to a well-filled order book. The factories of Bilimora are situated 20–25 km from Gandevigam and Chikhligam, a distance that can only be bridged by landpoor men - at least by those who are willing and able to bear the risk of vainly reporting each morning. Halpati women whom I encountered on the industrial estates all came from villages within walking distance, i.e. a radius of 7 kilometres at most. In comparison with the male and female labourers belonging to this landless caste, many more Dhodhiyas have succeeded in gaining a foothold in the industrial estates. This result, derived from my fieldwork in Chikhligam, is confirmed by a study of employment of labour in Vapi which, during the last twenty to thirty years, has developed into the largest industrial centre in the southernmost part of south Gujarat bordering Maharashtra. Their origin as small peasant farmers has given the Dhodhiyas a head start in finding employment away from the village. Members of this caste who have succeeded in this respect have also done far better than landless Halpatis who have managed to make the same outward move (Lal 1982).

A common factor among this type of commuters is that, in addition to regular work, they have a fixed workplace to which they travel daily. In this they are distinguished from their equally peripatetic caste mates who earn their living as casual labour. Within the course of a few weeks or even days, the latter will visit numerous locations, situated near or further away from the village, to perform the same or even different work each time: as helper in the building trade, loader-unloader on a lorry, navvy or road worker, or as agricultural day labourer. The absence of a steady daily routine and of occupational specialization so characteristic of their existence is also shown by the lack of fixed working hours.

The distance and mode of travel by commuters are dependent on their earning capacity. Halpatis who have permanent and relatively better paid work travel the furthest and comfortably by public bus. Regular use of such transport is too expensive for those who depend on work outside the formal sector. People who work regularly for the same employer but without protected employment conditions aim at buying a bicycle to save on daily travel costs. This durable conveyance, in the summer of 1991 owned by 21 of the 169 Halpati households in the two villages, enables the owner to qualify for employment at an hour's distance from his village. The radius within which casual workers have to seek a living is smaller. They travel on foot, seldom covering more than 5 or 6 km daily. Their restricted range entails, for example, that they cannot be present between 7 and 8 a.m. when prospective workers and employers or their agents meet each other in the bazaar of neighbouring urban centres. The distance is too long to cover on foot, while the bus fare is out of proportion to the meagre wage that, as unskilled labour, they will be paid when the job is finished. It sometimes happens, however, that employers utilize this reservoir of surplus labour by seeking Halpatis in their home milieu, particularly in Gandevigam where the localities inhabited by the landless are situated along the highway. They are collected by lorry in the early morning and dropped close to their home in the evening. The initiative is taken by transporters who need loaders-unloaders, or by building contractors who require temporary labourers for digging or haulage. The distance covered by daily commuters among the Halpatis seldom exceeds 20–25 km. Unskilled labourers do not earn enough to travel a longer distance. There are a few exceptions, one of which is a Halpati woman, the only breadwinner in her family, who is almost ceaselessly on the move in order to sell vegetables in distant Surat. Out of the 24-hour day, she is unable to spend more than six hours at home with her small daughter.

My work day actually begins at 8.30 p.m. I take the night shuttle to Surat every day. I carry with me chikoos, mangoes, datan [twigs to brush teeth] and occasionally vegetables like drumsticks. I buy my goods wholesale from different producers in Palsana [the research village]. The train reaches Surat at about 11 p.m. All of us vendors sleep on the platform until 4 a.m. Then we leave for market. By about 10 a.m. we finish selling our goods, and return to Surat station to take the Passenger back. We reach Udwada by 1 p.m. I reach home at about 2 p.m. If there is food I eat and rest a while. Otherwise, I cook. Between 2 p.m. and 5 p.m. I rest, bathe, wash clothes and meet women who sell their produce. Then I pick my dinner and start on the journey again. (N. Desai 1990: 91)

Two brothers in Chikhligam lead an existence that is hardly less peripatetic and demands perhaps even greater effort. One brother leaves his home in the dark of the night to cycle to the main town of the *taluka*; from there he takes the bus to Bilimora and continues his journey by train to Surat. He walks from the station to the powerloom workshop where he arrives early in the morning together with other members of the day shift. The journey back and forth occupies a total of six hours. Together with the expense incurred, this can only be made profitable by doubling the working day, i.e. from the twelve hours that are standard for this branch of industry to twenty-four hours at a stretch. When one brother leaves the workplace the other arrives. By relieving one another in this way, they keep the looms working night and day. At home the brothers hardly meet. The half-day that is left to them is mostly spent sleeping. Would it not be more attractive for the brothers to move to Surat?

Sojourners

The landless frequently change their place of domicile. On marriage, most Halpati women move to their husband's village, where the couple set up a new and independent household. Nevertheless, a fairly considerable number of Halpati men have traditionally settled in the village to which their spouse belongs. In my estimation, this category of sons-in-law (*ghar jamai*) includes from one-quarter to one-third of all household heads in the neighbourhoods where Halpatis live. In this way, each generation becomes accustomed to the coming and going of relatives, neighbours, and other caste members. Such migration takes place over a limited distance, however, since the marriage of a landless labourer is usually arranged with a partner from a village in the same *taluka*, and brings little if any change to the social and economic identity of the people involved. It is neither the aim nor the consequence of such movements to escape from the prevailing rural way of life. But when Halpatis leave the village in search of work, whether or not with the intention of settling down elsewhere, the case is different.

Surprisingly few members of landless households leave the village for any prolonged time or even permanently, driven by economic motives. Experience shows that migrants who leave together with their families are soon forgotten by those who remain behind. However, the risk of such under-registration is actually not very great. For more than thirty years I have been able to keep track of the drift of people belonging to the bottom class of Chikhligam and Gandevigam. During that long period I have seldom come across cases of landless households who left in their entirety to seek a new life elsewhere. This agrees with another factual observation, namely, the under-representation of 'scheduled tribes', including Halpatis, in the urban centres of south Gujarat. This part of the population has remained rooted in the rural milieu as can be illustrated with figures derived from the 1961 Census (see Table 2.5). Sixty of every 100 inhabitants of the villages in the region formed by Surat and Valsad districts belong to scheduled tribes, but in the urban areas they drop to 15 per cent or less. In the case of Halpatis, the ratio drops from 1:8 villagers to less than 1:16 town-dwellers.

Between 1961 and 1991 the urban population of Valsad district almost

Table 2.5. *Distribution of scheduled tribes in urban and rural areas of south Gujarat in 1961*

Social categories	Males	Females	Total
Rural			
Total population	950,545	958,884	1,909,429
working	513,855	399,340	913,195
non-working	436,690	559,544	996,234
Scheduled tribes	575,843	570,223	1,146,066
working	331,444	295,690	627,134
non-working	244,399	274,533	518,932
Halpatis	116,416	117,406	233,822
working	67,115	60,506	127,621
non-working	49,301	56,900	106,201
Urban			
Total population	280,873	261,322	542,195
working	141,735	32,819	174,554
non-working	139,138	228,503	367,641
Scheduled tribes	41,269	37,624	78,893
working	22,383	11,816	34,199
non-working	18,886	25,808	44,694
Halpatis	17,381	16,210	33,591
working	9,629	5,297	14,926
non-working	7,752	10,913	18,665
Grand Total			
Total population	1,231,418	1,220,206	2,451,624
working	655,590	432,159	1,087,749
non-working	575,828	788,048	1,363,875
Scheduled tribes	617,112	607,847	1,224,959
working	353,827	307,506	661,333
non-working	263,285	300,341	563,626
Halpatis	133,797	133,616	267,413
working	76,744	65,803	142,547
non-working	57,053	67,813	124,866

Source: 1961 Census for Surat and Valsad districts.

tripled, from 181,655 to 530,788. This acceleration signifies a relative increase in the percentage of town-dwellers, to a quarter of the total population of the district in 1991. Lack of numerical data, due to the fact that post-1971 censuses omit any division into caste categories, means that little is known with any certainty about the participation of rural tribal castes in the continuing urbanization process in the region of my fieldwork during the last two decades. It is my impression that scheduled tribes as a whole are gradually making up for their enormous arrears in the urban milieu. This trend seems to apply to members of landowning rather than landless castes, however, probably because the latter neither have the financial means nor the social capital needed to obtain a foothold in the urban economy. A survey held among 165 heads of Halpati households in Surat city at the end of the 1970s showed that only one had completed secondary education. Three-quarters were illiterate or had attended only the first few standards of primary school (Vyas 1979: 239–40). Subsequently some progress has no doubt been made in this respect but access to employment in the formal sector of the economy remains exceptional for these underprivileged. In contrast, Dhodhiyas who leave Chikhligam are assured of the support of members of their household who stay behind. Most of them are equipped with some or even advanced education and, moreover, have the necessary contacts to get and hold on to more qualified work in the urban centres. For all these reasons, they manage to secure a disproportionate number of jobs in the public sector reserved for members of the lower castes. Halpatis, on the other hand, do not meet the preconditions needed to gain much profit from this reservation policy. In their case, the greatest handicap seems to be lack of any resource base whatsoever and lack of an adequate bridgehead through which newcomers could make their entry into the urban work arena. The trouble is not so much ignorance of the various niches of employment as the inability to bridge the intervening gap other than in the spatial sense.

In the past, Halpatis have reached urban destinations in the domestic service of masters belonging to higher castes:

Dubla tribals were carried to Bombay as early as mid-nineteenth century by their Parsi *Dhaniamos* and were made to drive their horse-cart as well as to work as their domestic servants during the day hours . . . The Parsi *Dhaniamos* also made their Dubla servants to work as compositor in their printing presses, especially during the night hours. Similarly, the Dubla tribals were carried to cities and towns of south Gujarat by their *Dhaniamos*. Thus, in Surat city the arrival of Dubla tribals is not a recent phenomenon. (Vyas 1979: 91–2)

The source for this quotation is based on an empirical survey among Halpatis living in Surat towards the end of the 1970s. Of the interviewed heads of households 80 per cent had already been staying in the city for more than thirty years, and only 3 per cent had come during the last ten years. These figures indicate that it is quite difficult for members of this landless caste at the bottom of village society to get access to the urban economy. In the course of my fieldwork I have several times come across Halpatis who have become urban without ever having left their rural place of residence. Due to the expansion of municipal boundaries their village quarters have been transformed into localities within a growing urban agglomeration.

The metropolitan economies of Bombay, Surat and Baroda are too distant to be reached by more than a few Halpatis from Gandevigam and Chikhligam. The nine males who have managed to do so left their families behind and only return home for short visits to celebrate festivals, or a marriage, birth or death in the family. Even among those who have been absent in this manner for many years, very few have moved their families to their new place of settlement. This is due first and foremost to appalling housing conditions. The wife of a Halpati from Chikhligam who has worked for twenty-five years in a bakery in Bombay has not even once been to visit him. 'Where would she have to sleep?' he replied when I asked why this was so. For their first urban job the rural landless usually have to rely on a contact willing to recommend them to an employer. For this they seek the assistance of members of higher castes, as well as relatives, friends or neighbours. Some Halpati men and women from the villages of my fieldwork who have managed to reach Bombay or Surat start work in domestic service, from where they then try to find better paid jobs, making use of self-made contacts. In checking on their career in the place of arrival I have noticed that they usually operate on a solitary basis, while maintaining their ties with the household in the village of departure. Analyses dealing with the so-called informal sector also attribute strongly individualistic behaviour to the migrant worker. However, such self-centred conduct usually is not a question of choice but is rather imposed on those who enter at the bottom of the urban economy and often are stuck there for the rest of their working lives. Their narrow and uncertain economic base precludes the presence of dependent family members such as small children or a non-working partner. A few cases yield to the desire to live together, even without the most elementary form of privacy:

Kikabhai has been working for 18 months as house servant in Bombay, a position obtained on the recommendation of an Anavil Brahmin in his village. At the end of the long working day he retreats to the space allotted to him: under the staircase by the entrance to the apartment. A short while ago his bride joined him there, a Halpati girl from Chikhligam. She works as maid servant in various households during the day and in the evening helps Kikabhai with cooking and washing up. In exchange for her services she is given food by the landlord who also allows her to share the landing with her husband. The couple keep their few belongings in this shelter and unfold a sleeping mat here when all the work is done. The master lauds his own kind-heartedness in not deducting rent from the meagre wage paid to his servant. After all, he said to me, this saves him the expense of a night watchman. Kikabhai guards the entrance and has to get up a couple of times each night to do the rounds of the house. His wife is determined not to become pregnant, fearing that she would then be sent back to the village. The houselord has said in no uncertain terms that the shelter would immediately be withdrawn if she should have a child. (Fieldwork notes)

Kikabhai longs to have work that would release him and his wife from a life in his master's shadow. He has been offered a couple of jobs, as shop assistant and as helper in a laundry. The wage was better, but on the other hand he would have to find accommodation. So far, he has vainly tried to find something suitable for the two of them, preferably also with a baby. If nothing can be found his wife will have to leave Bombay and thus end her life as a sojourner.

On the basis of Kikabhai's experience and that of other Halpatis, I am inclined to refute the persistent assertion made in the more conventional informal sector studies that migrants have little difficulty in establishing themselves at the bottom of the urban economy. The neglect of public sector housing for the poor, one of the many fields in which the government has chosen to remain inactive, prevents the working class from withdrawing into a collective domain of its own and increases its vulnerability. I am inclined to see the refusal to implement a housing policy as a conscious effort to keep the lowest ranks of the urban economy mobile and to shift their reproduction cost as much as possible on to the rural hinterland. Even Halpatis who are settled in Surat for some few decades still live mostly in slums, on land that does not belong to them, and in one-room hovels built from waste material. Their miserable homes typify their poverty-stricken circumstances. A survey in localities inhabited by Halpatis shows that the majority of them belong to the lowest income categories in the city (Vyas 1979: 115–16). The same conclusion arises from the findings of a recent study on the process of socio-economic change in a village at the outskirts of Surat. The author reports that, contrary to other residents, most Halpatis have benefited little, if at all, from the urban employment opportunities in their near vicinity. They are perhaps a little better off than their caste fellows in rural areas, but the Halpatis form the most deprived part of the population of the towns of south Gujarat (D. S. Punalekar 1992: 235–41). Is it surprising that migrants who operate in such a milieu are unable to consolidate their loose foothold and eventually return home empty-handed?

Babubhai has returned to Chikhligam after 18 years in Bombay. As a young boy, he ran away from home together with a friend. He thinks he was about 10 years old. In Bombay he at first was engaged as house-boy and finally ended up working in a rubberware factory. The owner appreciated his hard work and appointed him foreman. He kept this position of trust until a labour conflict broke out, instigated by a trade union to which he belonged. Babubhai joined the strike and even played a fairly active part in it. The *sheth* was very angry and dismissed him after work had been resumed. It was not easy to find anything else but his expenses continued. Life in Bombay is very expensive. Everything has to be paid for: not only the roof over your head, but also wood and even water. Babubhai realized that after having worked so hard for such a long time he had not made any real progress. Even when he had earned a good wage it had not been sufficient to allow his wife and children to come to Bombay. He no longer wanted to go on living in the city without them and therefore decided to return to the village. For the last five years he has been together with his family and that pleases him more than his former lonely existence. He does not regret having returned to the landless hamlet, however difficult it is to keep his head above water. Bombay had been a hard training school where Babubhai expanded his social horizons and acquired a proletarian consciousness that expressed itself in a daring and even rather rebellious attitude towards work bosses, slum lords, authorities and other powerholders. He now earns an independent living doing plastering and painting work in the neighbourhood of Chikhligam. His craftsmanship is undeniable. If no work is available in his own branch, he does not hesitate to take on any odd jobs that will pay a decent wage. He refuses, however, to work as agricultural labourer for far less than the minimum wage. Never again, he has assured me more than once, will he accept such treatment. (Fieldwork notes)

The difficulties experienced by Halpatis in penetrating into the urban habitat confirms their identity as members of a caste that seems to be stuck at the bottom of the rural economy and society. This is all the more noticeable in view of the far greater mobility of high-ups in the village, in a pattern of migration that goes even beyond national frontiers. The leap outwards by Anavil Brahmins from Gandevigam and Chikhligam was started by the last generation. A dozen males of fairly young age and all related, literally went out into the world. Their followers in the present generation have also let their wives join them in such countries as the USA, Britain, New Zealand and Canada. Settlement in the prosperous West is confined to members of the caste that belongs to the elite in my research villages. On the whole, these overseas emigrants have had to remain satisfied with rather inferior positions in the labour system of the society where they have settled and where their economic and social advancement has only just started. In the eyes of the family they left behind, however, they lead a wonderful life, shared with all who belong to the rich and secure section of the global population.

A few people at the middle level have also managed to go abroad, although temporarily rather than permanently. Six Kolis from Gandevigam have been working for the last few years in the Arabian Gulf states, for which only men with some technical skills are considered. They work long days and lead a bachelor's existence in conditions which leave much to be desired. These drawbacks are more than compensated, however, by what for local standards is a fairly high wage, a large part of which is brought back home in the form of savings. This explains why some Dhodhiyas are even prepared to sell their land in order to obtain money for the fare. They do so in the anticipation that after a few years they will have earned enough to enable them to buy more and better land than they previously owned. Members of high castes are not interested in such contract labour, but for the lowly-placed Halpatis it is still a far away dream.

Babubhai of Chikhligam, mentioned above, is the only person in the district of landless labourers who knows how a man can be taken on as contract labourer in the Gulf states. A recruitment agent in Valsad was willing to put his name on the list of applicants, but demanded a down-payment of no less than Rs 900 for the favour. Babubhai could have paid that sum but not the far greater amount needed for the long journey and for passport and work permit fees, about Rs 10,000 in all. Not without pride he showed me the application form that he has had for rather more than a year. In the eyes of the illiterate Halpatis, these papers radiate such an authority that they must be treated with care. We both knew that Babubhai would never obtain the documents that he covets so much. Nevertheless, by preserving the form so carefully he can pretend to himself and others that its completion is all that stands between him and being sent abroad. (Fieldwork notes)

The conclusion is obvious. A man's position in the economic stratification of the village is the prime determinant of who will be considered for work elsewhere, in urban destinations or even abroad. Those who have capital, skills and contacts will go farthest and be the most successful. In all such aspects, the landless Halpatis lag behind, and this label of backwardness explains why so few of them are able to apply for work that is available elsewhere on a fairly continuous basis. It does not mean, however, that they are left in a state of complete immobility.

Seasonal migration

Insufficient local resources for subsistence in rural south Gujarat force part of the proletariat to leave their homes to seek temporary work as seasonal migrants. This does not apply to Gandevigam, however, where agriculture is practised more intensively. The village is in a fertile region where irrigation water is available throughout the year. Up to now rather more than half of all Halpatis have earned a living from cultivating the fields. Moreover, non-agricultural work is accessible nearby. Male members of this landless caste have little difficulty in reaching Gandevi, the *taluka* centre, or the railway town, Bilimora, where many industries have been established. In Chikhligam, however, there is less employment available locally. The agricultural area is small, less fertile, and dependent largely on rainfall. The cropping pattern is consequently not very labour-intensive, while the spread throughout the year is more irregular, with the agricultural cycle peaking at the beginning and end of monsoon. The urge to leave the village is thus far greater for Halpatis from Chikhligam, but they also have to spend more time and money to cover the distance to employment sites alongside the railway, where they meet their caste fellows from Gandevigam. Many landless from the hinterland, even further away from urban nuclei and industrial estates, have no other choice than to leave their homes after harvest at the end of monsoon and to stay away until shortly before the next rainy season, almost seven months later. The size of this annual migration can be measured by the fact that in Chikhligam in 1986–87, 67 of the total of 167 working Halpati males, i.e. 41 per cent, were labour migrants. They all had similar destinations: employment in one of the hundreds of brickworks in the neighbourhood of Bombay or along the highway and railway line running from Bombay via Surat and Vadodara (Baroda) to Ahmedabad. Bricks are baked in the open air and this cannot be done during the monsoon. By the beginning of June at the latest, all workers return to their villages.

This seasonal work started in the first half of the twentieth century. Informants told me in the early 1960s that their grandfathers already used to travel to Bombay to seek such employment. That is confirmed by Mukhtyar who, in 1927, did fieldwork in a village situated close to Chikhligam. He wrote that, at the end of the monsoon, eight of the 53 Halpati households left Atgam to work during the winter and summer months in brickworks or saltpans adjacent to Bombay (Mukhtyar 1930: 160–1). They must have been more numerous, however, because a few pages later he reports that Halpatis who worked as bonded servants (*halis*) also took part in the seasonal migration. By giving them permission to do so, the landed gentry avoided being held responsible for their livelihood in the slack season (Mukhtyar 1930: 168). This pattern of dual employment still existed at the time of my initial fieldwork. Big landowners used to hire temporary farm-hands during the monsoon, thus ensuring themselves of sufficient labour for activities involved in rice cultivation. The bonds with the employer had become looser and more contractual, however, than in the case of the *hali* a generation earlier. The temporary arrangement came to an end when paddy had been harvested and grass on dry land cut. At the end of October, the laid-off Halpatis together with their caste mates who had continued to work as day labourers, again started out for Bombay (Breman 1974: 131–2). Nowadays, farmers in Chikhligam do not need such seasonal hands. In my renewed fieldwork in the village I have not come across a single case. After their return, seasonal migrants offer themselves as agricultural or non-agricultural labourers and form one occupational category of casual workers with Halpatis who remained in the village throughout the year.

During the rainy season, men are recruited from among this workforce for the new season in the brickfields. Other landless labourers who had joined the stream of migrants in the preceding year also may come forward again, while some of those who have just returned will stay in Chikhligam to earn a living as casual labourers after the monsoon.

Since Independence, Bombay has developed into a metropolis in a manner that would not have been possible without a steady increase in the production of bricks. A large number of landless labourers and small peasants from the villages of south Gujarat take part in the annual cycle of migration. At the time of my first fieldwork in 1962–63 not less then 55 per cent of all Halpati males left Chikhligam for this purpose. A quarter of a century later the percentage of Halpati seasonal migrants had dropped somewhat. Among the Dhodhiyas the decline has been greater. The fall is due to the extremely onerous life led by migrant labourers away from their village, which will be discussed more extensively in later chapters. Even in the past, male members of small peasant households tried to leave their wives and children in the village and ultimately many of them dropped out themselves once progress in the family's economic situation made this feasible. Among the Dhodhiyas it is principally the landless who still go to the brickworks. In 1986–87 this was the destination of four out of every ten Halpati males in Chikhligam. In fact, this figure does not sufficiently illustrate the significance of seasonal migration for members of this caste. Women and children in the landless milieu migrate together with the males so as to make their labour power maximally productive. In the village, these family members function rather as a labour surplus, only to be used at peak times and then laid-off again as redundant. In the brickworks, however, every migrant of whatever age or sex, is mobilized unmercifully and continually. A detailed account of the total days worked per year by all Halpatis in Chikhligam would undoubtedly have shown that more than half were spent in far away brickworks even during my latest fieldwork.

While this labour migration was almost entirely in the direction of Bombay at the beginning of the 1960s, greater dispersal has occurred in subsequent years. This shift has been brought about by the enormous expansion of building activities, particularly in the urban-industrial corridor running north–south across the central plain of Gujarat. The periphery of Bombay continues to attract brick-makers from my fieldwork village, but the seasonal employers there now have to compete with various other destinations: Surat, Broach, Vadodara and even distant Saurashtra. I have visited a number of these new worksites during the last thirty years, several of them on more than one occasion.

Brick-making is not the only form of temporary employment for which part of south Gujarat's rural proletariat has been made mobile. From other villages in the vicinity of Chikhligam seasonal migrants go to stone quarries that have been opened in various places in south Gujarat, partly due to the boom in building activities since the 1960s. Saltpans along the coast in the neighbourhood of Bombay have long offered work in the dry winter months to migrants, some of them from my fieldwork region. A government report on these activities, based on a survey conducted in 1947–48, clearly shows that Halpatis even then formed an important part of the workforce (Report of the Salt Pan Industry, Bombay Province 1950: 4), a finding which was already reported by Mukhtyar at the end of the 1920s (1930: 160). The situation was still the same early in the 1970s (van der Veen 1979: 50). Patterns in the recruitment of labour for seasonal employment established several generations ago can be recognized even today. The deployment of migrants is determined largely by routes that were opened almost incidentally and which run from the home village to sites of temporary employment many hundreds of miles away.

In Chikhligam and its surroundings, this has long been the journey to brickworks and saltpans. These are not the only destinations, however, whether nearby or distant, to which the men, women and children of villages in south Gujarat migrate for part of the year. In the months before and after monsoon, these seasonal migrants can also be found in the urban casual labour markets, as discussed earlier. In Valsad, the Clock Tower is such a meeting place. In a publication devoted to informal sector workers in this district town in the early 1970s, I have described how, early in the morning, job-seekers get in touch with employers or their agents. Supply and demand are almost invariably for unskilled and low-skilled labour, needed for all kinds of building projects, for transport of goods, or for other activities that require little more than physical strength (Breman 1994: ch. 2). Twenty years later, that situation shows little change. Valsad now has more of such market-places in different parts of the town, e.g. close to the bus station and along the exit road. In January 1993 I found that the Clock Tower is still the busiest contact point. Between 7 and 8 a.m. the open space before it is crowded with hundreds of waiting men and women. In a large city such as Surat, this floating workforce may be thousands strong. Formerly, the men came alone or in small groups to the *majur* or *chakla bazaars*, but in recent years they have been joined increasingly by women and even children. An investigation into the operations of thirty-one such labour markets in six towns of Gujarat, including Valsad, has shown that in 1988 they were attended by men, women and children in ratios of 6:3:1 (Punalekar and Patel 1990: 41).

Such casual labour markets do not supply only the urban economy. Employers from the surrounding countryside go there as well to seek extra workers. In the harvest season in particular, farmers from distant neighbourhoods will travel by tractor to such markets in Valsad and Bardoli, for instance, to hire gangs of workers to harvest their crops. During summer months the agricultural co-operative in Gandevigam hires dozens of casual labourers to sort and pack *chikus* and mangoes and to load them into lorries. Many such workers come from neighbouring villages and are thus recycled into the rural economy via the urban markets. This mode of circulation clarifies that the market for unskilled labour cannot be understood solely or mainly on the basis of the contrast between town and countryside.

People who commute daily on foot to the casual labour market seldom travel more than seven or eight kilometres. Those from further away come for a longer period, varying from some weeks to months. These sojourners bivouac temporarily in the town, spending the night close to the market, in open spaces or along the roadside. They are often men, whether alone or in small groups, but entire families will also undertake the journey. Those who come for a whole season will punctuate their stay with short absences in which to visit their homes. Urban bazaars experience the largest numbers of job-seekers in the dry season, between *Divali* (October) and *Holi* (March). As the hot summer comes to an end, the regular seekers who stay on are usually people who have come to accept the town as their home. Over time, this category has grown considerably. Nevertheless, much of the work that has to be done is in the open air and comes to a halt during the rainy season between late June and end of September. During this interval migrants from the hinterland then have no choice but to return to their villages where they must depend on agricultural labour for a living.

The situation in south Gujarat is certainly not unique. In other parts of the state as well the rural (semi-) proletariat has become mobile during the last few decades.

Within Gujarat seasonal out-migration of labour from districts of Panchmahals, Vadodara, Surendranagar, Banaskantha and Ahmedabad has now been accepted as a way of life by the labouring poor in these areas. A study of seasonal rural migration from one of these districts had shown that 89 or 90 per cent of the 956 households in three villages covered in the study were found migratory, in the sense that at least one member of each household had migrated during the preceding year in search of employment. (B. B. Patel 1987: 143)

Patel ascertained that of every 100 children in the first form of primary school in a sub-district of Surendranagar 76 had disappeared a year later, and afterwards only five remained in the highest class of elementary education (B. B. Patel 1987: 151). Such figures corroborate that seasonal migration and illiteracy are narrowly intertwined. Young children who accompany their parents on the trek outside are destined to continue this type of roaming life at a later age.

Why is it necessary for a substantial part of the rural proletariat in the hinterland of south Gujarat to cover long distances each year, either for short or long periods of absence, in order to supplement the deficient income earned in the village? An obvious reason could be that work inside or outside agriculture is not available nearer home, while there is a simultaneous need for temporary labour elsewhere. This point is succinctly formulated in an overview article on the subject:

One would expect seasonal migration to be most evident where the timing of seasons in the sending and receiving regions complements one another. (Rempel 1981: 212)

However, the assumption that the landless Halpatis in south Gujarat are forced to trek to other destinations because of lack of local employment for part of the year is highly questionable. The region of my fieldwork is, actually, characterized not by stagnation but by impressive dynamism of the economy as a whole and the non-agricultural sector in particular. Then why is it that Halpatis and other landless are able to gain little if any access to the employment that accompanies such economic growth? The answer to that question is that employers in various branches of industry, in the villages as well as in the cities, show systematic preference for alien over local workers. Why that is so will be shown later. Before starting on a survey of the labour inflow into urban and rural south Gujarat, I wish to state that the departure of Halpatis to distant sources of employment, more temporarily than indefinitely, is caused by the fact that a growing number of workplaces within the region are occupied by labourers brought in from far away destinations.

3   Inflow of labour into south Gujarat

Urban order and economy

During the last few decades south Gujarat witnessed an urban growth rate far above the average for the state and also for the whole country. This is particularly the case for the age-old trading centre and harbour of Surat. After colonial stagnation and even deterioration lasting some centuries, this city has in recent times undergone phenomenal development. The acceleration started shortly before Independence and increased in intensity between 1971 and 1981, when its population climbed to over three-quarters of a million, nearly twice as much as at the beginning of that decade. This made Surat the second largest city in Gujarat after Ahmedabad. Since then, the rate of growth has continued unabated. In 1991, according to the provisional results of the latest census, the urban agglomeration included more than 1,500,000 inhabitants and expansion is still going on, reaching nearly two million residents in the beginning of 1995. The pace of population growth during the second half of the twentieth century reflects the emergence of Surat as one of the most important industrial growth poles in western India. Its dynamics are due mostly to two industries: diamond cutting and polishing and artificial silk production, together estimated to provide work for roughly 40 per cent of the total workforce. Immigration has been the main cause for the exceptionally rapid growth rate which seems to be sustained into the current decade. Most people nowadays living in Surat were not born and bred here. The city attracts newcomers like a magnet. Most of them do not even belong to Gujarat but have their place of origin outside the state, in Maharashtra, Uttar Pradesh, Orissa, Rajasthan or Andhra Pradesh. Around 60 per cent of all aliens arrive unattached, i.e. as lone individuals. For this very sizeable category in the urban landscape family life is not the regular basis of cohabitation. Surat's demographic profile lacks balance. The average migrant is a male worker between 15 and 25 years of age. The resulting gender and age distortion gives a particular flavour to the social climate of the city. Young children and

49

Surat unfriendly to women (handwritten margin note)

elderly people are under-represented and so are women. Surat is unfriendly to females of all ages. While in 1961 there were still 910 women to 1,000 men, this had declined twenty years later to 840. The inflow of migrants has remained strongly male-biased also during the last decade. Consequently, in 1991 the sex ratio had dropped one more point to women's disadavantage, i.e. to 839, by far the lowest figure for all urban centres in Gujarat.

The informal sector dominates the urban economy of Surat but the formal sector of production is substantial. Since the 1980s this sector has received a strong impetus from development of the petrochemical industry in extracting and processing natural gas obtained from drilling the rich reservoirs of the Bombay High Plateau in the Arabian Gulf. A number of major national business corporations, including Reliance, Larsen & Toubro, and Gujarat Essar, have opened branches directly on the coast, at a distance of 15–20 kilometres from Surat. Kribhco, set up in the co-operative sector, manufactures artificial fertilizers in a large industrial plant. The Oil and Natural Gas Commission and the Indian Oil Corporation are state-sponsored enterprises. The location of these public and private corporations in what used to be a purely rural landscape is further marked by a strongly formal appearance: walled-in grounds, guarded gate entries, modern buildings, high-grade technical installations and other infrastructural features that evidence the capital-intensive and complex-organized nature of the production process. The employees of these enterprises, mostly highly skilled and well-paid, form a real labour aristocracy accommodated in separate townships built in the immediate vicinity of the workplace.

A few have only just been completed or are still being built. But the Kribhco colony has already existed for a number of years. It is a spacious compound for 1,200 families whose houses are surrounded by attractive gardens and pathways. The little neighbourhoods reflect the industrial stratification: bungalows for executive staff, apartments for middle management, and simpler houses for the lower ranks. All of these make use of the same communal facilities including shops, post office, bank, small hospital, sport fields, a swimming bath, two club houses (with separate membership for officers and workers), a water tower and an electric generator. It needed some effort to gain entrance to this comfortable and well-protected enclave. Why had I come and whom did I know? The residents have little inclination to leave their domain of apartheid. They only make the trip to the city centre, using their own transport or the company's bus, by way of change or to make some special purchase. (Fieldwork notes)

Surat's untidy neighbourhoods contrast sharply with these neatly planned townships. Around the old city centre numerous new districts have grown rapidly which are not divided into separate zones for living and working. To say that the two spheres overlap one another would not do justice to the extreme subordination of the former to the latter. A large part of the population lives in the shadow of the workplace, not from choice but necessity. The combination of jerry-built sheds, workshops and other industrial tenements interspersed with slum areas dominates the urban landscape. According to an inquiry held in 1990 Surat had nearly 300 slum localities with nearly four and a half *lakh* people, representing 30 per cent of the total population (Das 1994: 40). Most of these slums are of recent origin. About one-third sprang up less than ten years ago and four out of five slum dwellers are non-Surthis by birth. These habitats are locally known as *jhoopadpattis*, hutment areas built from waste material. The roofs and walls are made of asbestos, rags, packing boxes, flattened drums, tin sheets, plastic wrappings, mud and rejected bricks, patched close together in all sorts of combinations. A second characteristic is that these neighbourhoods are over-populated and that the densely packed shelters are constructed on ill-favoured sites that lack even the most elementary facilities such as sanitation and water-taps. Slums are at least a recognizable part of the urban horizon. Less visible are the temporary shelters erected by the reserve army of transients for a few days, weeks or months along the roadside or on open terrains close to and within the municipal boundaries. Finally, there is the segment of the labour force – 10 to 15 per cent – which does not have a proper living space at all but seems to be inseparable from the workplace. The diamond ateliers in operation during day time are converted into dormitories at nightfall. Similarly, buildings under construction are utilized as night shelters by the transient workers employed at these sites. Day and night shifts at work in petty industries are accommodated in a lean-to behind factory walls or in sheds close to, and hardly distinct from, the sites of their employ. The absence of toilets in many *galas* adds to the general dirtiness of the surroundings. In these twilight zones labour has no social identity which would give it a presence in the industrial process clearly apart from other factors of production. It is a mere commodity that seems to lack both room for manoeuvre and a self-timed regulation.

Also, the slums proper are not just residential areas to which inhabitants return at the end of the workday or night. The hutment colonies double as industrial and business centres – where commodities, broken up in small quantities, are processed and traded – as well as meeting places for labour demand and supply. In fact, it is only in formal sector enclaves that working and living are demarcated into different spatial spheres with a distinct rhythm and space of their own. To these more regulated parts of the city belong the modern and multi-storey office buildings. From these high-rise vantage points the more down-to-earth informal sector economy is overlooked and controlled. The formal economy landmarks stand well apart from the neighbourhoods in which the social classes belonging to the higher income brackets reside. These living quarters of the more prosperous segments among the urban population culminate in the skyscrapers of expensive apartments and colonies of spacious bungalows for the super-rich. The elite districts are virtually no-go zones for most slum dwellers and for the transient army floating in and out of the urban arena.

Capital is certainly not absent in the informal landscape of work and employment but does not determine its basic character. The city's economy is dominated by the enormous mass of small-scale *galas* with only modest technology and at the most twenty or thirty employees with little if any formal training. The very high labour occupancy is one of the most noticeable features of this dominant circuit of the urban economy. Even large industrial buildings which, from the outside, seem primary examples of formal sector activity, prove on entry to have a completely informalized pattern of business organization.

The dyeing and printing mills, more than 150 in the mid-1980s, illustrate how such enterprises are run. In these large-scale industries the rough woven material that comes from the powerlooms is turned into finished products, in particular *saris*. Each such factory requires a sizeable capital investment and employs some hundreds of labourers. But there is still evidence of extensively informalized production. Personnel lists show no names other than those of the administrative staff, a few technicians, and overseers. The greater majority of workers are not employed by the works-owners but are taken on and dismissed by *mukadams* who act as sub-contractors. The various parts of the work process in the dyeing and printing works are contracted-out to these middlemen. It is they who convert the formal management of production into informal conditions of employment. (Fieldwork notes)

One characteristic of informal sector employment is its defective registration in government statistics. It is for that reason that I am only able to give an approximate estimation of the size of the workforce. Enquiries at municipal offices and specialized government agencies have shown both the incompleteness and the unreliability of official data. Statistical material regarding the formal sector is of far better quality. But even officials who are specifically charged with monitoring the size and flow of capital and labour outside the formal sector have little perception of what actually goes on. Even if they have such information as, for example, the Labour Inspectors do, it is often not to their own advantage to say so. For those who possess such information it is a form of capital providing income that has to remain hidden. Long and numerous talks with personnel in many state agencies, however, have led me to conclude that ignorance of the size and nature of employment in the informal sector, to a large extent, is not simulated but sincere. When I asked for an estimate of the labour force in the city as a whole or a more specified breakdown according to economic sector and branch of industry, I usually received a totally inadequate reply if any at all. Application to employers' and employees' organizations also made me little wiser, and basically for the same reasons.

My own familiarity with Surat's economy, based on lengthy fieldwork experience, brings me to calculate that two out of every three people in that city depend wholly or partially for their livelihood on paid work. This share is far higher than the 40 per cent which is the estimated workforce reported in most quantified accounts. The larger figure which I propose has to be understood by considering the extremely skewed demographic composition of the urban agglomeration. As has been observed before, the productive age cohorts between 15 and 40 years constitute a disproportionately high percentage of the total population. The majority consists of young male migrants who, if already married, have usually left their family at home. The implication is that households and other units of cohabitation have many more productive members than non-working dependants.

Organized efforts to live and eat together were also seen in Surat especially amongst the Oriya textile workers. Such 'communes' are operated by one or two individuals who have lived in the city for long and have acquired some space in these slums. They put up huts where there are berth-like platforms for the male workers to sleep. They also bring cooks from their own regions and feed these workers living in the huts owned by them. Such joints help them to lodge and board at the same place where at time of crisis they can still continue to live and eat on a credit basis. (Das 1993: 15)

Women and children from outside, to the extent that they have managed to accompany their male relatives, have no other option but to join the workforce in order to add to the income necessary for surviving in Surat, which is one of the costliest cities in the country. The participation of women in the labour process is quite low in the formal sector, and also informal sector workshops and ateliers have in general small numbers of female employees. Their marginal presence is clearly reflected in official statistics of Surat's workforce. Decennial occupational censuses, moreover, report a widening gap in gender distribution, a ratio which in 1981 had sunk to as low as 68 female workers to 573 male workers per 1,000 inhabitants (Agrawal 1992: table 13). However, Omvedt has questioned the thesis of increasing marginalization of women in income-earning activities. Their very substantial economic performance is made

Table 3.1. *Working population of Surat city, 1991*

Number of inhabitants	1,500,000		
Total workforce	1,000,000		
Formal sector occupations	300,000		
• employees		150,000	
• employers and their agents, free professions, businessmen		150,000	
Informal sector workers	700,000		
• 'self employed' street and home workers		225,000	
• industrial labour		475,000	
• textile workers			285,000
• diamond cutters/polishers			90,000
• other small-scale workshop labour			100,000

Source: estimates based on fieldwork data and secondary sources.

invisible by not recording their status as 'helpers of male earners' as domestic servants and own-account workers at home. This author comments on

the readiness of poor women to do any kind of work to maintain the survival level of the family. And it is precisely this fluidity that makes the women workers of the unorganized sector the base of cheap labour everywhere, the ultimate 'reserve army of labour'. (Omvedt 1990: 70)

A further correction is necessary in order to compensate for the failure in official counts to register child labour at the bottom of the urban economy. Independent socio-economic surveys of Surat's workforce have shown that in a large number of industries and trades as well as in all branches of the service sector children of less than 14 years represent 7 to 8 per cent of the total workforce. Such young ones are certainly not less, and possibly even more, numerous among the ambulant mass of street workers. Also in this non-registered and floating segment of the working population boys at all ages seem to outnumber girls.

Based on the results of the census held in early 1991 and on observations made above, I conclude that in early 1991 there were one million workers in Surat (Table 3.1). The next guestimate is that 700,000 of these depended on the results of their labour in the informal economic sector. My further assumption is that roughly 50 per cent of the remaining 300,000 belong to the category of formal sector employees. In addition to skilled and comparatively well-paid workers in protected employment with large private enterprises, these include employees in government offices and a great variety of public services, including transport (bus and train), education, post and communications, health care and the police. The other half of the 300,000 in the higher echelons of the labour hierarchy consist mostly of employers and their agents (sub-contractors, jobbers, overseers) and of all sorts of occupational groups who, with regard to education, status and income, enjoy a lifestyle that is at least equal to that of formal sector employees. For that matter, it should not be assumed that this privileged section of the working population have only formal sector earnings at their disposal.

At the beginning of 1991, the greater part of the city's workforce, perhaps 700,000 out of the total of one million, was employed in the informal sector. My estimate is that 20 to 25 per cent of the working population, roughly 225,000 in 1991, made their living in the street or as paid home-workers. They include the men, women and children who attend the casual labour markets. According to one study, around 15,000 job seekers came daily to eight of the ten *bazaars* that operated in Surat in 1988 (Punalekar and Patel 1990: 27). These streetworkers were increased by the army of transients who live in small but numerous concentrations on the agglomeration's periphery and bivouac in or near the building sites where the majority are employed. During my wanderings along the urban boundaries I frequently came across such gangs of migrant workers. They arrive almost unnoticed and settle for a shorter or longer period in the twilight zone between city and countryside. These casual workers are mostly channelled temporarily into urban employment by contractors or jobbers, who hire them in advance before they leave their villages or intercept them along the roadside or at crossroads when they reach the urban outskirts. The first arrivals especially have little chance of penetrating into the casual labour markets held at various places in the town. Such highly mobile workers certainly double the number of men, women and children who daily seek employment at the regular informal labour markets. The building industry and all its preliminary work (preparing the ground, digging for pipelines and electricity poles, road construction, etc.) is the principal sector of employment for this entire workforce, which I estimate at no less than 60,000 labourers.

The same category of 225,000 informal sector workers further includes all those who earn their living on the streets. They do so in various kinds of retail trade, selling a large assortment of wares at fixed points or going around in the streets. To this colourful collection of stationary or itinerant traders and craftsmen belong: shoe cleaners, lottery sellers, barbers, washers, tinkers and other repairers, porters, prostitutes and their pimps, knife-grinders, car-park attendants, petty thieves, gamblers, *bhangars* (buyers of second-hand goods), alcohol distillers, car cleaners, refuse collectors, beggars, etc. Finally, there are various kinds of transport workers: *hamals* (coolies or bearers of headloads), loaders and unloaders who ride with trucks, owners or renters of handcarts and rickshaw pullers and drivers. In my opinion, this heterogeneous mass of streetworkers equals or even exceeds the army of workers employed on building sites.

An equally numerous third segment in this category of my classification consists of paid domestic workers. These include in the first place those servants who continually, daily or for a few hours, are occupied in households which enjoy a formal sector standard of living. The domestic servants, mostly women and girls, total some tens of thousands. The same category also includes those who do paid work at home for others. For example, there is a sizeable group of textile workers. Brocading and embroidery were started long ago as a typical household industry in Surat. Notwithstanding the increasing tendency to transfer production to fully-fledged ateliers, a survey carried out in 1986–87 showed that in south Gujarat numerous men and particularly women still earned their living as home-workers in this branch of industry. In the city of Surat at least 12,000 to 15,000 embroiderers work at home (S. P. Punalekar 1988: 7–9). Lastly, a large range of products are made at home from raw materials or recycled material, while various services are supplied when ordered. Although all household members have to be prepared to undertake such varying activities, the women's contribution is once again disproportionately high.

I have calculated that the sub-categories described above total 225,000 workers. It should be realized, however, that such activities are not undertaken exclusively but rather in combination or interchangeably with one another. How does this massive army of street and home-workers manage to earn the income with which to meet their cost of living? Many work for their own account and at their own risk, usually referred to in informal sector literature as 'self-employment'. This is a somewhat ambiguous concept. 'Self-employed' is often used for want of a better term and hardly conceals the fact that the person in question has not been able to find permanent or even casual wage-employment. The relationship with a patron or buyer of the results of his or her efforts is of a different nature, one which, for convenience sake, is indicated by stressing the principle of autonomy in the mutual contract. Such an interpretation fails to appreciate the dependency suffered by the majority of such workers. In my opinion, what is called self-employment is in fact usually little more than a disguised form of casual wage labour. These modes of payment will be discussed extensively in Chapter 6.

The largest proportion of the working population in Surat – 475,000 out of one million at the time of the last census – is best described as industrial labour, with the proviso that conditions of employment are not of a formal but an informal character. As we shall see, these workers have had little education and have acquired their training on-the-job. Approximately 100,000 are distributed over a considerable diversity of small-scale production units and repair works. Next to these I estimate that, at the beginning of 1991, there were little less than 285,000 workers in the textile industry and another 90,000 in the diamond cutting and polishing industry. My research in Surat was concentrated on these two categories, a choice connected to the fact that they dominate the city's economy, in terms of the economic value produced. Even more important from my point of view is that one out of every three members of the working population in this urban agglomeration is employed in these two branches of industry. Together, they absorb more than half of the enormous numbers who depend on the informal sector for their livelihood.

Moreover, the large majority of these workers are newcomers to Surat. In effect, local labour is a minority and has had to accept living and working in the shadow of aliens. It was actually this migrant status of most textile workers and diamond cutters–polishers which drew my attention. These areas of employment are clearly not set aside for those who have been born and bred in the city. Yet, the rural proletariat and semi-proletariat of south Gujarat have not managed to penetrate in large numbers into these booming branches of industry. The inflow of hundreds of thousands of people from other regions and states into the informal sector, where demands for knowhow are not high, made me wonder why employers have systematically ignored the presence of large reservoirs of labour in the immediate hinterland of Surat. Why do they stubbornly persist in recruitment from far distant parts of the country?

Industrial labour in the informal sector

The textile industry

For centuries past Surat has been famous as a major centre for manufacture of silk and fine cotton materials, both for domestic and foreign markets. Fashion changes caused production to decrease, while the high price of materials also hindered the search for new sales possibilities. When the import of silk thread came to a halt during the Second World War it seemed that the industry would never recover. In post-war years, however, the crisis provided an incentive for changing to the use of artificial fibres. Instead of further decline, the industry began to flourish. A precondition for this, however, was that the industry convert from hand-weaving to machine-weaving. Mechanization of Surat's textile industry was a sluggish affair. The first powerlooms were introduced in the early decades of this century, but even in 1930 a mere 185 were in operation. It was only from the 1950s onwards that handlooms fell into disuse. The transition to artificial fibres caused an industrial upswing that was expressed in the rapid increase of mechanical looms: 5,100 in 1946, 10,000 in 1951, 15,000 in 1955, 39,000 in 1968, 48,000 in 1972. In an effort to protect the village-based hand-weavers and later also to counter the threat of this competition to the long established factory production in Bombay and Ahmedabad, the Gujarat government has frequently tried to halt further expansion of the powerloom sector in Surat by refusing to grant licences for the installation of new machines, but without success. By the beginning of the 1980s there were 105,000 authorized and non-authorized powerlooms, about half the total capacity in the entire country at that time, installed in sheds called *galas*. The rise then continued without interruption and reached the 175,000 mark in 1986. Insiders have told me that, in 1992–3, at least 250,000 powerlooms were in operation. The phenomenal development of this industry in Surat was directly related to the dismantling of textile mills in Bombay and Ahmedabad during the same period. Factory owners there complained about what they described as the excessive cost of labour, a consequence of strong trade unionization in the formal sector of the economy, and seized upon this argument to substantiate their refusal to make new investments. The closure of these factories explains the remarkable fact that in the 1970s no less than 70 per cent of the powerlooms operating in Surat were second-hand. Nowadays, these machines and their spare parts, formerly got from Bombay or even abroad, are manufactured in Surat and other towns along the railway line in south Gujarat. The steady demand for new looms has caused the metal industry to become another important source of industrial employment.

In the middle of the 1980s 60 per cent of all artificial silk in India was claimed to be produced in Surat on powerlooms which represented half of the total installed capacity countrywide. These figures imply that the closure of factories in the formal sector has indeed caused a higher return to invested capital. However, the considerable reduction in overheads caused by transferring production to new growth poles such as Surat, has been achieved primarily by exploiting labour more intensively. Organization of the powerloom sector is chiefly noticeable for the small scale of enterprises. In 1957, 41 per cent of these petty firms owned at the most four powerlooms, while an almost equal percentage owned from five to nine machines. Most of these petty industrialists have gradually succeeded in increasing their plant capacity. One should be careful, however, in taking these figures at face value in view of the strategy of entrepreneurs to keep a low profile by operating more than one workshop. By the mid-1980s roughly half of these *galas* were still equipped with not more than ten looms. Only 5 per cent had fifty machines or more. Powerloom owners are almost all Gujaratis, most of them original inhabitants of Surat. It follows that, as owners of capital, many of them managed to expand their business together with the rise of the city as an industrial metropolis. Fibre and other basic materials represent three-quarters of all production costs. Although the total amount paid in wages in this highly labour-intensive industry is a large sum of money, this expenditure represents a minor part of all costs of production, not more than 10 to 11 per cent of the sale value of grey fabric (Mehta and Gandhi: 124). Until the mid-1970s the larger part of the woven product was sold to factories outside Gujarat for further processing. This loss of value added was stopped, however, when more and more dyeing and printing mills were set up in Surat. Around 1960, forty such units were operating in the city, which together employed not more than 500 workers (*Gazetteer of India*, Gujarat State 1962: 426). In 1985 there were already 150 enterprises of a much larger scale, with an average of 250 employees each, and with a combined capacity amounting to half the total national product of this particular commodity at that time. The workforce has since increased to at least 40,000, almost exclusively male, spread over more than 250 dyeing units. In later years, the progressive trend towards vertical integration of the industry in India's principal artificial silk centre was further articulated by the transfer to Surat of the wholesale trade in semi-finished and finished products. A number of huge skyscrapers were built in which traders and producers or their agents bargain for terms and conditions.

Today the entire stretch of land on both sides of the Ring Road between the Sahara gate and Udhana gate has been studded with markets of all commodities but mainly textiles. It is estimated that at present there are over 20 markets in this area housing 3000 shops. (Mehta and Gandhi: 83)

The earlier mode of production of artificial silk firms, i.e. domestic manufacture by owners who depended primarily on family labour, was retained far longer in the brocade industry. Surat has always been the centre for this century-old *jari* handwork, i.e. the application of gold and silver thread to fine textiles, which used to be the monopoly of a few local castes. In 1877, the *Surat Gazetteer* mentioned that some of these artisanal castes had a working tradition that dated as far back as the time of the Moghuls. In the past, the limited clientele for this luxury product came from the highest echelons of the population. This situation has changed due to the growing prosperity of the social middle classes during the last few decades and to the reduced quality of the materials used (copper and artificial silk). *Saris* in which precious metal thread is used and of which the most expensive may cost some tens of thousands of rupees, now form an essential part of the wedding trousseau for the relatively well-to-do. Surat, with 80 per cent of the total annual production in the country, has managed to maintain its position as principal place of manufacture in the strongly increased national and foreign demand for *jari* articles of varied quality. Towards the end of the 1980s, brocade and embroidery firms in the town provided work for 30,000–35,000 people, of whom 70 per cent were women. The combined labour force in smaller centres elsewhere in south Gujarat is almost as large (S. P. Punalekar 1988: 7). Small producers who manufacture the metal thread and apply it to textile, working at home and using their own tools, are known as *akhadedars*. If the labour power provided by the household, including women and children, is insufficient, they will employ outside workers. In selling their products, they are bound to the traders who provide them with materials. A recent enquiry shows progressive concentration of capital. Among the women and girls employed in this branch of industry, 81 per cent are no longer unpaid family labour but nowadays work for a wage. Some of them are taken on as extra workers in the homes of small producers, but far more are employed by big owners who have transferred production to separate workshops employing 10–60 labourers. The latter category is dominated by 40–50 families who also act as wholesalers. They deliver raw materials to the *akhadedars* who return the processed textiles to them. Surprisingly, however, the increasing conversion of self-employed home-workers into wage-labourers has not been accompanied by any change in the social identity of the workforce. During the last fifty to sixty years the work has remained almost the exclusive monopoly of one caste: 'A striking feature of the industry is its inbreeding and restricted entry from outside the Rana community' (Desai and Tiwari 1985: 291).

In his report on an extensive enquiry into the employment of women in the *jari* industry, Punalekar mentions that his respondents in Surat included only a handful of people who belonged to castes other than the Ranas (also known as Golas). None of these belonged to the tribal castes who formed such a large part of the population in the city's hinterland (S. P. Punalekar 1988: 13–14). It is of interest to note that what nowadays seems a time-hallowed caste occupation has a tradition of not much more than one century. According to the 1884 *Bombay Gazetteer* Ranas used to crush paddy and spices in the houses of people belonging to higher castes. Patidars and Banias who ran the *jari* business at that time started to employ them as labourers:

Gradually the Ranas learnt the art and skill of this industry. So now one finds the traders, the karkhanadars and the worker – all from the Rana caste. The Patidars have completely withdrawn themselves from it. The reason for withdrawal of Patidars and Banias is that these higher castes found the physical labour involved too much. (Soni 1990: 134)

The first generation of workers in the artificial silk industry also came from Surat's own population. The most recent issue of the Surat District Gazetteer left no doubt as to their dominance at the end of the 1950s: 'Khatris, Mohamedans, Harijans and other backward class people were engaged in this industry. Most of labourers were illiterate and spendthrift.' (*Gazetteer of India*, Gujarat State 1962: 450).

The enormous expansion which has since occurred in this branch of industry has been coupled with the substitution of migrants for local workers. Any estimate of the total workforce can only be guesswork. The degree of under-registration in official industrial statistics cannot be established even by approximation. The data are simply worthless. In the absence of trustworthy sources, we can only base ourselves on the meagre information provided by the Surat Art Silk Cloth Manufacturers Association. This producers' organization gives a workforce for 1983–84 of 180,000 distributed over an estimated 15,000–20,000 firms – a significant variance in range. In that same year, at least 150,000 workers were said to be employed by the weaving units. At a conservative estimate, the production phases that precede and follow the weaving process would increase this by another 30,000 (*Working and Living Conditions* 1984: 15). Assuming an exponential growth rate an estimate of 245,000 workers in the art silk industry (170,000 in powerloom workshops, 45,000 in dyeing and printing mills), i.e. nearly one out of four wage workers in the city, seems not to be an unduly high figure in the beginning of the 1990s.

The workforce is predominantly male, more than half in the 15–25 age group. Only one in ten powerloom operators is older than forty. The labour process is so exhausting that very few are able to perform adequately after middle age. Once the ability to maintain production drops below the required level, older workers are discharged without mercy. There is no shortage of young people willing to take their place. Women and children are also present in the workshops, in roughly equal proportion, and together represent 12–15 per cent of the workforce employed in the powerloom sector. They are usually involved in the various preparatory processes that synthetic thread has to undergo (winding, twisting, beam passing) before weaving can commence. The powerlooms are in operation twenty-four hours per day, with two shifts of twelve hours each. If a worker of the new shift does not turn up, it is customary for his predecessor to continue and to operate the machines for thirty-six hours.

The report from which I derive these data gives the results of a survey held in 1984 by staff and students of the south Gujarat University among 1,635 textile workers employed in 435 workshops and mills. Interviewers visited them in sixty-two localities of Surat city. By far the majority were long-distance migrants: from Orissa 42 per cent, Andhra Pradesh 12.5 per cent, Maharashtra 8 per cent, Uttar Pradesh 5.5 per cent and Bihar 1 per cent. The inflow was slow at first but has grown increasingly in recent years (*Working and Living Conditions* 1984). The spread in recruitment over a variety of catchment areas in different parts of the country is confirmed by other publications.

The regions like eastern Uttar Pradesh, northern Maharashtra, Orissa, Bihar, Rajasthan and Andhra Pradesh supply the bulk of the labour to these industries. It may be noted that Gujarat workers constitute only one-fifth of the total workforce in the textiles industry. (Barik 1987: 168)

Barik has also investigated when Oriya workers first entered the weaving sheds of Surat. Their share in the workforce has increased rapidly and is estimated by Barik to have numbered 90,000 at the start of the 1980s, barely thirty years after the first had reached the city. The newcomers were gardeners according to the tradition of their caste, and were taken on as such by the industrialists. Only when this fairly incidental and modest occupational demand was satisfied, were their caste mates taken into the workshops, with the result described above. Although policy-makers in Gujarat are naturally aware of the presence of a large alien workforce in Surat city, they do not seem to realize the huge numbers involved. The army of Oriyas is particularly impressive. Nine out of ten are migrants from the Ganjam district in Orissa and even within that region the majority hail from a single sub-division. They belong to intermediate and lower castes and are landpoor and landless peasants who have been forced into migration for economic reasons. Low-caste landless labourers are, in comparison, less mobile because of their greater poverty and for that reason remain entrapped at the bottom of the village economy (Barik 1985: 8; see also Sahoo 1985: 7). The outcome of migration further aggravates the already existing condition of inequality. The sons of small peasants who manage to get access to better paid jobs far away from home send back money which helps to improve the economic situation of the households which they have left behind. However, their economic gains have to be balanced against the loss of status. The migrants may have left the village as peasants but there can be no doubt whatsoever, even in their own mind, that they end up in Surat's metropolitan economy as proletarianized labour. An indication of the lonely life they lead in the city is that 85 per cent of the more than 200,000 Oriya labourers at work in the textile industry in 1992 stayed in Surat without spouse or parents (Pathy 1993: 10).

Workers born and bred in the city were rapidly overtaken or even replaced by people from elsewhere. However, it is not only local workers who are poorly represented nowadays in this sector dominating the urban economy. Migrants from the immediate hinterland of Surat also experience difficulty in gaining access to the textile industry. The share of members of the tribal castes, who make up 60 per cent of the district's population, is less than 9 per cent of the total workforce in the powerloom sheds (*Working and Living Conditions* 1984: 25). The entrance threshold is almost insurmountable for Halpatis in particular. This barrier did not exist in the past. Before the great boom began the large majority of the workforce in the powerlooms were local people, either from Surat proper or the immediate rural hinterland of south Gujarat. According to a survey reported in 1975 one-third belonged to scheduled tribes and among them Halpatis stood first. Members of the latter tribal caste who were already settled in the city made up 18.5 per cent of the total number employed in the industry (Mehta and Pathak 1975: 60–61). The handful of Halpatis working as powerloom operators that I managed to trace fifteen years later were no newcomers to Surat. They themselves, their parents or grandparents have come there in search of work. These Halpatis hailing from the immediate hinterland can be distinguished from migrants from further away, 82 per cent of whom have lived in Surat for less than eight years (*Working and Living Conditions* 1984: 99). Artificial silk weaving units have also been opened in other urban nuclei along the railway which runs to the south, particularly in Navsari and Bilimora. The owners of these mills make more use of labour from the immediate neighbourhood, although migrant workers are also found. As a result, Halpatis and other landless labourers living in or nearby the smaller urban nuclei have a slightly better chance of becoming weavers, just as more of them are to be found in the diamond ateliers in these secondary towns than in the Surat metropolis.

But is the life of a powerloom operator an attractive one? Working and living conditions are wretched. The objective of a survey undertaken by a team of staff and students of the University of south Gujarat in 1984 was in fact to marshal factual evidence required for filing a complaint that could be submitted to the High Court of Gujarat against the scandalous conditions prevailing in Surat's largest branch of industry. The workers derive no security at all from their employment. Only a quarter of them are listed in their employer's administration under their true names (see also Barik 1987: 170). They are paid on a piece-work basis, and their monthly income is dependent on the degree of self-exploitation that they achieve during a twelve-hour day or night shift. Women workers are paid less than the men. They are all debarred from allowances and fringe benefits that secure the lives of workers in the formal sector. As single migrants, the majority of men are separated from wives and children who stay in the villages and to whom they send a maximal part of earnings whenever possible. In 1984 this averaged less than 100 rupees per month. According to calculations in a later report this amount ranged from Rs 400 to Rs 2,000 per year (Mehta and Gandhi: 130). The manner in which textile workers spend their non-working hours can be seen from the fact that three-quarters of them live in accommodation of less than 49 square feet; a quarter even has to make do with nine square feet (*Working and Living Conditions* 1984: 84). Many bachelors among the migrants huddle together in a congested space. I have visited a number of these billets, so small that the eight, ten or even more inhabitants could not all be present at the same time. They sleep in turn, the night shift preparing a meal for day shift workers before starting their own work, and vice versa. The nature of such housing makes it understandable that the two Halpati brothers from Chikhligam who alternate on the powerloom, continue to live in their own village. Notwithstanding the extra fatigue of the long journey they hang on to their urban workplace, for the same reason that masses of migrants submit to their miserable existence in Surat. This proletariat has no alternative. They all have come to Surat to escape the acute lack of work and income in their home milieu.

Diamond ateliers

The history of diamond cutting and polishing in Surat illustrates the way in which local workers have been superseded by migrants from other districts. In the mid-1950s the city had slightly more than 100 ateliers employing about 500 workers. By the end of the 1960s these had increased to more than 1,000 cutting and polishing establishments with 20,000 workers. Persistent drought from 1966–68 drove thousands of young Kanbi Patels, belonging to the locally dominant peasant caste, out of the villages around Bhavnagar in Saurashtra to the diamond ateliers in south Gujarat at the opposite side of the Gulf of Cambay.

The school-going youth were forced to leave schools and they came to Surat and Navsari in search of jobs in this field. It was an exodus on a very large scale. These youths were apprenticed for three years on very meagre wages – only their food bill. (Desai 1985: 3)

Once the connection was made the expansion continued and even accelerated in the next decade. In 1978–79 there were almost 5,700 workplaces with a registered workforce of 41,000. Punctuated by short-term recessions, the increase has continued. On the basis of similar data, Pathak calculates for 1982 a total of over 9,000 units with workers totalling 57,500. According to official statistics, unit size throughout this period remained very modest, averaging six or seven workers. The explosive growth in the number of units was caused by the fairly small amount of cash needed as starting capital. Wages formed no less than 86 per cent of all production expenses. Good relations with traders are a more important precondition for setting up an enterprise than the availability of cash money. This also explains why the majority of new owners are former cutters. The workers, *hiravalas*, are mostly young persons in the 18–25 age bracket as shown by the fact that only 2 per cent of entrepreneurs have inherited their business from an earlier generation.

These impressive growth figures only approximate the actual situation, however, and need to be adjusted upwards. Research based on sample surveys has shown that government registration leaves a great deal to be desired. There are more diamond cutting firms in Surat than is officially known. The number of workers is also very much higher than the average given of six or seven per unit; according to Kashyap and Tiwari, at least 25 per cent more (1982: 20). Taking these adjustments into account, I calculate a total of around 90,000 workers in the industry at the beginning of the 1990s, a magnitude which makes it understandable why Surat is called the Diamond City of India.

Even an average of ten to twelve workers per workshop makes no real difference to the small-scale nature of production. Ateliers are situated mostly in the densely populated city centre, in accommodation that is so small that association with sweatshops easily springs to mind. Women are conspicuous by their absence. The male bias in employment has to be underlined since in Trichur, a town in southern India where the industry was introduced more recently, the employment of women has become quite customary (Kapadia 1995). About half the diamond cutters in Surat live in one-person households, indicating their bachelor status. They may rent accommodation singly, but usually do so in small groups. It is a type of lifestyle to which slightly skilled and relatively better paid migrant workers, who form the majority of the workforce, are also accustomed. Less than one-third were born and grew up in Surat. More than half of all diamond cutters at work in the city come from far away, from Saurashtra or the north of Gujarat, and nearly without exception are Kanbi Patels, originally a peasant caste. This finding contrasts strongly with the situation at the inception of the industry, when the workforce consisted solely of inhabitants of Surat. These were soon joined by incomers from the direct vicinity who in turn were forced into a minority position by the progressive expansion.

Migrants that trickled down in the initial phase from the neighbouring areas have become perennial flows from more distant lands in recent times. Two regions – Saurashtra, and Mehsana and Palanpur - have been the major contributors to the more recent phenomenon, accounting for about 70 per cent of the migrant workforce. (Kashyap and Tiwari 1982: 102)

Although migrants now form the backbone of this important segment of the urban proletariat in Surat, as in the textile industry there are few landless among them who originated in the surrounding countryside. Halpatis who have penetrated into the diamond industry are not so easy to come by. In localities where members of this caste are concentrated I found only a handful of cutters-cum-polishers, adult men who have lived in the city since childhood and have not made their way there especially to seek work.

It seems that the chance of finding Halpati workers would have been greater during the second half of the 1970s when more and more diamond ateliers were opened in the direct hinterland of Surat. Navsari emerged as a secondary nucleus for the industry, while units varying in number from a few dozen to some hundreds were set up in most principal towns of the sub-districts in south Gujarat. During the first phase, the initiative for this expansion was taken mostly by cutters who had gained some expertise in well-established urban workshops and now, with support from traders, took the risk of starting up for themselves in small towns close to their home villages. Many were sons of Kanbi Patels, members of a dominant peasant caste in rural south Gujarat (Breman 1985: 45–6). At first they recruited workers from their own milieu. Tribals came later, and even they were mostly limited to members of landowning households. Halpatis were only considered in years of explosive growth, when atelier owners were prepared to train people as cutters whom they would have refused in normal times. The presence of nine Halpatis from Chikhligam and Gandevigam in cutting workshops located in the towns of these *talukas* has to be seen against that background. Close to their own milieu, the inclusion of Halpatis is rather less exceptional than in Surat city. Their share in the total workforce in this labour-intensive branch of industry, however, is extremely small, and they were the first to be discharged when a major slump occurred in the late 1980s.

At the end of the 1980s the diamond industry of Surat started to lose some of its former buoyancy. Competition and recession both resulted in a cut-back in the number of jobs, which had gone up to more than one *lakh* a few years earlier, by some tens of thousands. Many Kanbi Patel boys who had been trained in Surat as diamond cutters went back home in Bhavnagar to set up their own workshop. In addition to this shift away from the capital of the diamond industry in Gujarat, the international economic slump has undeniably caused a fall in demand for this costly product, whether for industrial purposes or for jewellery. Even more significant in the somewhat longer term is probably the increasing competition by new centres of production elsewhere in the world, particularly China, North Korea and Vietnam. I have been told that in these countries, where processing costs are even lower than in India, the quality of cutting is superior. The immediate result is that the number of diamond workers in Surat and other places in south Gujarat has fallen considerably during the last few years.

Rotation in the urban work arena

The majority of diamond cutters and powerloom operators are what I have described as semi-permanent workers. Contrary to casual labour in the informal sector they report each day to their employer, but without being able to derive any security from their regular service. It would therefore be incorrect to suggest that they settled down in the city to which they have migrated. To be taken on as diamond cutter or textile worker in Surat is just an initial step in an occupational career that continues to be characterized by very high mobility. This applies in particular to those who were not born and bred in Surat. At least one-third of the diamond cutters who have come to the city from elsewhere report having changed their job within the space of a year. After the second year this increases to almost 50 per cent. And this figure does not even include those who could not be interviewed because within that time they had left their job and probably also the city. The study from which I have derived these data gives the reason why diamond cutters change so frequently from one employer to another at the prospect of a somewhat higher wage and the wish for a more harmonious work environment. Another consideration may be lack of sufficient work or closure of the business (Kashyap and Tiwari 1982: 108). In all events, explanations for high mobility should not be sought merely in the rapid expansion of the industry. The phenomenon can still be found although the last few years have seen a decline in growth in the number of workshops and jobs. Another researcher who has noticed the rapid circulation of labour has considered the motives of diamond workers in some detail:

there is a high turnover of labour in the industry, with the workers frequently changing jobs. It is common for workers to shift from one factory to another every 2 or 3 years. The ready availability of jobs, especially for those known to be highly skilled, only partly explains this frequent job shifting. Workers expect to be treated well and may quit their jobs if bossed over. Some workers have an exaggerated notion of their skill and expect to be advanced substantial loans due to a highly skilled worker. When these hopes do not materialize, they try to save face by quitting. The ability of a *karkhanedar* (factory owner) to retain his workers also depends on whether he has enough contacts with merchants to obtain a steady supply of good quality raw diamonds. If he is unable to retain a steady supply, or if the diamonds are of poor quality and difficult to work on, the workers may look for jobs elsewhere. (Kalathil 1978: 100)

This passage suggests that the initiative towards breaking off the relationship is taken by the employee who apparently has considerable latitude. Such a situation can indeed be found, but only when the worker is known to be an excellent craftsman and, moreover, comes from a similar social background milieu as his employer. That applies particularly when both parties are Kanbi Patels. In that case the cutter will consider himself the equal of his patron and in fact intend to set up a shop for himself. A few pages farther on, Kalathil emphasizes that the few diamond cutters who belong to a low caste of agricultural labourers evince no assertiveness in their behaviour. When they leave their jobs it is for quite different reasons:

Workers from such a background are submissive to their employer and rarely talk back. They blindly carry out the jobs assigned to them and are apt to harbour animosities rather than give them free vent. As a consequence, animosities sometimes build up to such a level that it becomes impossible for the worker to continue in his job. (Kalathil 1978: 104)

Nevertheless, even this observation suggests that the worker takes the decision, although due to dissatisfaction or other reasons of dubious rationality. My own appraisal is rather different, and gives greater weight to the employer's motives. By giving cash advances (*baki*), he assures himself of a permanent core of cutters, supplemented by a few to whom he attaches less value and on whom he calls when the supply of stones offered him by traders is sufficiently large. These reserve workers are treated less considerately. It is never inconceivable, however, that even his most trusted and experienced workers will leave him if a competitor entices them away by offering a large cash advance. Diamond cutters of lower castes who entered the profession in later years, who have not yet acquired much routine and who have few of the contacts necessary for finding a new patron, can only count on obtaining sufficient work when times are good. If the industrial scene is less favourable, as at the start of the 1990s, they are the first to suffer. Members of tribal castes, especially the landless Halpatis, are particularly vulnerable.

Surat's textile workers can also be classified at best as semi-permanent. Their employers are so negligent regarding them that they do not even record the most elementary personal particulars in their business administration. This situation was publicized dramatically in the summer of 1981 when an illegally constructed dyeing and printing mill collapsed just as the day and night shifts were being changed. Most of the 1,200 workers were fortunately pulled out alive from the wreckage. The lack of official record, however, prevented many of the dead from being identified. An emergency committee of volunteers stated that migrants from Orissa who died in the disaster totalled more than the number made known by Gujarat's government (Barik 1987: 174). The report by a team of researchers referred to earlier, mentions that only 8 per cent of the 1,635 workers interviewed enjoyed a status that could be described as permanently employed. Another study shows that a quarter of all workers in the artificial silk industry move to another factory within a year (Desai 1981: 117). The analysis of work profiles shows that in most cases a change is made more than once and that it is not restricted to the initial period after arrival in the city. Only 28 per cent of textile workers had remained faithful with their first employer, at the time of interview. More than half had changed employment two to eight times, and a small percentage did so even more frequently. Under such circumstances, links with the place of employment cannot be other than extremely slight:

there is such a rapid turnover of workers, especially over small weaving units, that in several cases the respondents are not sufficiently familiar with their current workplaces to provide details like the number and background of other persons employed in the workplaces for various operations in different shifts. Even some veteran workers were unable to remember the total number of different units they had worked in during their careers and perhaps no amount of probing could have helped in such cases. (*Working and Living Conditions* 1984: 20)

The reason given for high mobility is similar to that given for the same phenomenon in the diamond industry: the prospect of a higher wage or bad relations with the former employer. But in my opinion, these arguments again incorrectly suggest that it is the employee who takes the decision to leave. In fact, a worker is frequently dismissed for very diverse reasons: fall in production; reduced output on the part of the worker; his or her absence due to illness; disinclination to grant leave; or displacement in favour of recommended newcomers. More than one-third of the workers said that they had been discharged once, twice or even thrice, summarily and without compensation. I found that this is the case, for example, when a migrant wishes to visit his family in the home village.

The notion that rural migrants refuse to fully commit themselves to industrial work and life because they stubbornly prefer to keep one foot in the village and in agriculture has remained a recurrent explanation in the literature on the high rate of turnover in urban employment. Reports sponsored by Surat employers' associations suggest a similar tendency among the footloose proletariat employed in textile production:

Labour shortage is felt in summer seasons where migrant labour takes leave to go home. Moreover some workers do have agricultural interests and they also proceed on leave in this season. Due to high absenteeism work suffers both quality wise as well as quantity wise as temporary untrained workers are engaged. (Mehta and Gandhi: 109)

This interpretation overlooks the possibility that the murderous work pace, still to be discussed, leaves the migrants no option but to go home for some time in order to recuperate. Another reason is that the uneven rhythm of production over the year makes it attractive for the employer to lay off part of the workforce during the slack period and, conversely, to recruit more hands when demand picks up again. Urban employment in the informal sector is marked by a cyclicality that is usually only associated with an agrarian–rural economic lifestyle. Employers refuse to guarantee that workers who absent themselves or are sent off will be taken back on their return. The industrialist is motivated by a single interest: to keep the looms in operation day and night and for as many days per year as possible. That ambition has priority over maintenance of labour relations based on stability. Given the abundant labour supply, employers consider that their *modus operandi* is more advantageous than detrimental.

I would estimate the army of workers who earn their living in the informal sector at 700,000, more than half of whom form part of the workforce employed by large industries, i.e. producers of artificial silk in various processing phases and diamond ateliers. The industrial nature of work for which these mainly long-distance migrants have come to Surat does not alter the fact that they frequently change employers although not their trade. Both diamond cutters and textile workers voluntarily or from necessity regularly seek other employment, but when they change their place of work it does not often happen that they change their occupation as well.

The case is different for informal sector workers who can seldom afford the luxury of specialising in a particular trade and who more frequently circulate through various stations of employment. For a start, there is the horde of migrants who settle on the urban periphery and are to be found on building sites. Their incursions into Surat are brief, lasting no more than a few weeks or months. Once the job for which they have been taken on is completed, they return home. This does not apply to another sizeable category of outdoor workers who came for a longer period and have found shelter in one of the city's many seedy quarters. They undertake all kinds of odd jobs for a multiplicity of employers, whether as wage labour, on a sub-contracting basis, or on their own account and risk. Their precarious existence in the urban arena is based on casual work and diverse sources of income. Another threat to their security has to do with their hazardous life as slum-dwellers. As squatters they have invaded private or public land which is not their own. The only hope of the illegal occupants is that their colonies will be regularized after some time. However, slum-dwellers are a removable lot and many such city residents have been evicted more than once. The threat of eviction remains a prime concern in this milieu, as Lobo reports in his case study of a Surat slum:

the people do not have any individual permission or something to certify that they are legal residents of this place, such as a house tax, ration card, etc. Hence, even if people want to improve their house they don't do it because it can be destroyed at any time. Respondents are caught up in a dilemma: they cannot leave the place for another as it is unavailable and at the same time cannot build a *pucca* house. People feel that it is better for them to invest in a good house back in their village. (Lobo 1993: 7–8)

Not only space for a tenement but also material to build it is difficult to come by for the urban poor. The slum is not an open arena nor has everybody free access to the waste which is lying around. There are regular traders who deal in recycled plastics, asbestos or corrugated iron sheets, rejected bricks, old wood, etc. as there are also specialised workers using such second-hand material for the construction of all kinds of slum dwellings (Das 1993: 31). Housing conditions such as these explain why circulation remains such an important feature in the life and work of the very large part of Surat's population who belong to the down-and-outs of the informal sector.

Influx in the rural hinterland

However important the urban economy has become during the last thirty years or so, the massive inflow of labour into south Gujarat is not only directed towards these industrial growth poles. A similar invasion sweeps through the countryside, clearly attuned to the rhythm of the seasons.

The sugarcane campaign

This tidal movement can be illustrated with the example of the huge army of harvest workers who trek through the central plain each year, to cut sugarcane in the fields. An initial study, started in 1977, into their coming and mode of employment throughout the campaign, showed that the majority of the 50,000 men, women and children had been recruited in the border state of Maharashtra (Breman 1978/79: 42). Ten years later, repetition of that research showed that the army of workers had doubled in the meantime. Since then, the acreage of south Gujarat that is planted with sugarcane has continued to grow. Taking my earlier data as a point of departure I was able to state with reasonable certainty at the end of more recent fieldwork towards the end of the 1980s that seasonal migrants mobilized for the sugarcane harvest in south Gujarat then totalled 150,000 (Breman 1990: 549).

Around the middle of this century, farmers belonging to the dominant Patidar caste in the Bardoli region took the initiative to set up a co-operative sugar mill. This laid the basis for an agro-industrial development that has contributed greatly to the growing prosperity of the large landowners. Most *taluka* towns in south Gujarat now have their own sugar co-operative, set up for the purpose and owned by farmer-members who have bought one or more shares which give them the right to deliver cane to the mill. The factories operate twenty-four hours per day, milling the cane brought in from the surrounding area in quantities ranging from 1,500 to 10,000 tons per day, during six or seven months of the year. A precondition for such large-scale production was construction in the 1950s of a system of irrigation canals that criss-cross the plain. This sugarcane crop that now dominates the local agricultural economy to such an extent, is by no means a new commodity. Sugarcane is said to have been one of the most successful crops in Bardoli already around the mid-nineteenth century (Breman 1985b: 32), and early survey and settlement reports mention its cultivation in other parts of south Gujarat as well. Farmers of that time pressed the cane in their yards in order to make jaggery (*gur*), which was then put into pots and sold to traders (Mukhtyar 1930: 95–7, 181–82, 187–93). These old sources show that the very labour-intensive cultivation and processing of sugarcane was the main motive why the landowning village elite employed landless Halpatis all the year round as farm-hands:

In this village, and, in point of fact, in the whole of Southern Gujarat, there still obtains a system of labour called the Hali system in which a labourer mortgages his labour to the farmer for a loan he takes for celebrating his marriage. A capitalistic cultivator keeps one or two Halis for performing field operations. He is bound to maintain them whether he exacts work from them or not. He, therefore, deems it wise and profitable to occupy them in sugarcane-cultivation. (Mukhtyar 1930: 97)

The quotation suggests that the moral economy of the time more or less obliged landowners to grow certain labour-intensive crops with the explicit intent of guaranteeing local agricultural labourers their basic subsistence. Informants from the older generation within the dominant caste of landowners in Chikhligam assured me that Mukhtyar's report was correct. They, too, said that there was a close linkage between sugarcane cultivation and the *hali* system which had continued until the completion of the struggle for Independence, and the remnants of which I encountered during my initial fieldwork. This also applied to Gandevigam, the second village of my fieldwork. It is interesting to note that between 1942 and 1945 a factory in the main town of Gandevi *taluka* produced white sugar, for which it employed only local labour. Informants assured me that in those days care for the entire growing cycle, from planting to cane-cutting and transport to the factory, was left entirely to local Halpatis (Breman 1990: 560).

I have digressed briefly into the history of sugarcane cultivation in south Gujarat to illustrate that the decision by managements of the new farmers' co-operatives to discontinue employing members of the largest landless caste in the region cannot be explained as due to the latter's non-familiarity with this kind of work. Although Halpatis were employed in former times, they have had to make way for outsiders since the modernization of crop production in the last few decades. Replacement took place not gradually and to some extent, but suddenly and completely. I have devoted a number of publications to the recent development of this flourishing agro-industry, to the exclusive use in the harvest campaign of migrants who work in gangs led by jobbers, and to the conditions under which these labour nomads have to live and work, and therefore refer to them here only briefly (Breman 1978/79, 1985b, 1990). Within their own rural domain and in their own tested field of employment, the local landless have been replaced by alien workers coming from distant destinations. I shall discuss the logic of this pattern of circulation in subsequent chapters.

Road construction and production of building materials

The building and repair of roads is a speciality of tribal labour originating from the Panch Mahals in Central Gujarat, and of the Kathiawadis from the western peninsular of the state. In the environs of Chikhligam and Gandevigam and during the dry winter and summer months, I have repeatedly come across gangs of road workers from those regions. It is my impression that the composition of this workforce is now more diverse than in the past. Over the years, recruitment has been extended to other regions. However, the hundred labourers who, in January 1986, asphalted the main road between Chikhli and Valsad were all tribal Bhils from the

Panch Mahals. The men did skilled work, the women and children acted as their helpers. They ate and slept along the roadside, in a bivouac that was moved as work progressed. The group was divided into two gangs of fifty workers each, led by a foreman. These *mukadams* recruited their gang members on the contractor's orders and stayed with them throughout the season. It was a big job and it looked as though the workers would be there for some months. But that would depend on the contractor. The *mukadams* have roved through all Gujarat together with the contractor, but their work gangs differ each year in composition. The manner of building these primary roads demands some degree of training: laying the gravel, pouring the asphalt; a few skilled workers operate the tar-spreading machine, steamroller, etc. This labour division does not apply to workers who widen or harden country roads on the orders of local builders, but even they are often seasonal migrants from other regions. Early in 1972 I met such a group not far from Chikhligam. In my diary I described this meeting as follows.

The road from Atgam to Dungari is closed for repairs. On both sides, down the slopes, men are breaking the ground with pickaxes. Women carry away the clods of earth in iron pans. They clamber with their headloads up the verge to where others stand ready to spread the material over the road surface and to pulverize it. There is no machinery, which perhaps explains why there are so many people. Four foremen-labour contractors are in charge of gangs totalling 200 workers. Two-thirds of these come from Saurashtra, the remainder from Dharampur in the eastern hills of south Gujarat. The former belong to the untouchable Vankar caste, the latter are tribal Kuknas. The work is paid on a piecework basis and is carried out by the entire family. Each day the *mukadam* measures the ground that has been covered by each work team. That amount is the basis for their payment, depending on the total labour power of husband, wife and children. Each week they are paid an advance, calculated on the amount of work done, with which to meet their primary necessities. The balance that remains after deduction of such advances and loans is not paid out until the end of the season. The contractor cannot keep them for long. Everyone wants to return to the village to cultivate the land before the first rains fall. Once they reach home, they at least have a roof over their heads. Then also they can enjoy the intimacy of family life. Here, everything has to be done in the open field – not only cooking and sleeping, but also making love or quarrelling with one another.

Stone is needed not only for road construction but also for the foundations of all buildings, and is quarried in numerous places throughout south Gujarat. In 1972, 1982, 1984 and 1986 I visited some of them in the sub-districts Chikhli, Valod and Pardi. Over the years, I have made the quarries near the main town of Chikhli my special target. When I first went there I found approximately ten quarries being exploited by private concessionaries. Previously, only the Public Works Department had obtained stone from there. The development of the region's infrastructure necessitated a greater volume of material, however, and more and more contractors started to open up their own quarries. Those encountered in the neighbourhood of Chikhli were all road builders who operated on a small scale and rarely accepted work outside south Gujarat. The quarries were located next to one another and each employed about fifty men and women. These were Dhodhiyas and some Halpatis, marginal peasants and landless people from the surrounding villages who came in the morning and returned home at night. Open-cast mining meant that work had to be stopped in the rainy season. This was convenient, however, because these small peasants were then engaged in growing crops, and it would have been impossible for the quarry owners to find labour. The workers reported again only after having harvested paddy in October.

The method of extraction was very simple, depending chiefly on manual labour. The only machine was a compressor which provided the power necessary to drill holes in the rock face. Dynamite was then placed in the holes and exploded. The quarrymen wrenched loose chunks of rock which they then broke up with sledge-hammers. Their wives carried these smaller lumps to a level stretch of land where they and the children hammered them to pieces. This was all done on a piece-work basis, paid per *brass*, i.e. the contents of a filled bin equalling a weight of four tons. Two such bins filled the trucks in which the crushed stone was taken away. Looking down the hill from above, I saw a crawling mass of some hundreds of men, women and children all working together in family groups. In each quarry a contractor's agent kept an eye on production and administered its progress. The *modus operandi* was similar to that observed by Koelen almost ten years later in a quarry in Valod (Koelen 1985). There, too, the stone-hewers were men, helped by their wives, for whom this work was additional to their agricultural work in the neighbouring village. In 1984 I visited another quarry in Valod, sited alongside the river where I found a contractor from Saurashtra who had hired stone-hewers from Maharashtra for the season. He had brought them that year because, in his opinion, the local workers were no good. They reported for work very irregularly and stayed away for days or even weeks at a time. He found the migrants satisfactory. They lived in an isolated bivouac at the worksite and, if only for that reason, were readily available throughout the season. In the stone-crushing mill just outside the chief town of Valod, where the product of several quarries was processed, I found fifteen tribal workers from the immediate neighbourhood. With the exception of the machine operator and the man who dropped the big chunks of stone into the crusher, they were all women and young girls.

When I returned in 1986 to the quarries near Chikhli I found that they had increased to over thirty, and that output had expanded considerably. A proud manager showed me high-tech equipment operated by two men, which could do the work for which nearly 100 men and women were previously needed. Stone production has become big business, a scale extension emphasized by transfer of the concessions to large entrepreneurs. Ashok Brothers from Vadodara, road builders who contract projects throughout all west India, belong to this category. To save on transport costs, they exploit a number of quarries situated as closely as possible to their various worksites. Trucks ride back and forth, tractors with excavator buckets remove the top soil and open up the hillside at two or three levels. The rock face is punctured with pneumatic drills. The increase in capital intensity in this quarry has brought a complicated division of work and a prolonged season. Work is only halted when rainfall is heavy, to be resumed immediately afterwards on the top level which is least affected by flooding.

The most significant change from the viewpoint of my research was the complete replacement of locals by migrant workers. The specialized machine operators all belong to higher castes and enjoy formal conditions of employment. This does not, however, apply to the approximately 150 migrants who, as seasonal workers, have set up camp on the open plain at the foot of the quarry – a collection of huts made of reed mats. They are members of low castes from Sholapur in Maharashtra, while others have come all the way from Karnataka. They have been working in this quarry for some years now, brought in by the same contractor for whom they had done road-building work nearer their home village. The male stone-hewers and their female helpers together with working children are divided into gangs led by a *thekadar*. These gang bosses are responsible for recruitment in the home area as well as for supervising the work.

I found a similar change in business management in the quarry south of Valsad, of which Western Railways is a major and regular customer. In 1986 the new owner of the modest quarry which I had visited much earlier proved to have spent a great deal of money on technological improvements in order to meet the rapidly growing demand for stone. For example, he had installed movable rails along which stone could be brought in tilting carts from the quarry down to the road, and an air pressure pipe runs upwards to the top of the hill to power the pneumatic drills. Production is stopped for two months during the monsoon, just because work is hindered by flooding. It is not stopped in order that local workers may devote themselves to agricultural work. They are no longer needed since the coming of about 150 migrants from Khandesh in western Maharashtra. Elsewhere in India also, stone quarries are surprisingly often operated by long-distance work migrants. The workforce for open-cast mining in Madhya Pradesh, for example, originates in Tamil Nadu. Similar enterprises in Haryana use migrants from Madhya Pradesh, Maharashtra, Rajasthan and Bihar. The stone quarries of Allahabad in Uttar Pradesh also work with such outside labour (Das 1990: 23).

I have already mentioned that there are now far more brickyards in south Gujarat than previously. Just as in the case of quarries there is not much literature available on these major rural industries which can be found in widely different parts of India. A common feature is that they operate on a seasonal basis and seem to depend each and everywhere mainly on migrant labour (see Das 1993). The brickfields in the region of my research are situated mostly near the principal urban and industrial centres: between Surat and Navsari, on the road from Valsad to Vapi, and around Bilimora and Bardoli. I visited all these worksites between 1972 and 1991, usually to meet Halpatis from Chikhligam who travel to these destinations as seasonal labourers. The majority of these brickyards are not registered, and those located further from the roadside are not noticed by the passer-by. On my frequent journeys by motorbike through the western plain area I never failed to come across new brickfields, some of which proved to have functioned for many years. At the beginning of the 1960s, according to the Surat District Gazetteer, the industry provided work for approximately 3,000 workers in south Gujarat for eight months per year (*Gazetteer of India*, Gujarat State 1962: 455). Even at that time, this must have heavily underestimated the workforce, whose size can now only be guessed at. If, on the basis of my research results for 1990, we assume at least 750 brickyards, each employing from 40–50 workers (with considerable deviation on either side), this gives a total workforce of some 30,000–40,000.

Brickyards can be divided into two categories, based primarily on the technology applied. *Bata* is the name given to small units whose owners do not need much starting capital. Land is the principal resource and has to be sufficiently available at or near the workplace. Cash advances then have to be made to hire a sufficient supply of labour for the entire season. Finally, a number of other production costs have to be met: the possible digging of a well, the ordering of some truckloads of coal ash and rice husks. Adequate financial means, as also sound technical know-how of all manufacturing aspects, have to be available if the business is to run successfully. This is immediately needed in making a suitable choice of worksite, and is further shown in experience with production methods and work organization. Understanding the market and knowledge of how to do business with customers are also prerequisites for successful entrepreneurship.

The raw material is mixed and kneaded, and bricks are shaped, by a work gang consisting of nine to eleven men, women and children. The bricks are taken wet from the mould and left in rows to dry for some days. They are then piled tightly in alternate layers and coal ash is mingled with rice husk. This heap forms the oven, the actual *bata*, which is then fired. When the pile of bricks has burned out and cooled off, the end product is ready for sale in the market. The oven thus consists of the bricks themselves and has to be built anew each time. The volume of the *bata* ranges to a maximum of 75,000 bricks. The time necessary to prepare this quantity varies with the number of work gangs, each producing 2,500–3,000 bricks per day.

Work in the second type of brickyard is similarly organized, but after the bricks have been formed and dried they are taken to a fixed oval-shaped oven built round a chimney. Manufacture is both larger in scale and technologically more advanced. The oven, which has a capacity of 300,000–450,000 bricks, is divided into sections. While bricks are being baked in one or more of them, using coal as fuel, other sections are simultaneously being filled or emptied. The smaller type of establishment allows flexibility. Within the margins of his workforce, the owner can react to changing demand by making more *batas* or less, thus producing in accordance with the flow of sales. Greater overheads and the need to maintain a more equal rate of production entail that a big entrepreneur will only decide to build a chimney if sufficient raw material is available nearby and if a large and above all regular turnover is likely at the end of the production chain. For the owner of a *bata*, the purchase of a lorry is of greater importance to his market position than a surge to greater volume, with all the risks that this implies. Giving priority to buying a motored vehicle counteracts the difficult accessibility of his business and makes him less dependent on customers who are able to come and collect the product themselves at the worksite. Most brickyard owners belong to local castes and have varying social backgrounds. The trade has great attraction for members of the Kumbhar (Potters) caste who nowadays present themselves as Prajapatis and mostly own small brickyards. The entrepreneurs owning chimneys include Parsis, Desais and members of other high castes. A few Koli Patels, clearly on their way up as industrialists, told me that their initial capital had been earned during their stay in the Gulf as contract labourers. Finally, an increasing number of owners come from Saurashtra in south Gujarat. Originally potters and members of related castes, they were attracted by the enormous growth of the building trade and in production of the necessary materials. Like the workers, these migrant entrepreneurs return home at the end of the season.

Does the setting up of more and more brickyards in south Gujarat mean that the marginal peasants and landless who form the workforce can now find employment close to home? To a certain degree, yes. Over the years, Halpatis and Dhodhiyas from Chikhligam who used to go to Bombay, can be met much nearer the village; but not near enough to enable them to combine this seasonal work with living at home. Even when labour is employed at sites only 10–15 km from Chikhligam, which seldom occurs, daily commuting is out of the question. At most, migrants who are employed within a 100–150 km radius may occasionally return briefly to their homes during a 7–8 month season.

M is a widow and only allows herself to be recruited for brickyards that she can reach from Chikhligam in a fairly short time. That is because her two children have to stay in the village. The eight-year-old daughter is old enough to work together with her mother, but not the four-year-old son. Both thus stay at home where the girl looks after her little brother. The neighbours keep an eye on them. M returns home once a month to put affairs in order and to bring money for the coming weeks. This year she is working near Surat, and travelling back and forth is a heavy charge on her meagre budget. She leaves the brickyard early in the afternoon, reaches Chikhligam in the evening, and then stays until late the following afternoon. In this way she loses as little work as possible. On the other hand, she has no breathing space in which to recuperate. When she returns at the end of the season, M is worn out. (Fieldwork notes)

The rapid expansion of the brick industry in south Gujarat has brought an influx of workers from far-flung areas. This is partly due to the complicated division of work in large-scale enterprises. Certain activities are reserved for workers who are thought to have a special skill. For example, chimney stokers invariably come from Uttar Pradesh, while the transport of bricks at the worksite from the drying place to the kiln and emptying the oven after the baking process, are entrusted to mule drivers from north Gujarat and Rajasthan. Even the brick-makers are increasingly brought from outside the region. Why? Again it is said to be due to reasons of industrial management. The local work gang of 9–11 members, called *surthi*, is vulnerable. If one worker is absent, the day's production falls. Employers try to counter this problem by replacing the *surthi*, wholly or partially, with Khandeshis from Maharashtra who work in teams of two or three. This system is sometimes called *hajaria*, which implies that a three-member team (man, woman and working child) account for the production of 1,000 bricks per day. That explanation is implausible, however, in view of the fact that many migrants are also employed under the *surthi* method. Wouldn't it be more logical to suggest that, due to the enormous expansion of the industry, the demand for labour is far greater than the local supply? But then this too lacks conviction, because the flow of migrants from central Gujarat (Vadodara, Anand) and Saurashtra to brickyards in the south of the state is countered by an outflow of similar labour, including Halpatis from Chikhligam, to those places. Seasonal work and labour migration are obviously closely linked and both phenomena have to be understood in the light of their interacting dynamics.

Agrarian labour migrants in Gandevigam and Chikhligam

The impression frequently given that by and large agricultural work used to be done until recently by local labour only is misleading. In the report on my initial fieldwork I discussed how landowners in Gandevigam assigned all digging work to Kathiawadis. In the dry season when there is little if anything to do in Saurashtra, these transients came to the villages of south Gujarat in search of work. Another example was the arrival of Biladias. These were mostly Halpatis from the neighbourhood of Bilad railway station, to the south of my fieldwork area, who were hired in gangs by mango traders to pick fruit that had been bought from growers sometimes long before harvest. It is a fact, however, that some twenty years ago the inflow of migrant labour began to increase strongly. In discussing my renewed fieldwork ten years after my first stay in Gandevigam and Chikhligam, I drew attention to this trend (Breman 1974: 245). Even then, the phenomenon seemed so significant that I decided to devote a separate study to it based on fieldwork carried out in Bardoli and its surroundings between 1977 and 1982 (Breman 1985b). The large-scale influx of temporary workers, mostly for harvesting activities, which I observed in this more northern part of the plain, has also occurred in Gandevigam and Chikhligam. The workers are almost all Dangis and Kuknas, tribal peasants from the eastern hills bordering Maharashtra. The need to earn more cash on the one hand and the increasing paucity of land – due to population pressure, and in particular to the felling of forests which had provided many sorts of subsidiary income – on the other hand, have caused increasing outflow of labour to the plains of south Gujarat which starts immediately after the monsoon. In my fieldwork diary in 1991 I wrote about these migrants as follows:

Informants told me that a persistent drought in 1973–74 had accelerated their outflow for part of the year. Acute starvation drove them from their homes, and Anavil farmers in Chikhligam found them prepared to work for a whole day for nothing more than a meal. In 'normal' years these migrant workers come in groups of 10 to 15 men and women around harvest time of the various crops in order, as they themselves said, to satisfy their need for money. They bring their own food for the duration of their stay. They can be met along the road, walking one behind the other in file. The adults carry pots and supplies on their heads and often a child on the arm. It is not a case of aimless wandering. The migrants go directly to addresses where they have been before and old contacts send them on to possible new employers. They do not migrate for an indefinite time but for a few weeks only, until the grain brought with them is exhausted. The gang then returns home, to make the following trip with the same or other people. Arrangements made long beforehand and sometimes sealed with a cash advance, contribute to the fairly tight rhythm that characterizes seasonal migration. This is a tidal flow that largely escapes the sight of outsiders. (Fieldwork notes)

These migratory groups take part in the harvesting of paddy and grass and carry out all agricultural work assigned to them by the farmers. But this is not all. In December 1989 I watched the arrival of twelve Kukna men, women and children at a brickworks situated on the main road near Chikhli, where I had spent the day. One man went up to the owner, leaving his companions waiting at the roadside. There was work for them to do: sifting a heap of coal that had arrived that same afternoon. The owner made a deal for the whole job, to be paid on completion. The group started work immediately. The owner told me that transient workers did not always accept his terms. If they did not like the offer, they went away without further negotiations. It is futile to try to persuade them to stay longer. They have their own time schedule and intended destination which, in his experience, could not be meddled with. Although unpredictable and intractable they are reputed to be very hardworking!

This can also be said of the Khandeshis who come to both Chikhligam and Gandevigam for cane-cutting. They do this heavy work on the orders of sugar co-operatives on the central plain, who contract them for the entire season. When all the fields in the neighbourhood have been harvested, they move their bivouac on to the next village. In this way they spend the period between early November and the end of May rotating over the canefields which are under the command of the Gandevi and Valsad factories. Finally, owners of mango and chiku orchards in Gandevigam are assured of the services of Dangis who arrive after the rainy season and stay until the end of summer. The number of these migrants is so large that, according to landowners, the supply of agricultural labourers available locally increases by one-fifth to one-quarter during that time (Breman 1993b: 290). The Dangis are tribals from the Dangs district to the east. The men usually travel alone, but sometimes with all their family, and set up camp in the dry bed of the Ambika river for the duration of their stay.

Given the predominance of agriculture in the area of my fieldwork, it is hardly surprising that seasonal migrants are mainly to be found working in the fields. That it does not end there can be illustrated with an example regarding Chikhligam.

When B was politically active in the Congress party at the end of the 1970s, he was also working as building contractor. Thanks to his connections, he and his Koli partner were given the licence to build subsidized houses for agricultural labourers in the *taluka*. To economize on building costs, B started to manufacture bricks. He appropriated a piece of land in the village for the purpose and kept a check on the gang of brick-makers who were contracted for the work. These were Kathiawadi from Bhavnagar in Saurasthra. Why did he not use the local Halpatis? B told me that he had relied on his partner who, as building contractor, was familiar with these outside workers. (Fieldwork notes)

Some time later it was proved that this was no coincidence. In 1984, at the end of the country road that links Chikhligam with the highway and barely 5 km from the village, I found a brickworks that had only recently been opened and whose workforce consisted entirely of seasonal migrant labourers. In the initial years these were principally Khandeshis. A new owner, whom I met on my return in 1986, gave preference to Kathiawadis, and had recruited about 100 workers from Bhavnagar. Paradoxically, the arrival of these newcomers was countered by the departure of almost an equal number of Halpatis and Dhodhiyas from Chikhligam to other destinations, including Bhavnagar, to seek work in the brickworks there! In the same way I found that the Kodinar sugar factory in western Saurashtra imports gangs of cane cutters all the way from the Panch Mahals district bordering on Madya Pradesh at the same time that a huge army of seasonal migrants has to leave the peninsula in order to survive during the dry winter months. The mechanics that sets this flow of similar labour going in differing and sometimes opposite directions for a season or longer, requires further explanation. The mass circulation of labour at the bottom of Gujarat's economy, which seems at first sight highly irrational, is a central theme of this study and will be examined further in later chapters.

According to a widespread notion the market for agrarian labour is distinctly local in character. This view is also upheld by Dasgupta without any reservation:

it has been observed widely in Indian villages that the agricultural labour market is closed, in that the hiring of labour across neighbouring villages is rare. Each village is an enclave. One reason employers may not wish to hire workers from a different village is that they are unknown commodities. Hiring them would involve large risks; 'foreign' workers may be unreliable, or simply incompetent. (Dasgupta 1993: 235)

It is not only that quantitative and qualitative evidence pertaining to south Gujarat tells a different story. I would even argue, as stated before, that the situation prevalent in the region of my fieldwork signals a trend which is manifest in other regions as well. Labour mobility, both rural-urban and intra-rural, is indeed a widespread phenomenon in South Asia. The inflow and outflow of migrants is part and parcel of a more general pattern of wage labour circulation and is not an almost incidental characteristic of the situation in the area of my research in west India. The authors of a recent survey of labour migration at the all-India level link the growing significance of this phenomenon with increasing disparities that mark the process of economic development in various parts of the country. They identify the rural army of unskilled and illiterate labour as being landless or landpoor from the agricultural-economic point of view, and as members of Scheduled Castes/Tribes or Other Backward Classes from the social viewpoint. Acute poverty forces these people to leave their villages, at least for a part of the year and frequently even longer (Shah et al. 1990: 7–17). Gujarat is identified as a state in which this process has developed to a strong degree. That verdict finds confirmation in another source which states that seasonal migration in various regions of Gujarat is now an integral part of the lives of the landless. A more detailed study in an 'outflow' district has shown that 50–85 per cent of total work-days per year are spent on locations away from the village and mostly also away from the district where the workers live. On the other hand, in a 'reception' district the percentage of migrant labour rose between 1964 and 1974 from almost nothing to about 20 per cent (B. B. Patel 1987: 143–5). Such data cause me to conclude that labour mobility such as I have observed in the countryside of south Gujarat has become the rule rather than the exception.

4 Contact between demand and supply

Labour market in a state of flux

South Gujarat is a clearing house for labour that comes and goes. In the course of the research reported on in this publication, Chikhligam and Gandevigam were my points of departure for moving around into the countryside. To find out how the rural proletariat is making its living I had to leave the villages of my fieldwork which only provide employment to many of the local landless for part of the year. In the first instance, this made it necessary to survey the sectors and locations in which the workers from Chikhligam and Gandevigam ended up, usually temporarily. Secondly, I could not avoid examining the question of why the marginal and landless peasants who represent the principal target group of this study, profit so remarkably little from the strong growth in urban and rural employment in the cities and countryside of south Gujarat. The purpose of this chapter is to show how people come into contact with employment possibilities away from the village. The chapter starts with a brief exposition of what I consider to be the principal characteristics of those who participate in labour migration.

The flow of migrants travelling to and fro can be divided on the basis of the rhythm of circulation: i.e. the period of time involved; the distance that needs to be covered between departure and arrival point; and finally, the principal personal characteristics of the migrant, such as sex, age, and social-economic status in the area of origin. Based on these three criteria I shall elaborate on the extensive labour mobility that is going on.

The circulation rhythm is shortest among labourers who leave the village early in the morning and return in the evening, daily commuting which is now more common than formerly. At the other extreme are those migrants who leave the village for an indefinite time but are, nevertheless, unable to settle permanently in the new milieu. In between is that sizeable category of seasonal workers which is again divided into those who take short trips lasting a few weeks and those who stay away for six to eight months. The period of absence is sometimes spent at one place of employment; others, however, such as cane cutters and other harvest workers, are obliged to move continually. Those who have managed to gain a foothold in the urban economy include many who frequently change employer, sometimes in a rhythm that hardly differs from that of the seasonal migrants.

The duration of absence from home seems to increase in accordance with the distance. Harvest workers from the eastern hills sometimes travel on foot to the villages in the plain, a journey that they make two or three times in the dry winter and summer months. Cane cutters, road workers and brick-makers, for example, usually migrate to more distant sites of employment and, in principle, do not return until the beginning of the monsoon. They remain sufficiently near home, however, to be able to return for a brief visit in between if this should become necessary. They are usually reluctant to do so more often not only in view of the travel expenses but also because of the difficulty involved in getting away from the work assigned to them, even for a few days. Semi-permanent migrants such as the powerloom operators and the diamond cutters in Surat try to take an annual holiday in order to spend a few weeks with their families who have stayed back in the village. Such an interruption in the work pattern, however, can mean the end of their present employment.

Most people reaching the city arrive straight from their village of origin. This does not necessarily mean that they have never been 'out' before. Various slum-dwellers whom I met in Surat had worked before in Calcutta or Bombay, destinations to which they went quite haphazardly. Typical for such personal case histories is the story told by a man from Uttar Pradesh who left his village as a young boy, after quarrelling with his father, on the spur of the moment.

I did not know where to go, but I knew I had to go away from home. I was on the railway platform without a ticket. I got in one train as many of our villagers were getting in. I came to know on the train that the train was going to Calcutta. After some time I met one *bhaiya* who was from my district. First, I told him that I was going to visit one of my relatives at Calcutta, but afterwards when we got friendly I narrated the true story to him. When we got down at Howrah station I was caught by a ticket collector. I had to give him all the money I had in my pocket. My friend took me with him. He was staying in one slum in the city and was selling fruits in a stall. I stayed in Calcutta only for 15–20 days. Everyday he took me with him to his fruit stall. I helped him in his work and stayed with him. As I had never gone out of my village during my childhood, I was feeling homesick. All the time I was thinking about my mother. I missed her so much that I felt like going back home. But when I remembered my father I gave up that idea. I did not like Calcutta. So one day when we were at the fruit stall I left him and ran away. (Lobo 1994: 50)

Nevertheless, 90 per cent of the inhabitants of this particular slum are first-time migrants who have come directly to Surat from their native place. It would still be misleading to generalize this finding. According to a survey which focused on the Oriya workers employed in the textile industry, many of the interviewed had already a migratory record before joining their countrymen in Surat. Not less than one-quarter had prior experience of working outside Orissa for which they went all the way to Kashmir, Maharashtra, Calcutta, Bihar or Assam (Barik 1985: 6). What most employers in the textile business assume to be fresh hands from the countryside are actually quite often seasoned sojourners who have been on the road not for the first time. Of course, Orissa is one of those areas from which labour has been extracted temporarily or permanently for more than one century, going in various directions within the country and also abroad. This large-scale and persistent mobility makes it all the more urgent to initiate further research on the social identity and occupational track records of workers who make a halt in cities like Surat but then also leave again.

Labour migrants travel individually or as families. The first of these is the pattern followed by people who continue to live in the village and commute daily to seek work in the close vicinity. These include both men and women, although the former are in the majority. This is not because women can afford to remain excluded from the daily struggle to maximize income but because they turn out to be less employable due to shortage of work. Women's mobility is restricted by the caring tasks assigned to them in the household sphere. That obligation also exists for divorced women and widows, but within the landless milieu they are, for lack of support, quite often forced to leave the home in order to make a living. Those who seek semi-permanent employment in the town also do so mostly on an individual basis. The reason why they do not lose the status of migrant, even in their own consciousness, is linked to their inability to allow family members to accompany them. It sometimes happens that single women and older children manage to reach an urban destination – to work mostly as street vendors, domestic servants or prostitutes – but this category of labour who leave the village for an indefinite period also consists mostly of men in the 15–40 age group. In contrast, seasonal workers frequently travel as family groups. The company of wife and children is generally indispensable if the family is to be assured of sufficient income. It does sometimes happen that married men go away for seasonal work while their wives stay at home, but in that case sufficient reserves must be available to provide for those who stay back. Though rarely, married women occasionally work away from the village temporarily while leaving their family at home, perhaps forced to do so by illness or disability of the husband. In such situations, parents may even send fairly young children to seek work without adult accompaniment.

A high percentage of the migrant masses who do casual work or who have no more than semi-permanent employment belong to the lower echelons of the caste hierarchy. In the rural economy they represent small or marginal peasants and landless labourers. As income from labour falls and, concomitantly, the use made of it is shortened, the proportion of landowners among the migrants declines and that of the landless increases. In this way, the gradual penetration of Dhodhiyas in Chikhligam to permanent and better-paid work outside agriculture and the village is accompanied by declining interest among members of this caste for the annual trek to the brickworks. Dhodhiya males who are not able to withdraw from such employment of the last resort at least try to spare their wives and children. But this option is actually available only to those who have a plot of land and a few cattle, property that needs care and which provides at the same time a sufficient livelihood for those who remain behind. It is not for altruistic reasons that men in the milieu of small peasants leave their families at home. This strategy is rather due to a combination of the need to supplement their income through work away from home, which necessitates their absence for a shorter or longer period, and the impracticability of permanently snapping their ties with the village. Women must remain in the village to compensate for the vulnerability caused by the absence of the men.

The mass exodus and influx of cheap labour is an outstanding characteristic of the economy of south Gujarat. This two-way mobility, which at first sight perhaps makes an extremely amorphous and diffuse impression, proves on further analysis to be not in the least chaotic but, on the contrary, well-structured. This can be illustrated with the aid of the strategy followed by labour migrants in my fieldwork villages. Their declining employment in agriculture is compensated by members of the local proletariat in Gandevigam by temporary employment in other economic sectors. They circulate, mostly as casual labour, through a considerable gamut of trades and workplaces outside the village which are to be found in or along the road to Bilimora. This booming town is situated close to the village, at a distance that can be bridged at little cost and time. Company buses that ply in the large urban centres are intended solely for formal sector workers. In fact, this mode of transport is one of the privileges reserved for higher echelons of the labour hierarchy. Entrepreneurs of industrial estates in Bilimora and other places along the north–south railway line have never even thought of picking up their unskilled workers by bus from the distant hinterland. And why should they? The supply of labour reporting voluntarily at the gate is already greater than their needs. Such an attitude explains why so few people from Chikhligam have managed to penetrate these more distant alternative sources of employment. As a result, the landless underclass in my second fieldwork village is compelled to continue the pattern of seasonal migration which originated more than fifty years ago. From Chikhligam alternative sources of employment are far less easily accessible. Halpatis in particular are thus forced to continue the pattern of seasonal migration which started several generations ago. The inflow of enormous numbers of long-distance migrants into the towns and cities of south Gujarat is definitely not the result of prior moving out to other destinations of surplus labour that otherwise could have been tapped nearer home in the rural hinterland. There is no such direct linkage between exodus and influx.

Mediation

How do the migrants find employment? By going to places where they have been earlier or where family members, caste mates, etc. have been before them. That simple rule needs further specification, however, by distinguishing between those who leave the village singly or with a small group of relatives or neighbours while retaining the right to use their own initiative, and those who do so in a more regulated fashion as members of a larger gang that is headed by a group leader.

Among the first category many will have been away before for a similar purpose. It seldom occurs that workers just leave on the spur of the moment and haphazardly, without any idea of where they are going and for an indeterminate period. Even the transients who called in at Gandevigam and Chikhligam more or less incidentally and who enquired of landowning peasants if they had any work, were on the way to a predetermined destination and adhered to a more or less well-defined timetable. The harvest workers who came to my fieldwork villages had often been there before and on their last visit had entered into a rather loose agreement with the farmers about their return in due course. In a number of cases a message went to or came from the migrants' home village during the rainy season preceding the harvest to clinch the arrangement by paying earnest money. The creditor then had the first right to the migrants' labour power when they reached their destination. Not until the work has been finished do the harvest migrants seek another job, frequently being introduced by their last employer to the new one. When incomers have worked for some time for one landowner to mutual satisfaction, as in the case of some *dangis* in Gandevigam's orchards, a more permanent tie may be formed which is renewed each year (cf. Breman 1985b: 226–30; 1993b: 289–90).

Introduction to an employer is more important when it concerns continuous employment for an unlimited period. Lack of sufficient contacts outside the village and their own work sphere means that marginal peasants and landless labourers face problems in taking the plunge. Halpatis from Gandevigam who, during the past few years, have managed to gain employment on industrial estates in Bilimora, have done so thanks to the recommendation of others. These are usually workers already employed by a factory and who are prepared to vouch for a newcomer's suitability and antecedents. If the latter prove inadequate or intractable, the employer not only shows his direct displeasure but can also bring pressure to bear on him through the person of the mediator. Given the fact that it is usually relatives, friends, neighbours and caste fellows who provide such a linkage, the presence of a collective bridgehead is of decisive significance for access to an arena of employment. The isolation, both physical and social, that characterizes the habitat of Halpatis in the countryside of south Gujarat is illustrated by the lack of such essential support. Those who turn to a potential patron in order to seek *olkhan* or *lagvag*, terms which imply recommendation and protection, are seldom the most vulnerable. Halpatis, especially, seem to lack the wherewithal, financial means and contacts which the relatively better endowed with these resources are able to mobilize. This is also the reason why members of the landless caste in my fieldwork villages are tardier in qualifying for alternative employment opportunities that have sprung up than the Kolis of Gandevigam and increasingly also the Dhodhiyas of Chikhligam. Halpatis usually do not have outside channels of their own and for that reason are more dependent on guidance by members of higher castes in their endeavours to find work away from the village (see also van der Veen 1979: 56–7). This applies to those who work as domestic servants in Bombay as well as to youths who manage to be taken on as apprentices in a diamond atelier. In the latter case, the leap away from the village is also a considerable forward jump from the economic point of view, and one which has to be paid for. In his research report on the spread of the diamond industry throughout the countryside, Koelen discusses the fairly exceptional case of a Halpati youth, the only one of his caste, whom he found in a workplace:

The cutter's father had worked for over 20 years as *rojio* (an agricultural labourer who comes daily) for a Kanbi Patel landowner who, a few years ago, had started a diamond cutting business in his village Butwada in Valod. Due to this long-term relationship the son was able to learn the trade and, exceptionally, to pay his apprenticeship fee in arrears. (Koelen 1985: 79)

This example can be supplemented with cases from my own fieldwork. Not only do landless labourers have to depend on vertical rather than horizontal contacts in their urge to make progress, but they also have to realize that ambition without being able to pay the price in cash usually asked for it. The advance made by landowning Kolis and Dhodhiyas over Halpatis, who have no form of capital, is due not least to the economic reserves available to the slightly higher castes of small and marginal peasants. A job in the formal sector has to be bought in most cases, but the co-operation of those who protect access to semi-permanent work in the informal sector also demands payment of a premium which fluctuates according to the level and regularity of earnings. The majority of landless households are unable to pay that levy for climbing over the barrier to a better livelihood. They are even obliged to refuse work if, instead of receiving a cash advance, they would not be paid until the job was finished. Koelen who, like me, found more marginal peasants than agricultural labourers from neighbouring villages at work in the stone quarries, gives the following feasible explanation:

A significant objection by the Dublas [a name that has fallen into disuse for Halpatis] against work in the quarry was that they were not given any cash advance; they said that they saw no possibility of bridging the period to the first payment – one or two weeks – without payment of an advance. (Koelen 1985: 107)

The social discrimination which rural Halpatis still continue to suffer in the economic transformation process pursues them into the urban employment arena. This finding, based on my fieldwork, is confirmed by Devyani Punalekar's study of the effects of the incorporation of a village on the outskirts of Surat into the agglomeration's municipal borders. While the prosperity of the other inhabitants, mainly Patidars and Kolis, improved considerably, this happened only exceptionally for members of the landless caste due to their virtual inability to penetrate to more skilled and better paid occupations. Out of 239 Halpatis who constituted the economically active within their households, 170 scraped a living as domestic servant or as casual labourer. Only a few dozen had been able to qualify as diamond cutter or textile worker, the predominant occupations in Surat. The women worked almost exclusively as domestic servants for members of the higher castes (D. S. Punalekar 1992). Vyas, who found a similar situation almost twenty years earlier in his research among the town's Halpatis, explained why more than half of all Halpati women did such work: 'Dubla females are normally preferred for this type of work as they are believed to be honest, hardworking and docile' (Vyas 1979: 110).

It will frequently be shown below that such 'explanations' are standard when an answer has to be given to questions regarding the relationship between social identities and occupational categories. Many Halpati males who, in Punalekar's study, had unconsciously been converted from villagers into urban inhabitants, made their living with casual labour. *Parchuran kam* is the term given to this sort of occasional work, and expresses the fact that those who thus earn their living have to be prepared to undertake any job that comes their way. Even the maximum possible flexibility that is demanded of them, however, cannot prevent them often being deprived of any income for days on end.

The absorptive capacity of the informal sector is not unrestricted. That conclusion refutes the optimistic reasoning that anyone who wishes can set up business in the urban streets. Competition is great, and those who have secured a niche for themselves will fight tooth and nail to defend it against newcomers. Such clashes occur at all levels, even between adults and children. Porters at Surat's railway station, for instance, chase away child coolies whom they accuse of 'stealing the bread from their mouths':

Often they complain to railway authority and on occasion they catch them and physically produce them before the railway police. The railway police admonish them. It takes usually two to three years for a child coolie to establish proper acquaintance with licensed coolies and railway authorities. Then alone he can get needed legitimacy and freedom to operate as a coolie. (S. P. Punalekar 1993: 110–11)

How do the migrants who pour into the town in such large numbers from other parts of India find any opening? Ninety per cent of the workers from Orissa who have invaded Surat's textile industry during the last twenty years came from just one district; moreover, half of them belong to the same caste (Barik 1987: 168–9). Newcomers are accompanied on their first journey or are met when they reach the city by relatives or fellow villagers who give them shelter, food and help in finding work. What goes together with taking care of 'our own men' in this way is that the employment niche that has been conquered is closed against competition from others. A survey of slum localities in Surat indicates that these habitats are based on the same lines of ethnic segmentation which give structure to the job market.

As high as 70 per cent of the Oriya workers are engaged in the textile sector mainly in the task of weaving. The Khandeshis are mainly engaged in jobs like carting, loading-unloading, unspecified casual jobs and wage labour in the construction activities. People from Uttar Pradesh are mostly found in various kinds of self employed and dyeing processing and related jobs in the textile sector. The fact that one can find Oriya, Andhra, Maharashtrian etc. slums inhabited almost entirely by people from these states suggests a mechanism by which the poor aim to develop defences against a possible urban environment by creating a similar structure that they leave behind. (Das 1993: 6)

Factory owners encourage this segmentation of the labour force along ethnic and communal dividing lines per industry by allowing 'loyal' and 'capable' workers to bring in a brother, nephew, friend or other close relation. This is not merely a favour but a conscious strategy on the part of employers for maintaining control over their present labour force notwithstanding a considerable and persistent turnover. Their reasons are illustrated by the following quotations, which refer to the workforce in the textile industry of Surat:

Selection and recruitment process is personalized. Generally close scrutiny is exercised as regards incumbent's past work experience, social behaviour and personal background. Queries are made as regards worker's behaviour with his supervisors, punctuality, state of solvency, etc. (*Working and Living Conditions* 1984: 65)

Nobody can get employment without proper recommendation, and the recommendation would normally go in favour of family members, immediate kin and villagers. Besides, the impression around here so far is that Oriya labourers are by nature hardworking, docile, sincere and submissive. (Barik 1987: 177, note 18)

The channel that is opened in this way includes a financial reward for those who mediate in the admission of newcomers. This may be a one-off payment but it can also be a percentage of the worker's earnings for some length of time (Barik 1987: 170). The owners of diamond workshops also use the services of such a fixer who for some years has belonged to their core staff of permanent workers. With the use of these confidants the industrialists not only take on apprentices but also temporarily expand their workforce in order to process an unusually large batch of diamonds on time (Koelen 1985: 82).

The role played by these mediators can become somewhat professionalized if entrepreneurs appoint somebody to take care of recruitment on their behalf. Such an agent is the jobber, called *mukadam* in my fieldwork area. He is then responsible for supplying employers with a prearranged number of workers at a given time. His task usually includes accompanying the gang that he collects to the workplace. This type of collective mediation is not coupled particularly to certain branches of industry but is to be found in all kinds of employment where systematic use is made of seasonal migrants. This is the manner in which large contingents of cane cutters, road workers, quarrymen, brick-makers and saltpan workers descend each year for a period of six to eight months on the plains of south Gujarat or, conversely, leave for similar destinations elsewhere. This catalogue shows that an enormous army of migrant workers is mobilized for a very broad range of activities which have already been discussed in previous chapters and which vary in scale of production as well. Cane cutting, for example, is agricultural work organized along industrial lines. In 1990 the Bardoli co-operative sugar factory hired about 15,000 workers for the duration of the harvesting campaign. On the other hand, most saltpans employ no more than a few dozen seasonal workers. A small brickyard can suffice with about twenty, while big establishments will require a few hundred men, women and children. Quarries and saltpans are found in rural surroundings, as is cane cutting of course. Road workers and brick-makers, however, come close to the urban milieu or even move right into it.

This survey is intended to show that seasonal migrants do both agricultural and industrial work, are deployed on both small and large scale, and do not let themselves be discriminated against in terms of rural or (semi-)urban destinations. They are governed by the fact that they are recruited by jobbers, and that they are moved to the worksite to be dismissed again at the end of the season. All these cases are concerned with work in the open air which is largely or entirely brought to a halt during the rainy season. That fluctuation determines the recruitment and dismissal of labour, and it is in that context that the jobber operates as mediator who bridges the gap that divides temporary employers and employees.

The jobber–gang boss as labour broker

The magnitude of seasonal migration in the landscape of labour in south Gujarat warrants special attention for the *modus operandi* of the jobber who also acts as boss of the work gang that he has recruited. Ambiguity is inherent to his role as mediator: he has the same origins as the workers but acts under orders from the employers.

During the rainy season, the co-operative sugar mills in the plain of south Gujarat use *mukadams* to recruit thousands of harvest workers for the duration of the coming campaign. In villages in the hinterland where the cane cutters originate, the jobbers hand out a cash advance to *koytas*, teams consisting of at least a man and a woman, sometimes accompanied by a child who also works. Several of these teams together – some ten, twenty or more – constitute the gang contracted by the *mukadam* and accompany him to the central plain when the rains are over. As gang boss he continues to be the link between the factory management and the migrants who have accompanied him. Work is allocated through his agency, he keeps a check on the daily state of affairs and organizes the distribution of the fortnightly cash and grain allowance; in addition, when the campaign ends, management settles the final account through him. He also holds absolute sway in the bivouac that the cane cutters set up for their night halt and which frequently has to be moved. I have extensively discussed the *modus operandi* of the *mukadam* in cane cutting in earlier publications from where more information can be gained about his key role in the work organization of this agro-industry (Breman 1978/79, 1990).

Within the framework of the present study, I want to focus primarily on jobbers who recruit gangs of outgoing seasonal migrants in the villages of south Gujarat on the orders of employers located elsewhere. Given its significance for members of the proletariat living in Chikhligam, I am interested above all in *mukadams* who recruit labour for the brickworks. Over time, in the course of my fieldwork, I have often watched from close quarters the activities of *mukadams*, not only in the home milieu but also in their role as gang boss at the place of employment. The profile that emerged has been rounded off with information gained by extending my fieldwork to other economic sectors marked by seasonality for which labour brokers form the linchpin. For this purpose I made frequent visits to villages in the neighbourhood of Chikhligam from where work gangs annually depart for the saltpans on the outskirts of Bombay, a type of migration that is just as old as that to the brickyards. These migrants and their headmen were also followed by me to their temporary worksites.

In all cases, recruitment starts during the rainy season when there is little work in agriculture. The consequent lack of income means that many marginal peasants and landless labourers have no other choice than to accept the advance held out as bait by the *mukadam*. They need money not only for food and other daily necessities, including alcohol, but also for such expenses which they can only meet once a year: a wedding in the family and repairs to the house. In the past, landowners were prepared to meet such needs by providing a loan that was repaid later in labour power, but they are no longer interested in binding labour in advance in this way. As a result, the jobber is one of the few whom the poorest people in the village can approach for obtaining credit, which they so desperately need in their struggle for survival and reproduction. The price they have to pay is the loss of any control over the hiring-out of their own labour power during the coming months. The jobber is given a lump sum by his sponsor to be used in this way. The distribution of that money, even when spread out over some months, is not without risk. I heard numerous stories about the unpredictability and especially the unreliability of labourers. In their attempt to get their hands on the highest amount of credit possible, Halpatis do not hesitate to accept cash advances from different and even conflicting sides. It sometimes happens that they collect earnest money without ever intending to go away and thus do not put in an appearance when the time comes to leave. This risk in itself shows how important it is that the jobbers are rooted in the same milieu as their catch. Only then are they able to assess the quality of the labour on offer, to judge who is suitable for heavy work and who will submit to management's rules without creating problems. It is also essential to be in close vicinity of the targets to ensure compliance with the labour contract. Finally, these considerations explain why *mukadams* recruit principally in their own village and its direct neighbourhood.

Most jobbers who have Chikhligam as their field of operations have themselves been employed in the brickworks from a young age onwards. What characteristics have caused them to be chosen for the advanced position that they occupy later in their migratory career? Thorough knowledge of the total work process through own practice helps the *mukadam* in keeping control over production in his role as work boss. The set of people he takes with him are contracted for particular tasks: invariably, the male brick-maker is assisted by nine to ten men, women and children who belong to his gang. In addition, there are men who accompany the truck or tractor as loaders–unloaders if the earth has to be brought from any distance, women who carry the ready-made bricks to and from the kiln, and a few other categories. The owner of a large brickworks will often keep contact with a number of *mukadams*, because only then is he assured of the right mix of men and women, older and younger, experienced workers and newcomers. On the other hand, it sometimes happens that an experienced and trustworthy *mukadam* will accept the obligation to provide the full complement for a brickworks or even for more than one.

Vallabh Kikhabhai, a Dhodhiya Patel in Chikhligam, is one of these. He brings no less than 450 seasonal migrants to a brickfield in Rander, close to Surat. Jobbing has made him a rich man. He is one of the few members of his caste to own a mango orchard in the village. In it is also a large bungalow of the same type as those owned by Anavil Brahmins. But this is not all. V.K. is now the owner of four lorries and has had a house built in the *taluka* town for one of his sons. It is all the result of the faithful service that he has shown for more than a quarter of a century to his patron who has grown together with him. He no longer calls himself *mukadam* but uses the English term 'labour contractor'. V.K. continues to use the village as his base of operations. Like a spider in its web, he organizes the recruitment during the wet season, assisted in his work by some dozens of touts who work for him as sub-agents. (Fieldwork notes)

The jobber has to be able to get on with the workers. That is to say, he has to know how to get them to work in a way that will satisfy the employer but without arousing any antagonism from among his work gang. He has to find the right mix of cursing and yelling, persuasion and encouragement. Harshness and forbearance alternate in a relationship that produces the maximum possible output. On the other hand, he is supposed to show utter deference towards the employing industrialist. Great patience and obedience are demanded of the *mukadam* in his effort to build up a reputation of reliability. Did he really arrive with the specified number of workers at the agreed time, did the migrants not run away during the season, and did they work to full satisfaction? Good performance on all these scores may be rewarded by the employer next time with the order for a more sizeable workforce and with more generous credit. On the other hand, the migrants must not get the impression that the gang boss is negligent in his care for their interests and systematically subordinates them to those of the employer. The latter usually avoids any contact with the migrants, neither can he be approached directly by them. The middleman conveys instructions from above to the workers, and passes on any request for favours from below, e.g. for a short leave, an extra allowance, permission for medical treatment, etc.

The *mukadam* must be able to maintain a simple handwritten notebook in which, at the time of recruitment, he writes down how much he pays to whom and when. Also, after reaching the brickworks, he records the size of the daily production, the cash allowances handed out every fortnight or ten days, and any other information regarding his work gang. The ability to read and write, however elementary, assumes some literacy. Few Halpatis are literate, which is the major reason why I found so few members of this caste among labour contractors. An even greater obstacle is that they do not possess any property. The payment of cash advances at the time of recruitment involves a considerable amount of money which the employer does not hand over without covering his own risk. He does this by making the jobber liable on paper and by demanding collateral, such as land, house, cattle or agricultural implements. In the event of *mala fide* practices, the jobber runs the risk of losing his property or at least can be put under pressure by the threat of such a consequence. Employers say that they are powerless against claims by their agents that the cash advance has been paid out to workers who subsequently proved to be dishonest. In such cases, I was told frequently they could do nothing other than to write off the amount. To avoid such bad debts, however, owners take precautionary measures. Nowadays, it is customary for them to visit the jobber's arena of operations while recruitment in the hinterland is proceeding. The jobber provides his employer with a provisional list which shows, in addition to name and domicile, the sort of work for which a man is contracted, his previous experience, family members who will accompany him, his need for credit, and so on. On the basis of these data, the second and larger instalment of the advance is paid in the patron's presence. The latter brings the necessary cash with him, and takes the opportunity to assure himself of the quality of recruits and, even more important at that time, of their reliability. To convince workers of the gravity of the contract, they are required to sign for receipt of the cash advance by setting their thumbprint. Those who are going away to work for the first time are only given an advance if someone is prepared to stand surety for them. The advance is then recouped from the latter if the new recruit does not turn up or if he deserts soon after arriving at the brickworks.

To be a *mukadam* is extremely lucrative. The jobber is paid a commission which not only varies with the size of the gang but also according to his service record. This is the way in which employers reward the loyalty and increased creditability of their agents. In addition, he is paid a premium for supervising the work during the season, expressed in a percentage of total labour costs paid in wages. A gang boss earns many times more than the migrants whom he brings along. His economic situation is different, however, if he is only at the start of his career as *mukadam*. As recruiter he needs means of his own to invest in brokerage. To prevent default, the employer tries to defer providing credit to the latest possible date, until far in the rainy season, and also keeps the amount as low as possible. The workers' dire need for an advance to be paid earlier forces the jobber to bind the people he wants for his gang by paying earnest money. Good workers often demand a larger sum which he is obliged to pay to avoid the risk of losing them to a competitor. If a new *mukadam* is unable to manage with the credit that an employer is willing to give, he has to provide the rest of the money from his own pocket. If he lacks sufficient cash-in-hand he has no choice other than to borrow from a local moneylender, who naturally demands the customary exorbitant interest.

The stronger subsistence basis of the landowning Dhodhiyas makes it understandable why this is the social and economic identity of almost all *mukadams* in Chikhligam and its vicinity. During the long period in which my fieldwork took me back to this village, I have only encountered two Halpatis who, notwithstanding lack of property and illiteracy, have managed to become and remain labour contractors. Both have to thank their modest advance to a sympathetic patron who helped them during the difficult starting phase and to whom they, in turn, have always remained faithful. A number of their caste fellows have had the ambition to improve their position to that of labour broker, but have not succeeded or soon became bankrupt.

L is again working as brick-maker after having acted as jobber and gang boss for two years. He was ruined by a couple of migrants who had agreed to go with him at the start of the second season but failed to show up at the time of departure. At that late date, he was unable to find replacements, according to him due to lack of solidarity of Dhodhiya *mukadams* in the village. These are prepared to help one another, but they spread a rumour about L that the brickworks' owner had no faith in his ability as gang boss. The patron was angry when L arrived with less workers than he had promised and deducted the advances given in the monsoon to the missing workers from his commission. But this was not all the damage. Two members of his gang returned home early due to illness with the result that the output of the others was reduced. The upshot was that at the end of the second year he was indebted to the owner of the brickworks. According to the calculations of the latter at least, with the result he had to return to the village without a penny in his pocket. (Fieldwork notes)

Various informers told me that you could only become a *mukadam* with the aid of others who already held that position. Some have been introduced to the business by father, uncle or brother, but protection need not necessarily be along lines of kinship. The big seasonal labour contractors build up a network of helpers who act as their eyes and ears in the neighbouring villages. The services provided by such henchmen are not restricted to finding new recruits but include reporting on their good conduct as workers, the sort of household to which they belong, and on their credibility. Not only are such touts given a premium for their job, but also a *mukadam* with a large workforce will choose some of them as his assistants to supervise the labourers in the brickworks. He gives them a proportion of his total earnings. By building up experience, a henchman may win the trust of the patron and permission to start an independent career as labour broker.

Most owners try to avoid becoming totally dependent on one contractor. The fact that the industry is often sited far from the area of recruitment makes them vulnerable to an adequate supply of migrants. A *mukadam* with a monopoly in bringing the workers will demand a higher price. It is more detrimental, of course, if he with his gang succumbs at the last minute to a more attractive offer from the owner of a new brickworks, for example, and switches to the latter at the start of the season. Owners cover themselves against such risks by using several brokers to recruit more workers than they actually need. It is my impression, however, that the *mukadam* is more often given the push by the employer than *vice versa*. The *mukadam* may be sacked, for example, if the enterprise closes down, if it is taken over by a new owner, if the new owner decides to change to a new recruitment area, or because the latter thinks he has found a better broker. Loyalty and integrity are the *mukadam*'s capital and for the sake of his advancement he is more dependent on good contact with his employer than *vice versa*. This is an ambiguous relationship. I was told in somewhat veiled terms by labour contractors that, without them, the *sheth* would never have achieved his prosperity. But in the same breath they praised their 'benefactor' humbly and profusely for the progress that they themselves had made.

In the landscape of labour, the *mukadams* stand out noticeably from the mass of migrant workers that they lead, but too great a detachment from their catchment milieu can also be counter-productive. They need to be sufficiently close to the clientele's world to remain alert to the limited space in which they have to manoeuvre.

How completely wrong things can go is shown by the case of D, an Anavil Brahmin and former village head of Chikhligam, who saw labour contracting as an attractive source of additional income. For many years he had witnessed the departure of seasonal migrants to the brickworks, whose owners regularly visited the village to gain information from him about the reputation of recruiters and workers. D reckoned that he was better qualified than anybody else to streamline this demand for temporary labour according to the requirements of modern times. After all, members of the low castes in the village trusted him and a man of his social background would find it easy to convince distant employers of his integrity and intelligence. D took matters up in a big way and, according to him, entered into a contract to supply some thousands of workers to the brick-making industry of Bombay and south Gujarat from Chikhligam and adjacent villages. He even took the trouble to accompany the first contingent of some hundreds to Bombay. However, the factory owners there, who had indeed provided him in good faith with a large amount of credit, were dissatisfied with the poor quality of the workers with whom he showed up. When these bosses continued to refuse payment of the commission which he had been promised on deliverance of the gangs, D loaded all his workers at night into lorries and took them to Surat. Some of the Halpatis still burst out in laughter as they told me about this adventure in which they had taken part. (Fieldwork notes)

Mukadams do not have a permanent gang of workers but recruit new members each and every year. The personal merits or demerits of the gang boss do play a role in this rotation, but other motives have priority in the choice that the migrants have to make anew each year. Their first preference is for a cash advance and as large and as early as possible. Some brick-makers from Ahmedabad whom I encountered in a brickworks close to Surat told me that the piece rate per 1,000 bricks in south Gujarat was lower than that in their own region, but that the attraction of working closer to home for this reason was nullified by the much lower amount of credit in their area of origin which moreover was only paid just before the season started. They simply had no other option but to attach themselves much earlier. A local *mukadam* confirmed this tale with the complaint that his own patron was always so late in paying the advance that he got hopelessly behind-hand at the peak of recruitment and had to incur extra trouble and expense, by taking high interest loans from a moneylender, to avoid being lumbered with the poorest quality workers.

I have described the jobber as a broker in seasonal labour who has his basis of operation in the rural milieu of south Gujarat in which he is rooted. Without fundamentally qualifying that notion I have to point out that the *mukadam* is not an unknown figure in the urban informal sector. For instance, he is markedly present in the early morning labour market held in small towns and big cities for casual workers. In that scene the *mukadam* acts as an agent on behalf of an employer with whom he has a relation of confidence. Usually this is a building or road construction contractor, the owner of a transport firm, etc. The jobber supervises the work of a gang (*toli*) which he himself has brought together and which he dismisses once the job is done. It happens that males and females who often come to the urban labour market are quite familiar with a particular *mukadam* and try to cultivate a regular relationship with him. They are the first to be selected and his favourites may also advise him whom to choose among the waiting crowd. Those who enjoy such a special treatment can get an advance payment. It is a form of credit which they repay by making themselves available at a later date with or without prior specification. The jobber receives a commission from his patron and in addition to that reward he takes his daily cut from the wages paid by him to the gang. The jobber is present in the shape of labour contractor in the dyeing and printing mills as the key man organizing the work process.

Due to contract labour system, the process houses' managements [note: i.e. the dyeing-and-printing mills] do not have to face any labour problems as contractor is responsible for quality and quantity of production. He exercises control over labourers and also recruits them or sacks them as and when required. He keeps on changing the workers from one unit to the other to nip the problems in the bud. (Mehta and Gandhi: 108–9)

Instead of being paid a regular wage the contractor makes his money by selling the output of the workers recruited by him to the owner of the mill.

On the basis of the discussion above I conclude that the jobber can be found both in the rural and urban economy. He keeps a high profile in circuits of seasonal labour, inside and outside agriculture, in particular, but he is present in other modes of employment which are low-skilled and casual in nature as well. We do not know much about the history of this powerful figure in all sorts of labour modalities. According to one source the jobber originated in the industrializing landscape of Lancashire (Joyce 1980). In his manifestation outside Europe he has been written up as a typical *comprador* of colonial work regimes. However, the *sardar*, *maistry*, *mukadam* or *serang*, some of the names by which they were known in British India, have a record as labour agents which antedates the colonial economy. Moreover, these intermediaries between workers and employers did not disappear when colonial rule came to an end. A historical essay of the jobber's role in past and present India or Asia at large would fall outside the scope of this study. I just want to add here that the jobber remains of prime importance in our understanding of the structure and functioning of segments of the economy clubbed together under the informal sector label.

Debt bondage

Recruitment is not organized along territorial lines. The *mukadams* of Chikhligam operate within a radius of roughly 15 kilometres from the village. This area is shared with dozens of other recruiters who also do not restrict their activities to their own home village. Does this give rise to fierce competition among them? To a certain degree, yes. It occurs quite regularly that a potential seasonal migrant is offered and takes an advance from a number of *mukadams*. Conventional wisdom is to blame the worker for the situation that is created. In his greed for credit, he had craftily taken advance payments from different sides, without considering the problems that his reckless behaviour would cause for others. This stereotyped explanation is not very plausible because, as we have seen, the recruiters keep track of what their catch is up to. It is the gang bosses themselves, busy to make up the required strength of their gangs, who unscrupulously use money to entice workers already contracted to another. There is a standard solution to the tussle that follows. The *mukadam* whom the 'swindler' eventually accompanies repays his competitor the amount that the latter had already paid, and claims the entire advance against the worker's earnings. The gang bosses know all too well that they are the losers when competition is drastic and especially open. They consult one another if they doubt the *bona fides* of a candidate and if necessary swap gang members, with or without payment of extra compensation, if one has too many of a particular kind that another lacks.

An interesting attempt was made in 1974 to establish a brotherhood of labour contractors. At the start of the rainy season, forty of them came at the invitation of a big *mukadam* to Khergam, a large village in the vicinity of Chikhligam, to try to solve the problems with which they all had to deal. The discussion, I was told by one of those present, resulted in a number of specific agreements: workers should not be shanghaied from one another, a blacklist of *mala fide* candidates should be drawn up and circulated, and a maximum amount set on the advance to be paid. Employers to whom I spoke some time later showed a mixed reaction to this initiative. They approved insofar as the rules laid down would restrict unseemly conduct on the part of the seasonal migrants. They were apprehensive, however, and not without reason, about a collective stand by their agents. Such a closed front would reduce the employers' manoeuvrability. However, the gang bosses were unable to clean up their practices, whether or not this was due to obstruction from above. In later years I have seen no sign of such concerted action.

As we have seen, recruitment puts seasonal migrants in a situation where they have no choice but to follow the commands of the *mukadam*. The relationship that they enter into is reminiscent of the way in which, in the past, the Halpati submitted himself to a landowner as a bonded farm servant. Naturally there are differences. *Hali*-ship had no time limit. The farm servant frequently stayed all his life by his master and the relationship continued in the next generation. Brick-makers, on the other hand, bind themselves only for the duration of the coming season. That limiting clause in itself gives the contract a less personal and more business-like character. The elements of patronage that I have called characteristic of the earlier *halipratha* (Breman 1974) are given little chance to develop in the case of the much shorter-term transaction between *mukadam* and labour migrant. Moreover, the social gap between the last two is far less than that which divided the traditional landowner from his landless serf.

In addition to these real differences, however, there are some surprising points of similarity. Like the earlier *hali*, the present seasonal worker puts himself in a condition of bondage by accepting a cash advance to be repaid in labour power. Seen from the viewpoint of the employers, advance payment is the price that they have to pay in order to ensure an adequate workforce. Rudra has this to say about labour bondage still practised in many parts of the country:

There is no law that ties the labourer to his employer and the police will not come to force the labourer to work for that particular employer. The labourer took the loan voluntarily, and knows full well the terms of the contract. He is bonded in the sense that he cannot leave the employer before repaying his debt in full. But debt is an economic institution; how can we say then that the lack of freedom of the indebted or bonded agricultural labourer is extra-economic in character? (Rudra 1994: 87)

Rudra makes this point in order to reject the suggestion that Indian rural society can be characterized as semi-feudal. I certainly do not want to dispute his conclusion, but it would show greater realism if it were accepted that these labourers are forced to become indebted because of their immense and perennial or even lifetime poverty, with the consequence that they are deprived of their freedom of movement. Contrary to Rudra, I am inclined to argue that debt is both an economic and a political institution by which labour is manipulated in a relationship of dependency. In that sense, a line can be drawn from the pre-capitalist past to the capitalist present. The impression that we are concerned with a related form of servitude is strengthened by the fact that, apart from himself, the seasonal migrant is frequently forced to commit members of his family to temporary employment away from home. This is unavoidable because the size of the advance rises proportionately to the number of productive workers who accompany him. The bondage of a farm-hand in former days similarly included the availability of his wife as maid servant and their children as help on the farm.

At the time of my first fieldwork in the early 1960s I repeatedly met with brickworkers who spontaneously suggested a parallel between their own condition and the *hali* system to which the earlier generation of agricultural workers in the village had been subjected. The connection drawn in this way became even more cogent when some brickworks owners in Bombay told me that they were sometimes approached by angry farmers seeking farm servants who had gone away for the season with a *mukadam* without asking permission. If a truant was found he was claimed by his first employer; if the brickworks owner refused to hand over the labour commodity temporarily under contract to him, the former master would demand payment of the worker's outstanding debt.

The acceptance of earnest money means that the migrant puts his own labour power and possibly that of the members of his household at the disposal of the jobber for the term agreed upon. Under that obligation, seasonal labourers are thus guilty of breach of contract if they prematurely withdraw from the work assigned to them. Measures taken by the employer to ensure their presence at the worksite for many months will be discussed in a later chapter. I shall confine myself here to discuss the pressure, which may even include physical force, that is brought to bear to compel them to leave the village at the agreed time. Getting the migrant mass into motion is a large-scale operation. I have discussed this extensively in my report on the annual trek of the army of cane-cutters to the plain of south Gujarat (Breman 1978/79: 59–60; 1990: 572–81). In a fashion that hardly deviates from that trek, large numbers of brick-makers and workers for other seasonal industries from villages in south Gujarat set off more or less simultaneously for their destinations. In the weeks preceding that departure, many factory owners come to the recruitment areas to ensure that everything runs smoothly.

L and K are brothers and partners in a brickworks on the outskirts of Bombay. In the middle of October they have come to Chikhli for three weeks, renting an empty house for their stay, which they first had thoroughly cleaned. They were accompanied by a servant who prepares their meals. The brothers take it in turn to go to Bombay for a few days, because life here is anything but comfortable. The one who stays behind, meets the gang bosses and travels with them by motorbike to the villages to prepare the workforce for the impending departure and to yield or not to requests for a last-term advance. This is also the opportunity to bind workers who have been held in reserve or to pass them onto another interested party after settlement of advance payments. The concluded contracts cover 170 migrants in total. It is quite a job to get all these men, women and children away on time. No one is given permission to come later, that cannot be allowed. The brothers arrange the transport to Bombay with their own lorries. Gangs for other employers go by bus to Valsad or Bilimora and then take the train, accompanied by their jobbers. What happens to those who do not turn up? One of the brothers together with a few assistants takes care of these suspects, going to their homes not only in the daytime but also late at night. Those who failed to appear due to illness will be sent on later or, in case of continued ill health, may send another household member who will take their place. The recalcitrant are tackled more harshly. Threats and curses are usually sufficient, but if they do not help then the aggression can result in beatings and kickings. The workers are well aware of this and often hide for days, counting on the fact that although the arresting team's behaviour may be violent, its readiness to take action does not last long. The presence of both brothers in Bombay is urgently needed to help get production going at the beginning of the season. (Fieldwork notes)

Later in the season, however, the absent workers are again in danger of surprise assaults. Requisition of their labour power is then no longer the objective, but repayment of the advance that they collected during the monsoon. When I returned to Chikhligam in 1986, I indiscreetly accepted from the *taluka* town a lift by jeep to the landless's neighbourhood. To their isolated hamlets such a vehicle seldom comes, and on the rare occasions that this does occur it bodes ill for the inhabitants. When a cloud of dust announced my arrival, a number of Halpatis fled panic-stricken into the fields, fearing that the *mukadam* and his patron were searching for them. A beating was the least that they expected. They were their enemy's primary target but if they were not at home then other members of the household would have to take the rap. The bosses' wrath seems to be a large part due to the fact that the migrants have little if anything at home which they can take away in lieu of compensation. The warrant given by someone from the same social background is not taken seriously and is no remedy for the default.

The migrants offer themselves voluntarily, but they are no longer free once they accept a contract with earnest money. That transaction reduces them to a mere commodity at the disposal of the gang boss. The moment of departure and the way in which it is arranged actualize the situation of bondage in which they have become enmeshed. Transport is supervised by the *mukadam* who never takes his eye off his flock during the journey. This is due not so much to the migrants' lack of familiarity with their destination, as to the fact that competitors lie in wait in depots and railway stations, hoping to entice away the volatile and untrustworthy workers with the aid of a generous offer of money. Strict surveillance is imperative to forestall this danger.

The extra-economic pressure to which labour migrants are subjected has lessened over time. To that extent Rudra (1994) was certainly right. Physical violence still occurs but meets more resistance from the victims than at the time of my first fieldwork. This change is made manifest by the fact that verbal and physical aggression is not always one-sided, from the top downwards. In recent years I have heard a surprising number of reports about *mukadams* having been beaten up. Does this warrant the conclusion that acquiescence has disappeared from the seasonal labour regimen? Not at all. Economic pressure still has exactly the same effect as in the early 1960s. Participation in the annual trek to seasonal industries is still based unrelentingly on the mechanism of binding with the aid of credit. Payment of money in advance continues to be necessary to enable the worker and his family to survive the rainy season. Those to whom it is paid accept the attendant obligation to leave the village. However, this does not mean in any way that the landless who are without income at that moment have internalized the enforced lack of freedom. The majority of labour migrants adhere to the agreement, turn up at the stipulated time and place, and do not run away from the worksite. They do not comply due to 'obedience', but because they have no other choice. The concept that it would be morally reprehensible to accept a cash advance and then not to report for work, is alien to them. The majority are urged to give in by the sober thought that in the last instance they themselves have to suffer in case of default. After all, who would accept them on the next occasion? An advance is indispensable to settle all sorts of small and big debts they have to incur, and they prefer to demand the largest possible amount. It sometimes happens that a brick-maker's family will sell their collective labour power to a gang boss for more than one season, for example to cover the costs of a wedding. In 1990 this needed an amount of Rs 5,000 – Rs 7,000. The yield of their work during a seven-to-eight month period is not sufficient for repayment of such a large amount. They have no other option but to go with the gang boss a second time and sometimes even for a third. In the view of migrants, their submission is not caused by their acceptance of an advance, but to the impossibility of escaping the annual trek to worksites far away from their own home. There is no alternative to subjecting themselves to the forced rhythm of seasonal work, because access to sources of livelihood nearer home is closed to them.

It is my impression that the position of *mukadam* has recently undergone change, motivated by employers' dissatisfaction with their uncontrollability. Some employers, indeed, have experimented by ignoring the *mukadam* altogether.

The owner of Remedios in Bombay has decided to do this. He will have nothing more to do with the gang boss from Chikhligam who introduced me early in the 1960s in these brickworks and who supplied it with migrants from Chikhligam and surrounding villages over many years. According to the patron, the gang boss had cheated him all that time. Repeatedly, a number of contracted workers would not appear and that had cost him a great deal of money. He had trusted blindly in the *mukadam*'s word that it was useless to try to reclaim those advances. But a couple of seasons ago he had discovered that the migrants who had left him in the lurch were employed by another brickworks. Together with the owner of that brickworks he had thoroughly investigated the matter. It proved that a number of gang bosses mutually exchanged some of their recruits but reported them to the employer as 'missing'. Not only did they themselves directly rake in the earnest money, but the rascals also claimed an extra premium for the timely provision of reserve workers. The employer had immediately sacked his *mukadam*. Since then, he does business only with the bosses of smaller gangs who make the bricks, who look after the firing process in the kilns, and who transport the bricks on the worksite. (Fieldwork notes)

An owner whom I met in Surat in 1986 told me that when he started his industry in the previous year he had also tried to bypass the labour contractors and recruit on modern lines. He had pamphlets printed and distributed on a large scale in the villages of my fieldwork region, promising migrants who directly reported for work a higher wage than was paid by other owners and a bonus at the end of the season. To his disappointment this experiment failed completely. He had made no allowance for the fact that the workers were illiterate. In his opinion, however, the opposition by the recruiters was a greater hindrance. The broker to whom he turned at his wit's end, told him that he had become the target of a secret boycott.

For the time being, the *mukadam* seems indispensable in the organization of seasonal industries. One strategy that has been adopted by some entrepreneurs is to narrow the gap between the middleman and the industry's management. While retaining the payment of commission for recruitment, they pay the gang bosses a regular wage to act as overseers at the worksite; moreover, 50 per cent of that wage is also paid during the months that work is at a standstill. In practice, it proved unfeasible to do away with mediation altogether. It is more advantageous to establish direct contact with leaders of smaller gangs in the hinterland,

and that method of delegation also augments the factory owner's grip on the migrants after their arrival. At the same time, however, the employers' limited span of control in the area of recruitment makes them vulnerable in the critical phase preceding the resumption of work each year. The majority of brickworks owners told me more or less with resignation that for them the *mukadam* was a necessary evil.

The manager of the Remedios firm in Bombay has reached the same conclusion. I met him again during the 1986 monsoon when he was staying with the owner of a petrol pump sited on the main road from Chikhli to Valsad. Here he meets the migrants who have been recruited for him by a new gang boss. In exchange for placing their thumbprint on a paper they are given the first instalment of the promised cash advance. But the patron has armed himself against the deceit with which he had formerly been victimized. He takes a photo of each contracted worker. The flash that accompanies the making of the portrait is not really necessary, but its use dramatically stresses the importance of the proceedings. In a loud voice he then also says that this evidence will be a great help to the police if the workers tried to defraud him. In an aside he tells me that he turns down anyone who refuses to follow his order to look straight into the camera when he is taking the photograph. (Fieldwork notes)

The *mukadam* is not a necessary evil for the employers only. The seasonal migrants also cannot manage without him. He leads the way to work far from home that would otherwise be inaccessible to them. Of course, they know quite well that the gang boss makes money for rendering service to the owner and also pockets a share of what is really theirs. But without him, they would in all probability be worse off. All said and done, the gang boss comes from their own milieu and will need to find workers again in coming seasons. Therefore, he cannot be absolutely ruthless. After all, who else is there to solve their problems, to protect them against the patron's displeasure, to ask for favours if the opportunity should arise? One gang boss may defend their interests more vigorously than another, but there is not much difference between them. Given the inevitability of annual migration and all the misery that it entails, the *mukadam* is the one who herds them to the work site, acts as buffer, and finally brings them back home when the season ends.

A sense of realism dictates that those who attend urban casual labour markets should accept the jobber as a work-provider. It would be an exaggeration, however, to deduce that they see him as a benefactor. In his research among women who depend on such markets for their livelihood, Punalekar heard quite different stories:

'When he [*mukadam*] gives us employment, he behaves as if he has obliged us for whole life. Moreover, he goes on scolding us. If we show slight independence or autonomy, he threatens that he would not employ us again.' One female labourer said: 'He [*mukadam*] shows such an authority and power over us. Even our husbands do not show so much of dominance.' (S. P. Punalekar and Patel 1990: 149–50)

If the jobber pesters, abuses or ridicules them, the workers can do little but remain silent, fearing boycott in future. This would not only be by their own *mukadam* but also by others of his ilk, incited by him to shun such intractable people. They cannot afford to expose themselves to such a risk.

5   Quality of the labour process

Informal training for work

The main characteristic of the work done by the majority of workers in whom I am interested is that they lack skills and have to depend on little more than their own physical strength. Learning by doing is common practice from early age onwards. This type of training is standardized particularly in the case of those who are taken on for an indefinite period but who at the start lack the necessary knowledge that will help them in due course to become experienced workers. One of the workers already employed – perhaps the same one who mediated in finding employment – will then show the newcomer the tricks of the trade.

Apprenticeship in the diamond industry is undoubtedly the longest, i.e. six months, but still too short to teach the newcomer how to use the lathe and all stages of diamond cutting. Old hands at work told me with pride that their generation needed two years in which to become fully skilled. It will be clear that only young males who belonged to a household already firmly above the poverty line went for that training. For the landless it would have been impossible to carry the subsistence burden of adults or adolescents who, instead of contributing to family income, invested in their own future. Nowadays, instruction is restricted to a single part of the cutting process. Most of those who finish this short training period are not given, or do not take, the chance to expand their knowledge to other parts of the work process. At the time of my fieldwork in 1986–87, a boy had to pay Rs 500–700 to the workshop owner if he wanted to learn how to cut diamonds. That charge was said to be to compensate the employer for the devaluation of stones that became damaged during the learning period. This explanation is not at all convincing, nor is the argument that it costs time and money to supervise the pupil. For an experienced worker, it is an investment that will begin to show profit after only three months. That is when the trainee is considered to have learned the cutting technique. The full wage for the stones that he processes during the following three months is paid to his instructor, who is thus generously compensated for the loss of income suffered during the time that the pupil demanded his constant supervision. A more plausible argument is that the obligation to pay a tuition fee discourages those who show little interest and patience in becoming proficient diamond cutters. One result, intended or not, is that the charge for entering the profession inhibits youths from the lower social-economic milieux. To members of the tribal castes, payment of such an amount is almost equivalent to the amount of dowry:

a woman who offers her future husband the chance to become a diamond cutter is a good match and on that basis can enter into marriage with the son of a large farmer; in addition, she then marries a man with the prospect of earning a good income. (Koelen 1985: 83; see also Kalathil 1978: 99–100)

The modest number of Halpatis who have entered the diamond cutting profession usually have to thank a beneficent atelier owner for their induction. Instead of paying the fee in cash and in advance, he might permit them to pay it in arrears by working for a longer period for nothing or for a nominal wage. From the viewpoint of labour attachment, this is an attractive arrangement for the patron. It means, however, that the parents of these young adolescents must have sufficient means to maintain the favoured son or brother for even a longer period than that of apprenticeship. In the preceding chapter we have seen that for the landless labourers and marginal landowners this depletion of meagre reserves is an almost impossible burden to carry. Job training without pay is usually beyond the capacity of such households. A Halpati friend of mine in one of the fieldwork villages had run away from home as a young boy because his father forced him to leave school to help him in his daily work as bricklayer.

The textile industry lacks proper training facilities for beginners. According to some sources, textile workers from Andhra Pradesh are brought to Surat owing to their traditional experience in weaving, particularly in the Warangal region. That reputation was probably the reason for importing labour from those parts, but it does not signify that the young men who come to Surat have ever worked in that industry. This background does not apply to the greater flow of migrants recruited from a peasant caste in the countryside of Orissa. Their acquaintance with weaving looms starts only when, after reaching their destination, they first enter the factory to learn the work. One researcher reports as follows on industries in Surat where woven cloth is dyed and printed:

that new workers learn only by working with experienced workers. An unskilled worker is known as *begari* who in course of time becomes semi-skilled and is a 'helper'. As he gains more experience he becomes skilled and he is taken up as a 'printer' in the printing section when a vacancy arises. (Desai 1981: 115)

It is just the same in the powerloom workshops, as I observed. A beginner can only enter the industry and learn the trade by literally standing next to an experienced worker. He is present only in a marginal sense and has to make himself almost invisible where and when the manufacturing process takes place. The night shift is ideal for the purpose because the workplace is then peaceful. The surreptitious manner in which skill is passed on is characterized by the fact that the patron often does not know what is going on, or at least behaves as though he does not. His deputy, the weaving master, is in close touch with the workers and it is impossible to avoid him while teaching a skill to newcomers. His silence and collusion have to be bought because the errors that an apprentice makes cannot be hidden from him. There must not be too many errors, however, because then the prospective weaver is irrevocably shown the door and his instructor must take care not to suffer the same fate. Why, then, are the experienced workers prepared to accept such a burden? Apart from social obligations, i.e. to help a relative, caste fellow or inhabitant of the same village, financial gain is the principal motive. Actual apprenticeship lasts no more than a few weeks but it is continued thereafter for some time, varying according to the nature of the relationship, in order to compensate the instructor. The latter shares the yield of the production of his pupil with the weaving master. This state of affairs again emphasizes the principal reason why members of the landless castes are under-represented in the weaving industry. Men of these households cannot permit themselves to work for longer than a few days without wages. If an opening becomes available in the workshop, the apprentice may show that he has become a fully qualified worker. If this takes too long, then he may seek an opening in another establishment.

Halpatis from Gandevigam and Chikhligam who travel daily to the industrial sites of Bilimora are at first paid as 'helper' for activities that require neither training nor experience. In fact, the nature of their occupation differs little from that of long-term workers. In such cases, the term 'helper' indicates that he has been employed for only a short time, a sort of trial period during which output is remunerated at a lower level than the wage paid to older workers. Although there are no formal entrance requirements for this sphere of employment, my fieldwork data show that in practice employers only take on young workers who have attended at least some years of elementary school. This information seems to conflict with the assertiveness with which employers claim that they have no need for literate workers. Certain employers whom I met expressed that they considered the ability to read and write a handicap rather than a recommendation. Similar pronouncements are found in other studies concerned with my research area. For example, on textile workers in Surat:

Seven entrepreneurs informed us of having caught raw hands from nearby villages and of having trained them gradually. This took some time but entrepreneurs felt that old workers were trouble creators due to their contacts with trade unions and labour leaders. So they preferred raw hands from villages in spite of their limitations. (Bhatt 1979: 167)

On diamond cutters in the countryside of south Gujarat:

A few owners will find a couple of years of schooling favourable, but of secondary importance. An owner in Bajipura, on the other hand, found even the slightest amount of education to be disadvantageous because, in his opinion, it destroyed any ambition to do manual work; he gave preference to dexterous boys without any education. (Koelen 1985: 78)

The reasons vary, but in both cases the meaning is clear: education results in a mentality which, in the eyes of the employer, reduces rather than improves the quality of labour. The argument underlying the first quotation will be discussed more extensively in a later chapter. The veracity of the second quotation is doubtful. The statement ignores the fact that factory labour demands a certain amount of discipline and a sense of time that are difficult to adjust to for a Halpati boy accustomed to grazing the cows of a local farmer. Even a few years of schooling will teach, in addition to elementary literacy, a feeling for order and regularity, acclimatization to a rhythm based on the division of the day, week or month into permanent reiterative time periods. To work under a roof, to find shelter from the elements among four walls, in itself gives a higher status to the work that has to be done. But not all those who are privileged to penetrate such an environment are able to adapt to the demands that go with it. Not without gloating, farmers in Gandevigam told me about local landless youths who had fruitlessly tried their luck in the factories of Bilimora, but who soon had to resume their existence as agricultural labourers because they could not stand the rigour of industrial discipline. This encourages the local elite in their conviction that members of this lower caste are suited for little other than work on the land. And even in that respect, according to Anavil landowners, the Halpatis who formerly served them as *halis* compare badly with the harder-working migrants now coming to the village. A preoccupation with those who manage to work their way upwards from a situation of extreme poverty should not lead us to overlook those who are forced to drop out from this steep and slippery path to a better and more dignified life. They just seem to fade away in due course.

An Industrial Training Institute (ITI) has been set up in Bilimora, for imparting training in various trades and crafts. Students admitted to one of the vocational courses are given a certificate which gives them access to jobs in the formal sector of the economy. In my fieldwork villages a few youths from higher castes and more from the middle castes (Anavil Brahmins and Koli Patels respectively) have qualified as mechanics, motor mechanics, turners or fitters. But they include no Dhodhiyas, let alone Halpatis. Dhodhiya youths are increasingly exposed to secondary education but mainly to seek employment in the public sector where the government's policy of positive discrimination gives them more chances than in the private sector. Halpati children rarely attend even primary school and many of them drop out even at this elementary level (Breman 1993b: 345–6). In many cases their parents realize quite well the value of education but are simply not able to bear the cost of such an investment in the next generation. Even in villages located at a stone's throw from the town, disappointingly few children from the landless quarters ever attend school. When people are questioned about this fact, their replies are often quite bitter.

If our children are uneducated how can they hope to get better jobs outside in the city? People say that we Dublas are careless and irresponsible. We send them to field or tobacco factory or to *chayno larigallo* [tea-stall] rather than send them to *balmandir* [kindergarten] or primary school. We force them to work and live on their earnings, they say. It is a cruel joke they are heaping on us . . . We also have fatherly sentiments and we also know value of education. But when I am refused work in the field and my old mother comes back saying she too has no work on that day, we momentarily cease to be fathers and against our wish ask our children to go out and work. That is what is happening in Halpativas. (Cited in D. S. Punalekar 1992: 252)

The few craftsmen that I encountered in the Halpati quarters of Chikhligam and Gandevigam have to be satisfied with on-the-job training, under the supervision of their father or uncle. In view of the few tools at their disposal, they are only able to perform fairly simple and crude work, cheaper and inevitably of poorer quality than that of skilled craftsmen from intermediate castes who have gone through formal technical schooling.

Children born to landless households seldom have the opportunity to gain any knowledge of a trade at school or even in practice. The route through education is closed to them. Even the apprenticeship which they ought to undergo by an employer if they are to acquire technical or trade skills assumes that their parents or other guardians are willing and able to provide for them during that time. This is usually out of the question as can be seen from the report on an enquiry among children found working on the streets in four towns of Gujarat, including Surat:

Some car cleaning boys do try to learn servicing and repairing of two-wheeler auto [rickshaw]. Not many of them are always successful though. Servicing and repairs carried out at known garages require sufficient training background. That training is given without wages. Training period is at least three to six months. What would they eat during this period? (S. P. Punalekar 1993: 106)

Non-specialization, i.e. to avoid concentrating on and trying to learn a single trade, is the most commendable strategy for those who exist on the broad underside of the labour hierarchy. There are many slum-dwellers who seem to have drifted along a large number of employment sites on which they get information from neighbours, friends and their temporary workmates. Lobo has described such wandering occupational histories in his research on one particular Surat slum (Lobo 1994: 45–65). Progress in the art of survival is determined by success in the constant search for new sources of income. Street children, in an effort to scrape a living, learn that lesson at an early age.

Car cleaning activity [at the crossroads of busy streets,] is a transit occupation for many [boys]. They try to learn and do other jobs like selling dusters, flowers, etc. or do cycle repairing, coolie work, etc. (S. P. Punalekar 1993: 106)

Rajesh and Ramesh live on the platform at Surat railway station. The young boys, one from Bihar and the other from Maharashtra, clean railway compartments and are given small tips by the passengers. Both travel daily from Surat to Bulsar, and then Bulsar to Baroda. They prefer Gandhidam Express. Because, in this train they are sure to earn good money. All the same, they are not too happy with their life. They do remember their parents. But they do not want to go back home. They feel that once they are grown up and become adults then they have to change their occupation. That is why both are saving for buying shoe-shine kits.' (S. P. Punalekar 1993: B-5)

Their sheer survival is dependent on their will and ability to be as flexible as possible, to take on or to search for anything that offers. By preference they work close to home, but if there is no alternative they go farther or even far away. Such work is by definition unskilled, not requiring any experience; in short, work that everyone is able to do without having done it before. This is the commonly held opinion but it needs adjustment.

In the first place, not everyone has the physical strength to do hard, strenuous work. During my fieldwork I repeatedly met people who found it impossible to continue in the brickworks, cane-cutting, quarries or salt-pans. They simply could not keep up with the killing work tempo, were unable to cope with working during the night or for more than twelve hours at a stretch, and suffered too much from the abominable conditions in which they were forced to live and work. It was easy to see from their experience that complaints were by no means always due to weak physical stamina or to unsuitable age, i.e. either too young or too old. Some people had literally fled from such work because they obviously lacked the mental toughness that would enable them to acquiesce to the demands of the production process. Secondly, the fact that jobs in specific branches of industry as also the slum habitats are broken up in distinct social collectivities to which people belong with a shared identity along regional, communal or religious lines, conflicts with the notion of a total state of flux and an unstructured heterogeneity at the bottom of the urban economy. Ethnic segmentation is even an organizing principle of the urban labour market. The customary as well as superficial explanation given for this is that some people are traditionally familiar with particular work. Kathiawadis and Kanbi Patels in particular, for example, are deemed to be more suited than any other for the diamond cutting trade; Khandeshis have long been accustomed to cane-cutting; tribal workers from the Panch Mahals are known for their dexterity in road building; and in Bombay, but not at home, Halpatis maintain a reputation as brickmakers. My own interpretation of the division of the mass of unskilled labour into several segments, already discussed, will be examined further in a later chapter.

Members of the rank-and-file in the informal sector, which to an outsider seems to be an undifferentiated mass, have a strongly developed sense of their own diversity, which is expressed in a high–low interrelationship. The inclination of the toiling mass of street workers to place one another in a ranking that runs from untouchable to high (self-) respect, as though on a caste ladder, is learnt at an early age.

A female street child working as a domestic servant considered herself higher than a rag-picker . . . Nature and status of each street activity was judged by them and accordingly ranked socially. This is also true for male activities on the street. Male beggars were treated as lower in status by the male coolies or compartment cleaners working on a railway platform. The latter in turn were looked upon as inferior by shoe shine boys who in turn were rated low in status by teashop/hotel servants. Boys working in a garage or a small workshop on a road side took immense pride in their job and considered themselves higher to everyone else engaged in other street activities. They called themselves as 'skilled workers', 'technicians'. (S. P. Punalekar 1993: 153)

The unskilled labour scene is thus much less uniform than it might seem at first sight, while within each branch of industry the division of tasks is far more complex than an outsider might assume. A telling example is the elaborate work organization in the somewhat larger brickfields. The man who makes the bricks is surrounded by a group, called *patala*, made up of adults and children who each have a specific task: to knead and mix the earth in a pit with water; to dig it out in heaps that are deposited in front of the *patavala*; to give him a ball of mud which he smacks into a mould; to snatch the brick that he has formed from the slab under his feet; to carry away this raw product and to lay it in rows further away to dry. These are all separate activities that are allocated among nine to eleven different men, women and children. In addition to this there are other work gangs as well: to bring earth to the worksite; to stoke the kiln; to carry the bricks to the kiln; to pile the bricks on top of one another and, after baking, to empty the kiln again. These are all tasks carried out by the people concerned for an entire season and already specified in the contract when they are hired.

In the lower economic echelons the labour scene is thus characterized by strong differentiation which is horizontal in nature. The landscape is rather flat, by which I mean the absence of vertical stratification. As a result, the great mass of people are trapped in a work environment that offers almost no prospect of improving their position. The chance of obtaining employment that is a cut above that of others in terms of skill, esteem and income, is minimal. An exceptional case, for example, is that of a seasonal worker in the brickworks who, sitting next to the one skilled man on the job, learns how to drive the lorry and later has the chance to get the driving licence which makes him a licensed driver. A great deal is necessary for such social mobility, however: not only a cordial relationship with the tutor and the owner of the brickworks, but also good luck or just bad fortune. An obvious example is that of the *mukadam*, the jobber-cum-gang boss who is close to the workers whom he mobilizes but at the same time stands head and shoulders above them.

Finally, although there is very little vertical differentiation among unskilled labour, there is one type of distinction that is noticeable all along the line: that between man and woman. The former is invariably the focal figure: the cane-cutter, quarryman, road worker, brick-maker and, not to be forgotten, the overseer in all his variations. The woman, on the other hand, fulfils the classic role of 'helper' although the severity of her work gives no reason for that subordinative term.

It is definitely not profitable for informal sector workers to delay ingress into the labour process until after having completed lower and continued education, perhaps followed by some sort of vocational training that would eventually enable them to cross the threshold into formal sector employment. The minimum training that they need in order to find work is a question of practical experience, of imitating others, a manner of learning which soon enables them to earn an income. This can be further illustrated by considering the highly skilled personnel employed by two high-tech firms forming part of the petrochemical industry in the coastal town of Hajira, west of Surat.

Larsen & Toubro (L&T) is a heavy engineering plant which specializes in factory equipment and offshore installations. At the end of 1992, one-third of the almost thousand employees belonged to the managerial and supervising ranks, and there were 676 labourers. A man starting in this lowest rank had a beginner's wage of Rs 1,800–1,900 per month. This is preceded, however, by a long qualifying period as apprentice. To be accepted as such – there were 50 trainees at that time – aspiring hopefuls have to have a secondary school diploma and an Industrial Training Institute (ITI) diploma. This is followed by a three-year industrial training during which they receive a modest monthly allowance which just covers their cost of living. Only those who are prepared to subject themselves to this lengthy training – in effect they work as mature but low-paid labourers – can be given a permanent job afterwards, always provided that places are available. Kribcho is an extremely modern plant in the co-operative sector, daily producing 5,000 tons of artificial fertiliser (urea). Its employees, numbering 1,400 at the end of 1992, consist for 75 per cent of people appointed to the higher ranks as manager or officer, in salary scales that reflect their college or even more advanced education. Kribhco, whose administration is computerized and production is automatized, has little need for unskilled labour. Workers who are employed as operators, only 25 per cent of the total workforce, have completed Polytechnic School (Diploma Engineer) or at least have an ITI certificate. The latter have to work a three-year apprenticeship before being given the chance of permanent employment. During that time they receive a meagre monthly allowance ranging from Rs 675 (during the first year) to Rs 725 (subsequently), free hostel accommodation, medical care, home leave, work clothes, and a few other facilities. The rank of operator provides a starting wage of Rs 2,300 per month. (Fieldwork notes)

In view of the high demands for preparatory training and the low wage paid during the long induction period, it is clear that members of the proletariat have no chance at all of penetrating to this arena of formal employment. It is neither possible nor attractive for them to take even a step in this direction. Such an inclination does exist at a higher social level, however. Not because the wage paid to lower-ranking workers is so generous, but because of the security, the protective working conditions and the prestige that accompany permanent employment.

The extensive industrial terrains formerly belonged to inhabitants of surrounding villages. To persuade them to relinquish their land, the enterprises promised to reserve workplaces for the farmers' sons. To the intense indignation of the local population, however, little has come of that promise. The industry's management defends itself with the argument that local people were not sufficiently qualified for this work when the factories were opened. The village youth lacked the necessary training even for a job as operator. For the same reason, they were quite unsuitable for the less numerous but more lucrative officer ranks. Moreover, it is customary for such big corporations, with branches throughout India, to recruit their higher cadre on a national rather than a local basis. This explains the noticeable presence of non-Gujaratis in these enclaves of economic modernity. In the meantime, interest in advanced technical education has increased greatly in the villages. In most cases, however, the factory gates remain closed even to young men who have the necessary papers, due to lack of suitable vacancies. It is rarely that anyone with a permanent job will give it up, nor is there much scope for expansion of present capacity in these capital-intensive enterprises. Apart from lack of capacity, there seems to be some degree of reluctance on the part of employers to meet the reasonable wishes of the local people. I deduce this from the fact that non-technical personnel are also brought in from elsewhere: for example, the factory police who guard the gates and patrol the grounds, as also the cleaners and maintenance workers.

Use of technology

Hajira is a model for the high-grade industrial sector in which labour almost disappears from sight in a landscape dominated by capital. On the broader underside of the economy the opposite is true in the relationship between these two factors of production. The majority of the workforce do what is demanded of them each day with no other means than their own physical strength. Working principally with their arms and legs, but with the additional use of head, shoulders, back and hips, their work posture shows evidence of physical motions that demand much energy: various combinations of hauling, pulling, pushing, carrying, lifting, bending and squatting. In their research among women who sell their labour power each morning at the urban markets, Punalekar and Patel ascertained that 90 per cent of them have no other means of production than their own bodily strength:

They went to the casual labour market bare handed. Some of them felt that they should have had some tools like sickle, hammer, axe, etc. of their own. [Thus equipped] they could possibly have had an edge over other persons in getting work. (Punalekar and Patel 1990: 136)

Most of the rural army of labourers also have to do the work that is daily demanded of them with no other means than their crude labour power. Only a minority make use of tools, usually no more than one: a machete for cutting the sugarcane; a pickaxe with which the road worker can break up the ground; a wicker basket or iron tray in which the woman can carry soil on her head or hip; a crowbar and sledge-hammer with which the quarryman may dislodge chunks of rock; a two-handed hammer with which his wife can break them into smaller pieces; a spade for a navvy; a mould in which the man may form bricks; a small iron or wooden plate on which women and children may carry the wet or dry bricks away. The meagre range of tools used by craftsmen is their own property. Labourers are usually lent them by their employer. But if the cane cutter's machete should break, anything but a rare occurrence in its use during the many months of the campaign, the cost of repair or replacement is deducted from his wage. It also happens, however, that people who own nothing have to provide their own tools. Road workers take a pickaxe and basket with them, a *mukadam* will only recruit a man as brick-maker if he has his own mould and forming plate, while many quarries will not take on labourers who do not have their own crowbar and hammer.

The new owner of the quarry in Pardi explained this by saying that people who own little if anything are careless in their use of other people's property. In the past his workers left the tools lying around or took them home and then tried to get him to give him new ones. He had not been bothered in this way since he introduced the rule that workers who used tools could get them from him, but only on payment. (Fieldwork notes)

At a slightly higher level of production in the informal sector more progress has been made with the use of modern means of technology. This applies, for example, to the industrial workshops such as diamond ateliers and powerloom sheds which were the focus of my research in Surat. Nevertheless, even this environment seems to be dominated more by labour than by capital. Owners of such workplaces can manage with a limited assortment of tools and equipment. Their limited stock is usually, however, very intensively utilized. Labour is made to work for long hours and also the shift system is practised to maximize the exploitation of the capital invested.

The labour intensity of the sort of industries covered by my research is illustrated by the fact that only a small minority of the workers come into regular or even sporadic contact with machinery. They include diamond cutters and operators of powerlooms. Owners of such workshops can also make do with only a modest capital investment. A small diamond atelier requires nothing more than a turner's lathe, an electric motor, a couple of work benches, and a number of clamps with which to hold the diamonds. At the end of the 1980s this involved no more than some tens of thousands of rupees. In the same period, a powerloom cost Rs 20,000 at most. More important than the small size of this investment is that after only a year profits will equal the total investment cost. This does not alter the fact that the starting capital needed for acquiring these more advanced means of production is prohibitive for those who own little if anything at all. The yield of their labour power does not allow them to accumulate even the modest sum that would enable them to cross the threshold towards entrepreneurship. Nevertheless, the minority of workers who use tools or who operate machines are paid for their skills to handle such equipment a higher wage than the majority who have no assets other than their own bodily strength. It may be added that women are strongly under-represented in the first category and over-represented in the second. But even at that more inferior level there are signals of further marginalization. In her case study of gender employment in Surat's art silk industry Agrawal has observed that women have not been able to become loom operators. On the other hand, however, the abundant supply of alien labour has resulted in male migrants taking over jobs which used to be reserved for female workers: 'Thus, for women it is diffi- cult to enter into traditionally male jobs but men have sought an easy entry into traditionally female jobs' (Agrawal 1992: 258).

The technology used in the informal sector is generally not only of a fairly simple nature but also is rather obsolete. The first generation of mechanical looms to be installed in Surat, mostly still in use, were bought second-hand from traders who had retrieved them from shut-down facto- ries in Bombay and Ahmedabad.

For the weaving industry in Surat, it can be said that the technology employed is conventional, may be obsolete. Almost all the units use only plain looms even though they produce expensive synthetic fabrics. It goes to the credit of the workers and entrepreneurs that even on plain looms, they are able to produce fabrics of acceptable quality. Loom speeds are low compared to other countries such as Japan, for similar fabric using filament yarn both as warp and weft. Even simple attachments such as electronic weft feeders which have a short pay back are used by only a few units. Preparatory machines likewise are cheap and conven- tional type and no attempt has been made to use high speed, semi-automatic machines. (Mehta and Gandhi: 24)

The authors comment that the backward technology is all the more sur- prising since the industry is relatively young, and more advanced machin- ery was already available when production started to boom. The abundant supply of cheap labour which can be trained at no or minimal cost to the employer is in my opinion the main reason why industrialists are reluctant to replace this factor of production by capital. As has been pointed out before labour constitutes only 10–11 per cent of the sale value of grey fabrics. At the same time, however, powerloom owners are pre- pared to accept that wages are a major or even the most important part of the total cost of production.

In the diamond business as well wages paid to the cutters make up 87 per cent of all costs borne by the atelier owners (Desai 1985: 2). In these workshops the same modest range of instruments is used that I already came across during my fieldwork in the early 1970s. The only innovation is the recent introduction of a semi-automatic *ghanti* (an iron work-bench around which four diamond cutters sit on the floor). Few owners have so far acquired this new equipment because, in their opinion, it is only advantageous for the cutting of larger stones for industrial use.

The brick-making industry is a perfect illustration of the way in which employers have for many years persisted in hand-made production. The way in which this business used to be run at the beginning of the 1960s had undergone no change in later years, as spokesmen of the manufacturers' union in Gujarat acknowledged in front of a committee set up by government:

At no point in the process of making bricks any machinery, operated with or without power is used. All sorts of work are being done by human labour. Thus brick industry is a labour oriented industry. (Report Minimum Wage Advisory Committee for Workers Making Bricks 1975: 29)

On the basis of data compiled during the past fifteen years I have no reason at all to over-rule this statement. The technological stagnancy is all the more surprising in view of the enormous increase of production during the intervening years. This can be illustrated with the aid of a step-by-step description of how things are organized in the brickworks:

When earth at the worksite becomes exhausted it is brought in by truck or tractor from a distance of five to ten kilometres. Members of the gang who are charged with the transport use only a spade with which to fill the container with *mati*. Larger clumps are passed by hand or headload to a mate who stands in the container. Unloading is just as laborious. On the worksite the earth is distributed in piles at the places where the brick-making gangs are at work. The amount needed for a day's production is thrown into a pit filled with water. The two to three men whose chore this is have to mix the earth with water, coal dust and rice husk. For hours at a time they knead the mixture with legs and hands, standing in the pit from which they remove stones, pieces of wood and other flotsam. Two other men and/or women dig the resulting mash out of the pit with their hands and knead it once again. The partner of the brick-maker squatting next to the pile, seizes a ball of mud with both hands and passes it to the *patawala* who puts it into the mould. This linchpin of the group then smooths both sides of the mould, an action that he has to repeat 2,500 to 3,000 times each day. When the mould is lifted off, the wet clay remains in the form of a brick on the steel groundplate. Two or three children, dependent on their age, take turns to lift the plate with the brick and to run with it to an older child who carefully lays the bricks next to one another. The rows that are thus formed are left to dry for half-a-day. But then the occupied space has to be emptied for the next series. Members of the same gang carry the bricks a little farther away to pile them in rows so that the drying process can continue. Another work gang, almost all girls and women, then carry eight or ten bricks together on their heads to the kiln, where they are taken over by one or two men who specialize in the correct stacking of the half-product for the firing process. They also take the fired bricks out of the oven and pass them to the waiting women bearers. These then carry their heavy headload to the stockpile from where the end-product is transported away, or directly to a waiting lorry. (Fieldwork notes)

Are the entrepreneurs not aware that machines are available that wholly or partially replace the human labour power on which the production process now depends? Owners of small brickworks showed little if any interest in the question, but larger manufacturers were usually prepared to give a more detailed answer. A few had heard about a semi-automatic kiln in Ahmedabad. Others told me that a few years earlier a machine had been tried somewhere in the neighbourhood of Vapi which delivered the raw material ready-made. The bricks that were made with it fell to pieces during the drying process, however, and the experiment was soon stopped. I was told repeatedly that human hands were simply indispensable for the making of good quality bricks. This argument is easily refuted, as shown by the kneading machine that I found in 1962 in a brickworks on the banks of the River Tapti in Surat:

The Parsi owner proudly showed me around when I visited the works to meet a gang of brick-makers from Chikhligam. The motor-driven mixer stirred the earth with water, coal dust and rice husks in a large cement tank. Workers used their hands to pull the compound away from under the mixer and threw it by the armful from bins into tipper carts. These were pushed along rails through the yard to the place where the brick-makers and their gangs were busy. I found the innovations which I saw and the large scale of the production process very impressive. This entrepreneur was certainly taking the lead in a modernization process that would be followed by more and more owners. However, this was not the case. When I visited the now aged Parsi for the last time in 1984 I found him in his office enraged about the *mukadams* who could not be trusted. They always wanted a large advance in cash but at the start of the season they came with less workers than they had been paid for. He also vented his spleen about the authorities who sent him far too little coal with which the two chimneys had to be kept burning. He had had enough and was going to stop the work that year. When I returned two years later, I realized that that decision was connected to the old man's illness. After his death last year, a daughter and a son took over management of the business. (Fieldwork notes)

In 1985, after a great deal of trouble, I eventually managed to speak to the chairman of the *Surat Jilla Int Utpadhak Mandal*. Members of this local association of brick manufacturers, set up in 1974, are almost all owners of large businesses. The association looks after the interests of its members and mediates in the supply of coal which is available at fixed minimum price only for holders of an official licence. The chairman appeared not only a warm champion of the industry, but also one of the very few who were familiar with the machines used in Western countries. A couple of years earlier he had taken part in an international congress of brick manufacturers held in London. He had a photograph in his office of the mechanized firm that he had then visited in the United Kingdom. He was all praise for what he had seen. But according to him there is little chance of introducing that technology into south Gujarat in the near future. Why that should be so was concealed behind a stream of words. Apart from the extremely low wages, a subject dealt with in the next chapter, this seemed to be due to the manufacturers' wish to conceal their production from government as much as possible. This would be out of the question if they changed to a production system which demanded more fixed capital. In some way, machines are easier to register than working people. At any rate, owners would then be far more vulnerable to numerous legal or illegal depredations on their profits by government officials. Nevertheless, a point can be reached where it is economically unwise to continue production on a manual basis only. One example that has been discussed already is that of a number of road builders who started to mechanize the exploitation of the quarries for which they have a bought a licence. In seeking an answer to the intriguing question why the powerloom workshops and diamond ateliers dominating the industrial landscape of Surat continue to run on the basis of a backward technology, I earlier referred to the ready availability of cheap labour. However, the reluctance to go in for more capital-intensive industrialization may also have to do with fluctuations in the demand for the commodity produced. Most powerloom entrepreneurs have no or only minimal control over the source, quantity and price of the raw material their patrons are willing to deliver, while they also have to accept whatever conditions are imposed on them for marketing the grey fabric. In the same way the owners of diamond ateliers are bound hand and feet to traders who supply them with the stones, dictating the price of processing, and who may at any moment and quite arbitrarily decide to discontinue the business relationship. Such structural constraints, which were already a feature of the pattern of industrial development in colonial India, are not really favourable for persuading industrialists to invest in more advanced technology. It is not that the actual producers do not get a proper price – as a matter of fact profit margins are usually very high – but that they have to operate in an unregulated and unsteady market. Given these conditions of uncertainty and dependency it becomes attractive to pass on the entrepreneurial risk and to keep a less costly and more variable production factor than capital unstable, i.e. to expand or contract the workforce according to the need of the moment. It sometimes happens that employers bring up the mechanization argument as a threat with which to reject demands for higher wages or, more generally, to nip in the bud any attempts that are likely to result in increased labour costs. In south Gujarat, the management of the capitalist agro-industry uses these tactics to bring pressure to bear on government (Breman 1990: 605). Spokesmen for the brick-making industry in the state use the same argument. To members of a government committee charged with fixing a minimum wage, they had declared a long time ago that any increase in cost price caused by a wage increase would make it necessary for them to introduce machinery (Report Minimum Wage Advisory Committee for Workers Making Bricks 1975: 33). In the intervening years, as noticed, that threat has not been put into practice. In view of the increasing irritation shown by employers with regard to what they see as fickle and dishonest behaviour on the part of their workers, however, I do not consider it out of the question that such a trend will yet arise.

Together with his brother, J owns a tile-making workshop, one of such enterprises for which Bilimora has long excelled. Increased prosperity has caused many large and medium landowners to decide to modernize their houses into bungalows with the help of interior decoration, more specifically, by having the floors and walls of their rooms tiled. J has no lack of orders, but he has a great deal of trouble in keeping up the size of his workforce. At first he employed almost only local Kolis, but they took too many holidays or even stayed away without asking his permission. A couple of years ago he changed to using *bhaiyas*, the generic term given to people from Uttar Pradesh. These outsiders are hard workers and are always available. During the summer they sleep somewhere on the worksite – J nonchalantly pointed out of the window – and in the winter he allowed them to sleep indoors. The problem is that these workers, whom he has trained himself, return to their homes once each year and then he never knows whether they will come back. They could find similar work in Kashmir where the wages are higher. J is fed up with always having to instruct newcomers how to do the work. He wants to bring in machines as quickly as possible, though his brother is still against the idea. (Fieldwork notes)

Working hours

For the large mass of people who earn their living with unskilled labour, standardized working hours are an unknown luxury. The casual use of physical power is characterized by uncertainty as to when the working day actually begins and ends. Calculating according to number of hours is not so important as making sure of the income that the physical effort will provide. Factory labour brings an end to the unpredictable rhythm of daily workers who each day have to roam restlessly seeking work and trying to contact employers who will pay them a wage. Just as work performed under a roof increases a worker's prestige, the marking of a day into a regular and clear-cut pattern of work and non-work increases the dignity of labour. When, in addition, the work is interrupted once each week by a free day with pay, and a longer leave even is given once a year, working life takes on the character of formal sector employment. Such a situation is approximated by workers who serve the powerlooms in Surat.

However, they lack all those restrictive and protective conditions that make employment in the formalized sector of the economy so attractive. It would seem that the long hours of work in the weaving units go back to the time when this industry was still run as a family business and the monopoly of local craftsmen. All members of the household used to participate in the production process which went on in an uneven rhythm all hours of the day and night. A report describing the artisanal style of operation also draws attention to the importance attached to ownership of the means of production in this *petit bourgeois* milieu which prevailed:

All members of the family irrespective of age and sex participate in weaving as and when they get time. The single condition of work is that weaving is their bread and butter. Thus in the case of small units weaving is a way of life. It could be that the girl who is adept at weaving is a better qualified girl as a bride. She won't be a burden to the family, either as a daughter or as a wife. Perhaps the worth of a family might be measured by the number of looms it owns. (Mehta and Pathak 1975: 100)

The work regime has since become more capitalistic. The workers do not belong to the family or even the same caste anymore and the intimate relationship between capital and labour that earlier existed has been clearly cut. The loom operators are hired hands only who, however, have not been given the type of protection enjoyed by the workforce in the formal sector of the economy.

Although the Factory Act expressly stipulates a working day of no more than eight hours, almost all employers give their weavers no other choice than to stand behind the machines for twelve hours at a stretch (*Working and Living Conditions* 1984: 42). These conditions do not only prevail in the powerloom sheds of Surat as is made clear in a report on the regime in the same industry in Ichalkaranji, a town in Maharashtra.

'The twelve-hour shift is a real bitch. Gnaws at our lives it does!' . . . 'Twelve-hour shift? Not eight?' . . . 'Oh no! 8–8 full twelve hours. And you can't go off like in other factories because all pay is by piece-work. 13 paise per metre. We have to keep the loom going till the other shift arrives. Then we put our mark on the cloth and get up.' Another, a little older, said, 'That twelve-hour shift kills a man. By the time we get home after the shift we are like zombies. Some get drunk on the way home, some not. Put some junk in the tummy and go out like a light. Get up and come to work.' (Awachat 1988: 1733)

And if a member of the next shift does not turn up to take their place, then the workers have to continue operating the looms until they are relieved twenty-four hours later. Such an extreme lengthening of work time is not disagreeable to the powerloom operator. In line with the law of self-exploitation he makes use of each and every opportunity to maximize his income. This is naturally impossible without one or two brief intervals, but it is typical of the industrial climate in the informal sector that most workshops have no formal rules regarding intervals. The weaver who rests a little, eats something, or has to go to the toilet, remains responsible for anything that might go wrong during his short absence. Shortage of electrical power makes it unavoidable that workplaces in Surat close down for one day each week. That is the only reason, caused by the interrupted use of capital, that the workers are given a day off. It is a matter of fact that they are not paid on the day that the looms have to close down (*Working and Living Conditions* 1984: 44). This also applies when workers take any leave, which they have to do on their own account and at their own risk. A weaver is fortunate if, on his return, he does not find that his place has been taken by another.

The better life of the diamond cutters is also expressed in the greater latitude they are given in performing their daily task:

Diamond workers start and stop at their convenience. Workers who stay in the town may commence work as early as 7 a.m. Those who stay in the surrounding villages commute to work by cycle, bus or train. Buses and trains are not noted for their punctuality and travelling by cycle is problematic during the monsoon months. These workers report for work by nine or even ten o'clock in the morning. Workers also have their lunch break or noon rest at a time convenient to them. By five o'clock in the evening workers begin to leave, but some may continue working up to seven or eight o'clock in the evening. (Kalathil 1978: 100-1)

At first sight, this relaxed manner of employment, certainly as regards its flexibility, compares favourably even with the more comfortable working conditions that characterize formal sector employment. Piecework payment plays an important role, however. It sometimes leads to this type of more skilled labour taking an attitude that I am inclined to associate with the work mentality of *petit bourgeois* behaviour. Diamond cutters are paid per stone. The work tempo that they maintain – i.e. to come or not, to start and finish earlier or later, to work harder or more slowly – determines the amount of their earnings. If the work will not go right, if a stone is difficult to cut, the worker may decide to chuck it in for the day.

He may quit work early to watch a movie or roam about the market place. In the matter of leave too there are few restrictions on the workers. While some are considerate enough to inform the *karkhanedar* in advance, others fail to do so. In the agricultural harvesting season some workers who come from villages absent themselves to engage in harvesting. They say that this arrangement works out to their advantage financially. On the whole, the workers do not like a lean pay packet, and this is what keeps them on the job 6 days a week. (Kalathil 1978: 101)

This last remark is not in the least superfluous, even if only to avoid the impression that diamond workers form the sort of labour aristocracy that can be found in the formal sector of the economy. The owner of the work-place accepts such behaviour only from his best workers whom he does not want to lose. The others not only work long hours if the patron so wishes, but are also given little latitude to regulate their own presence or absence.

Piece-work is generally the customary method of payment of labour throughout all layers of the informal sector. It also applies to the power-looms, without even a small percentage of the workforce being granted any discretion as to their obligation to report for work. Weavers are paid per metre of woven material, and management bases itself on an average daily production per machine. The amount is based on what a hard and skilled worker can produce in twelve hours. If the output of a newcomer or an older hand remains below that norm, not incidentally but systematically, then he is discharged by his employer who thus puts an end to the underutilization of his capital investment.

The large number of workers used in all sorts of seasonal rural or semi-urban industry are also paid on the basis of piece-work: in cane-cutting, fruit picking, paddy harvesting, quarries, road building, brickworks and saltpans. An important difference with the textile worker or diamond cutter is that all these occupations usually have to be carried out by more than one person. All kinds of combinations occur, varying from work teams consisting of a few family members, to larger groups of adults with children.

Cane-cutting

The gang led by a *mukadam* which stays in the plain of south Gujarat for the sugarcane harvest is made up of 20 to 50 members. They are subdivided into smaller units, called *koytas*, usually made up of a man, woman and often a child. At the start of the working day the gang boss lines up the *koytas* at the beginning of the field. The members of each team have to cut the rows of stalks in front of them, remove the leaves, cut them into pieces, and bundle them. The area that all cover working in this way is the same, but the tempo depends on the labour power. This means that one work gang will finish its daily task earlier than another. The norm is high: approximately three-quarters of a ton, which demands an effort lasting nine to ten hours. Weak teams need so much time that the gang boss may decide to transfer part of their task, and its payment, to other teams that have extra capacity.

Brickworks

A gang of brick-makers consisting of nine to eleven members is expected to produce and stack 2,500 to 3,000 bricks per day. The amount of earth and other raw materials (coal dust and rice husks) with which they are provided at the start of the work day is attuned to that number. In my experience, the time in which the quickest and slowest gangs manage to process this quantity varies from ten to fourteen hours. Gangs that systematically fail to produce the required number of bricks are penalized for their shortcomings by reduction of the weekly allowance on which they depend for their sustenance.

The above examples show that the norm is based on an uninterrupted workload, of which only the strong are capable. Those who have difficulty in keeping to that tempo and in maintaining it until the end of the day, are discharged in due course. They have been judged and found inadequate, unsuited to take further part in the production process. The workers have their own unwritten rules, however, with which they try to defend themselves against their exploitation as a result of the piece-rate method. That defence is the subject of constant complaint by the employers to the effect that labourers absent themselves without valid reason and without making it known beforehand. Such behaviour, considered reprehensible by employers, is due to the long and severe work days and nights that are made even more taxing by the lack of any regular and paid intervals. Under such circumstances, absenting oneself from work is one of the few effective means by which to avoid complete subjection by the employers. The latter react angrily to the unexpected breach of their authority, thinking, often correctly, that it is due to sabotage by the workers. What is known in the employers' jargon as 'lack of discipline' is a logical consequence of the workers' lack of alternative for avoiding total hegemony over their labour power in any 'civilized' fashion.

There is yet another reason for scepticism about the indignation with which employers react to the unpredictable conduct of their subordinates. Employers do not show the slightest scruple in victimizing the workers for the many work stoppages that occur. The working rhythm is in fact very irregular. Therefore, the employers ensure availability of reserve labour which is not paid in the case of under-utilization. This applies both to all sorts of tasks that take place in the open and to manufacturing processes in a closed space. The entrepreneurial risks and the resulting costs are thus transferred from management to labour.

Cane-cutting

Day and night, a fleet of vehicles - lorries, tractors and bullock carts - comes and goes to bring cane to the factory. Management is in constant contact with the field staff so as to accelerate the work if the supply is insufficient and to slow it down if the factory becomes congested. Cane-cutting repeatedly has to be stopped because of machine defects in the mill, a transport breakdown, or other technical flaws. It means that on the one hand the army of cutters has to be constantly available, but on the other hand it is not paid when breakdowns occur in the process.

Transport

Loaders riding with the lorries are paid per run at rates that fluctuate according to distance. Like the lorry owner, they are concerned with loading and unloading as rapidly as possible because the number of runs they make will determine the wage they get at the end of the day. Sometimes, however, they just have to hang around for hours on end if the arrangement to pick up a load falls through or if the lorry breaks down. That enforced idleness is their problem and bad luck, according to the employer.

Weaving

The patron who yesterday had given a weaver a scolding due to absence without leave, now explained patiently why workers have no right to an income when production is interrupted. That this occurs fairly regularly can be seen from the underutilization of the looms, which run at rather less than three-quarters capacity (*Working and Living Conditions* 1984: 13). Confronted with complaints from his impatient workforce, the employer replied that he couldn't help it if yarn was not delivered, if there was a power cut or a machine broke down. And what could he do other than to send his workers away temporarily, with instructions to report daily, if he could not sell his product for a decent price?

Apart from staying away from work now and then the mass of unskilled workers have no other choice but to subject themselves to the dictates of the production process in which they have to earn their livelihood. Their submission is so complete that outside the work sphere they have almost no say even over their private life. The cane-cutters' working day is extended into the night by another three or four hours if they have to return to the fields to load onto lorries the cane that they have cut during the day (Breman 1990: 586–7). The same story of suffering can be told about labourers in the brickworks. Their work starts between two and four o'clock at night and continues until the end of the morning. They then have a break, when the women prepare a meal and do other household chores. In the afternoon it is time to clear the workplace for the ensuing night. Bricks that have been laid out to dry are stacked in rows a little further away. In the evening the water-soaked earth is taken out of the pit and heaped up close to the spot where the brick-maker will sit or squat a few hours later.

Altogether, the result is a working day lasting 14–16 hours, but that duration does not sufficiently illustrate the burden of the job. Unconditional surrender by labour is manifested in the complete subjection of the rhythm of life to the demands of the job, for twenty-four hours at a stretch. The smooth and efficient organization of agro-industry forces cane-cutters at night to load the amount of cane that they have cut during the day, because the mill's machines run continuously. But why is it necessary that the purely manual production of bricks should start at night and in the early morning? Brickworks owners were not unanimous in their reply to such questions. Many just said that this was customary in their branch of industry. The majority argued that drying is a very gradual process. If wet bricks are immediately exposed to the glaring sun, they would break easily even before being put in the kiln. Some employers say that workers are less distracted when it is dark, that they work harder in winter in order to keep warm, and that in summer they work at night to avoid the day's heat. Productivity certainly shows some fluctuations. In both cane-cutting and brick-making, daily production is highest between November and February. From then on the amount of cane cut by a *koyta* drops to little more than half-a-ton every 24 hours and the number of bricks made by a gang falls to substantially less than 2,500. The heat during the day undoubtedly plays a role, but more important is the exhaustion caused by the production process itself. The decline in performance does not mean that working hours become any shorter. Only the effort put into the work slows down towards the end of the season.

In general, the labour regime in the informal sector seems over the years to have been intensified. Women who wait long hours in the casual labour markets until someone may need them insist that they have to work both harder and longer now than ever before. They are expected to work until after dusk if necessary to complete a job. In most cases, the greater effort is not compensated by extra payment. This is a hidden wage reduction which indicates the increasing inequality between supply and demand.

Previously the contractors used to take work for 8 hours from the labourers. Now they take work for 9 to 10 hours a day. Many a time, they are not allowed to go home till the cement concrete mixing work is completed. The labourers engaged in slab-filling work usually start working in the morning and work till 7 p.m. Sometimes, this work is extended to midnight also. (Punalekar and Patel 1990: 126)

A common complaint is that members of the lower castes who come straight from the countryside into an industrial environment are not able

to work attentively and regularly for hours at a time. This stereotype is
further accentuated in the case of labour from a tribal background. Of
them it is said that, as carefree children of nature, they lack the self-discipline that is the basis of any successful performance in modern methods
of production.

In their traditional economic activities, the tribals have never been bound to work
in a routine manner. After doing some hard labour, they used to have relaxation
for as much time as they wished. Now in their new occupation it is required for
them to work for hours with a small break. They have not yet fully adjusted to this
sort of routine and hence some of them clamour for more recess hours.
(Lal 1982: 83)

The essay from which this passage is taken is concerned particularly with
Dhodhiyas and Halpatis who have penetrated to the industrial sites of
Vapi in south Gujarat from their nearby villages. Their employers were
dissatisfied about the lack of a steady work rhythm among these newcomers, a recrimination that I see as a variant of the lack-of-discipline complaint. As stated before, informal sector workers sometimes leave
unexpectedly, and inopportunely for their employer, in order to escape
the extremely heavy workload and other pressures. It would be misleading, however, to attribute erratic working behaviour at the bottom of the
economy exclusively to a more or less veiled refusal to toe the line. A more
important explanation is the lack of regularity inherent in the labour
process itself. The regime of the informal sector is characterized by the
sudden and unexpected alternation of peaks and falls, not only per season
but even in daily activities. Hours and days of almost unbroken drudgery
make way for shorter or longer periods of imposed idleness. This contrast
between maximum effort and forced inactivity reflects the logic of informal sector business and is not the manifestation of an uneconomic idio-
syncrasy which disqualifies the worker from a better existence. This mass
of men, women and children has to be present wherever, whenever, and
to the extent that there is a need for their services. A child working on the
streets expressed this as follows:

I have no fixed timings for my work. I go to Sardar Baug in the morning for selling
balloons, plastic toys, etc. In the evening either I do the same thing or engage
myself in selling water in an earthen pot. I am not always lucky. Often times, the
policeman or sometimes the garden watchman drives us all away. On some days
the area is cordoned off by the policemen if the procession (julus) has to pass that
way. So though we are ready to work all days, the situation is not always in our
favour. (S. P. Punalekar 1993: 127)

What seems at first sight a disjointed and irregular schedule is not due to
unwillingness or carelessness. Such an outlook does not do justice to

behaviour that shows the greatest possible flexibility in systematically attuning labour supply to the strongly fluctuating demand. Of relevance here is the point made by Thompson about the need of disciplining a labour force which is only partially and temporarily 'committed' to an industrial way of life (Thompson 1993: 352). However, time-thrift and a clear demarcation between 'work' and 'life' seem to presuppose an industrial environment in tune with the factorized urban capitalism that emerged and became dominant in the Atlantic world during the nineteenth century. It does not mean that lack of time consciousness is characteristic for the rural and urban proletariat which I have researched in India towards the end of the twentieth century. The daily rhythm of informal sector working classes is conditioned by the need to surrender completely to the unreserved claim made on their availability at all hours of the day or night, in all seasons of the year. That this potential demand is only partially and temporarily actualized has to do not so much with their faulty time-thrift but with the low and irregular demand that is made on their labour power.

Far more than in the countryside, the urban lifestyle is now regulated by time. A Koli woman from a village that has recently merged into Surat and which has long been exposed to the impact of its proximity, has expressed that type of pressure as follows:

Because of urbanization, our domestic tasks have become more complex. We have to take care of so many things in an orderly manner. Thirty years ago, we did not even care to have a wall clock. And when we purchased one, its novelty did not last long then. If it went out of order, we did not much bother to get it repaired. But now the situation is different. We have five wrist watches and two alarm clocks. We feel uneasy if we get up late. That upsets our routine for the whole day. Not only that, we cannot spend much time with our relatives and friends if they happen to visit our house on working days. That has created some misunderstanding among my relatives living in Olpad villages. They say that I have become *pucca* Surati and deliberately neglecting them. That way they are carrying wrong notions about me and my way of hospitality. How can I convince them that Piplod is not much different from Surat and our life must be run in clockwise precision? It is very difficult to convince them. They will only realize if they live in places like Piplod. (D. S. Punalekar 1992: 402)

However hectic daily life may be, the disciplined handling of clock-time apparent in this quotation is above all the prerogative of that small portion of the working population, to which this Koli household belongs, which may boast of subjection to punctuality in which formal sector activity is said to excel. However, time is also a strategic good in the hands of those whose intention it is to aggravate the task of informal sector workers by extending its duration. It is no coincidence that *mukadams*, as leaders of work gangs, are easily and immediately identifiable because they wear a wrist-watch. It is an article that forms part of the standard equipment for their profession.

Degradation in the labour process

In most branches of industry covered by my fieldwork, the labour process has such a degrading effect that, for that reason alone, employers feel forced regularly to replace and replenish their workforce.

This is, however, less applicable to diamond workshops. The term 'sweatshop' perfectly illustrates my immediate and principal impression gained from visits to these establishments in Surat, Navsari and Bardoli. In a small room with no ventilation, well-lit with neon tubes but without fresh air, ten or more young men sit cross-legged and close together on the floor around *ghantis*, work benches, closely watched by the owner from his air-conditioned cubicle. A towel hanging around the worker's neck is used to dry hands and face of sweat that runs profusely, particularly in the summer heat. The boss does not tolerate any fresh air to come into the atelier out of fear that his workers might rob him of diamonds by throwing some of the valuable stones given to them for processing out of the window or use any other opening to the outside world for that purpose. The textile workplaces occupied by powerlooms are larger, but the people working among the machines have hardly space in which to move. The enormous noise of the looms and the heat under the corrugated zinc roof are also sources of discomfort. Even employer-biased reports are somewhat critical of the appalling work conditions to which the industrial proletariat is exposed, resulting in a 'balanced' picture like the following:

largely due to insanitary living conditions, the health of the workers is affected and absenteeism from work is noticed. It is difficult to attribute all health problems to the working conditions or long hours of working as most diseases are not work-related. Diseases like chronic head-aches, stomach problems and skin affections could hardly be work-related. These are more likely to be due to lack of nutritious diet and maybe, to drinking habits. For hearing problems or deafness in the weaving industry, there is no solution. It is, however, true that if safety precautions are observed, problems like electrical shocks, chemical burns, physical injuries due to fall, etc., could be prevented. It is sad to note that, in the majority of factories, even first aid facilities are not provided. (Mehta and Gandhi: 128–9)

However bad conditions might be in the factories, those who work there find it rather less uncomfortable than most forms of industry that occur in the open air. Employers of the latter type frequently disagree. The manager of a sugar mill whom I accompanied on his daily round through the fields was quite convinced that the much lower wage paid to fieldworkers was compensated by their stay in the countryside. 'During the campaign they live in similar fashion to the sort of picnicking and camp life that you westerners enjoy in your leisure time,' he commented when we passed a cane-cutters' bivouac along the road side (Breman 1978/79: 66). This opinion was surpassed by the way in which the owners of saltpans boasted about the beneficial effect of this habitat on the physical well-being of their migrant workers. Their evidence before an official committee gave the impression that workers from south Gujarat came there every year to enjoy the delights of a health cure:

The employers further claim that the workmen who work in an atmosphere saturated with salt are generally free from attack of cold, rheumatism, neurology and similar other troubles. The preservative qualities of the salt account for a long life among these workers. (Report Minimum Wages Committee Salt Pan Industry 1976: 13)

I have seldom seen a more inhuman work environment from the climatological point of view than these saltpans during my fieldwork. Nature does not tolerate any living organism above water other than human workers. On the bare plain, not a single piece of shade can be found against the burning sun, and the saltish soil reflects the fierce light on the body. At the end of a day, my eyes were rimmed with red. During the hot summer months the morning temperature rises to such a high level that work has to be stopped at noon for a couple of hours. The work gangs who stamp down the soil of the pans at the start of the season accentuate their work rhythm with songs in which they sarcastically praise the mercy of the bosses who enticed them there, far from home, with their cash advances.

The stone quarries are just as ruthless. The workers who quarry the hills in the middle of the plain do not even have water nearby in which they could once in a while seek cooling during the hot summer months, as do the men who work in open mines along the river banks.

The work is done in the open air without any form of shelter. In the morning hours they work in the shadow of the rock wall; after about 1 p.m. this shadow disappears and work stops until 4 o'clock. Even then, it is exhausting just to stay in the quarry without working, with the sun reflecting on the now heated rock face. The men keep fit by regularly taking a dip in the river. (Koelen 1985: 104)

Not only adults but also children are victims of the miserable working conditions in the brickworks. Their labour power becomes indispensable while they are still quite young, and from the age of six they are wakened during the night to carry the fresh bricks made by their father. While wet, those bricks weigh roughly three kilos. The little children run with one brick each, away from the base plate and into the darkness. When they reach the age of about nine, they are promoted to carrying two bricks.

Sometimes their parents wake them up crying from the rags that form their beds. But at night they are the only ones who sing, trying to give themselves courage. If they run back quickly they can warm their hands for a few seconds by the wood fire which provides the *patavala* and *patavali*, the brick-maker and his female mate, with light and warmth in the cold winter nights.

Last night, while the parents were at work, a toddler was badly burned. The little boy, not yet three years old, had scampered to the kiln to seek warmth. There he must have fallen against the hot bricks in his sleep. Wet rags did little to stop the lad's screaming and crying.

A couple of days later, in another brickworks, I found a girl of about fifteen years old who lay on the ground under a couple of jute sacks, shivering with fever. Her younger sister came now and again and shook her gently, trying to get her to go to work, because she was unable alone to carry all the bricks away from the base plate. The labour power of her sick sister is needed to eliminate the backlog. When that has been done, she can lie down again although for no longer than ten minutes. (Fieldwork notes)

The sources of employment in which the toiling mass at the bottom of the economy is imprisoned not only provide poor earnings but also cause damage to health in ways that are obviously linked to the appalling work conditions. Independently or in combination, heat, cold, dampness, noise, dust and stench are noticeable risk factors in this debilitating working environment. Of all categories of labour to which I have directed my attention, the diamond cutters are undoubtedly the most fortunate. Although they complain that the constant peering through the magnifying glass is damaging to the eyes and that the diamond dust released during grinding eventually causes breathing problems, I have found no tangible evidence of these occupational diseases whether in practice or in the reports of other researchers.

On the other hand, I had no difficulty at all in corroborating the complaints of powerloom operators about their working conditions. Noise is the greatest evil. When streets are quiet at night, the continual rattle of the machines in buildings in many parts of the town is all the more noticeable. Investigations into conditions in this industry showed that 78 per cent of the respondents suffered from fairly serious health complaints, particularly hearing disorders, eye disease, bronchial complaints and chronic pain in the head or limbs (*Working and Living Conditions* 1984: 79). Even worse than the situation of weavers is that of workers in the dyeing-and-printing mills who have to handle dyes often with their bare hands and inhale the noxious smells of chemicals. And then there are those who, in a closed space with very high humidity, operate a machine with a high piercing sound, which treats artificial silk yarn in such a way that the threads are loosened and curled. Listening to the shouted explanation of this treatment and profusely sweating over my whole body, I have never been able to stay in such a workplace for longer than a few minutes. Reports which are the outcome of employers' sponsored research quite blatantly hold these industrial workers responsible for their poor health condition. Both statistics and research on work hazards, industrial injuries and occupational diseases which disproportionately afflict people in the informal sector, are sadly lacking.

The industrial townships on the edge of Surat, in particular Udhana and Pandesara, are bad places in which to stay, let alone in which to work. Environmental pollution, of air and water, is unimaginable. Dense smoke, soot and dust make it difficult to breathe, and I have often left this jungle of modern industry with my eyes watering and nose running. The same applies to industrial sites in other places along the main road and the railway, which form the connections with Bombay in the south and Vadodara/Ahmedabad in the north. Farmers in south Gujarat's western coastal plain complain about the damage to their crops and land caused by the chemical industry that has been set up here. Employment in any of these industries entails a considerable health risk, as labourers from Gandevigam and Chikhligam have experienced. They have to handle corrosive salts and acids without any protection at all for face, arms and legs. 'I can show you the wounds on my hands,' a Dhodhiya man said to me, 'but not the pain that I feel inside my body.'

Workers in the open air are perhaps less exposed to modern industrial pollution than are the factory workers, but they run other risks that may result in temporary or permanent harm to the body. Industrial accidents are a common occurrence on work locations in the informal sector. Building sites in particular are notorious for risks to which casual workers are exposed. The contractor refuses to accept any liability for injuries resulting in temporary or even permanent disability, and it is equally futile for the worker to seek redress from the *mukadam*. On the contrary, it is quite normal for the victim to be instantly dismissed without any form of compensation. Men and women frequently fall victim to the primitive modes of extraction that are still practised in the majority of quarries:

the feet and lower legs are particularly at risk because the labourers work with bare feet and legs. The greatest risks occur when large rocks have to be hacked into more manageable pieces with a sledge-hammer; the pieces are rolled into position and held there with the bare feet. There is always a great danger of rebounding hammers and mis-hits. (Koelen 1985: 104)

The arms and hands of the cane-cutters are not protected against the knife-sharp top leaves or against slips with the machete. On their bare feet they have to carry their heavy headloads out of the stubble that they leave in the fields after harvesting. The primitive or even non-existent medical care means that wounds on arms and legs, hand and feet, easily become infected. In the brickworks, precautionary measures of any kind are conspicuous by their absence. Injuries of all kinds are common occurrences in the handling of raw materials, operating the kiln and humping the bricks in the successive processing stages. The workers who stand in the mixing pits for hours at a time, the women who carry the bricks on their heads ten at a time with a total weight of about twenty-five kilos, the brick-maker and his partner who sit in a squatting posture for hours on end – they all complain about pain in their backs and other parts of the body. While discussing health hazards with a Halpati from Chikhligam, who has taken part in the seasonal migration for many years, he pointed out many knock-kneed children, a defect that is certainly caused by a combination of poor food, long working hours, and too heavy burdens at a young age. Brown lung disease seems to be another complaint peculiar to this branch of industry. It applies particularly to the *chapavali*, the women who each day and all day carry the baked bricks out of the kiln. By evening their faces are like masks, entirely covered in dust. Using an edge of their *sari* they do their best to cover their mouth and nostrils. But the stone dust even penetrates that veil.

As a result of the poor hygienic conditions under which seasonal migrants in particular are forced to live, they fall victim to all sorts of chronic disease, e.g. dysentery, TB, malaria, and take them home. An impression of this can be gained from the following description of conditions found in cane-cutters' camps by a committee appointed by the High Court in Gujarat:

Being compelled to use highly polluted, non-potable water for drinking purposes many a time, it is not surprising that there were large numbers of cases of workers suffering from dysentery and diarrhoea . . . it was obvious that the workers live in total destitution without even a minimum facility for staying, clothing, and nothing to sleep on, children of tender age without clothes were a common sight at the camps. Pregnant and nursing mothers also sharing the same conditions, all left without any clothes to protect themselves from the winter cold. (Breman 1990: 585)

'The Crushing of Cane and of Labour' was the sub-title that I gave to my first report on the employment of the huge army of migrant harvesters in the fields of south Gujarat (Breman 1978/79). Similar circumstances dominate most other branches of seasonal industry. From the mass of men, women and children who participate in this mobile workforce each year, a number always return back home blind, deaf, crippled or bent double with rheumatism. In discussing secondary labour conditions in the next chapter I shall further examine the fate of the workers who are forced to live a circulatory existence, temporarily or semi-permanently. Adults older than forty years migrate less and less frequently. Not because they can permit themselves the luxury of staying at home, but because their lack of sufficient fitness in mid-life makes them the last to be considered by jobbers. As the owner of a brickworks told me: the replacement of old labour by young costs nothing, but the replacement of old by new capital is expensive.

A well-known doctor in Valsad, whom I met occasionally during my fieldwork, has his medical practice in a neighbourhood populated by unskilled labourers. He attributes the poor health of the majority of his patients to the conditions under which they have to work.

How will they be able to do normal work when they have to inhale dust particles? They take cold and insufficient food. Over and above that they consume liquor to relieve themselves of tensions and exhaustion. Their lungs become weak and they begin to suffer from incurable diseases like TB and asthma. They suffer from sunstroke as they have to work in a scorching heat. There are some cases of cholera too. They suffer from boils because they sit in dirty, insanitary places. Some female labourers are compelled to have sexual relations with people in order to get work and other favours. That leads to venereal diseases. (Punalekar and Patel 1990: 101)

The brutal labour regime imposes an even heavier burden on women and children than on men. Boys and girls of 10–12 years of age frequently have to work the same long hours as the adults, but at their tender age they are less able to withstand fatigue. Their pace of strenuous work is not always adequate, and it is quite customary for employers and overseers to be harsh in disciplining them. Their greater vulnerability makes them an easy target for verbal or physical violence and for the continual threat of dismissal due to default (S. P. Punalekar 1993: 134). The same author states that three out of every ten children who earn their living on the streets suffer from hunger. Although extreme poverty is undoubtedly the principal reason why they have to seek work at such an early age, many obviously earn too little even to assuage their hunger. Nevertheless, even the most deprived among these young people maintain a work code of regulating what is decent or improper. The latter category includes the acceptance of free food (S. P. Punalekar 1993: 161). Mutual solidarity among fellow-sufferers in miserable conditions helps them to cope with extreme adversity. Children who not only work in the streets but also have to do so without adult protection will share the food that they earn and look after their sick mates. Street wisdom teaches them that help and distrust are not far removed from one another.

Pick-pocketer could be any of us standing here. How do we know? When living is expensive and when there is too much competition in earning money, some of us end up by earning only a paltry sum of Rs 5 or Rs 10 by evening. Day's expenses including tea-bread, potato, wada etc. cost us more than Rs 10 per day. When we earn less, we request our work mates to lend us money or food. Sometimes they oblige, sometimes they do not. In such eventualities, anyone of us can be tempted to steal away money even of our close friend. (S. P. Punalekar 1993: 146)

The women usually have to cope with a double burden of work. A few hours before starting their paid labour, they are busy with all sorts of domestic activities: preparing meals, caring for the children, washing and cleaning. They are the first to rise in the morning and the last to go to bed at night. The men come back tired from their work, demanding rest, care and attention. The women, who are equally tired, are expected as a matter of course to continue their work in the private sphere.

When we come back home, we feel already tired and exhausted because of factory work. We need some respite and rest. But our husband, children and in-laws, all expect that we must begin our domestic work as soon as we enter the house. They have little understanding of how much fatigue we experience in the factory. They think as if we come back from movie or marketing. (S. P. Punalekar 1988: 76)

We have already seen that working girls and women run the risk of sexual abuse. This may be forced on them in the household where they work as domestic servants, for example, by the *mukadam* who can select or ignore them for employment, by an employer or his foreman who can dismiss them if they refuse a wide range of sexual intimacies, including rape. Usually the only protest possible against such treatment is to leave the workplace. In order to avoid risks of this nature, which bring the whole family into disrepute, people are quite anxious to find out about employment opportunities for female household members in advance. This is the practice in the case of Surat's *jari* workers:

The women workers who are ignorant about all other things are very conscious about their safety. The mother will check whether a place is safe before sending her young daughter for a job. When a woman wants to change her place of work, the men in her family first check whether the new place is safe or not and then only the woman worker is allowed to go there. (Soni 1990: 145–6)

Those who are at the bottom of the informal sector cannot always afford to safeguard themselves against attacks on their code of sexual honour. I found, for instance, seasonal migrants going to the brick-kilns to be quite helpless in resisting *mukadams* and employers who took advantage of young girls or married women even when fathers or husbands of these victims were around. Similarly, young children scraping a meagre living on the streets are without protection against sexual assaults. A quarter of the street children questioned by Punalekar had been forced to have intercourse or named their friends who had experienced this (S. P. Punalekar 1993: 170). This is an alarmingly high figure for a subject that is taboo and regarding which the researcher gets to know little even after long acquaintance.

Informal sector workers have to survive in extremely cruel conditions. It needs all their resilience to cope with a continual series of setbacks. It is inadvisable to express anger and disappointment during working hours, but their bottled-up aggression regarding their miserable circumstances has to find an outlet. It is hardly surprising that the weakest members in their milieu are then victimized, as one regular customer to an urban labour market acknowledged:

Since last one month, we have been passing through very difficult times. We are not getting work. It has become difficult to buy even a cup of tea, not to talk of snacks or regular food. If the children cry due to hunger, we beat them and force them to sleep. What else to do? (Punalekar and Patel 1990: 141)

6   Mode of wage payment and secondary labour conditions

Wages

Wages paid to informal sector workers in south Gujarat show strong variations. A classification that I made early in 1991 (Table 6.1) of amounts paid to the principal categories of labour discussed in this study illustrates those differences. The survey shows that the lowest paid received five to six times less than the amount earned by the highest paid. These figures are for adult males. Children up to the age of 15 or 16 who work as unskilled labourers are paid no more than half the amounts mentioned for the first five categories, while the rate for women is at least 20 per cent lower than that paid to men for the same work.

Agricultural labourers earn least of all. Recent research nevertheless shows a gradual improvement in the economic conditions of the landless at the bottom of rural society which forms the largest working class in the country. First in the 1970s and even more in the early 1980s, the agrarian proletariat in various parts of India benefited from a real wage increase. The same source mentions, however, that this favourable trend seems to have come to an end in 1984–85 as far as Gujarat is concerned (Report NCRL, vol. 1, 1991: 61).

On the basis of fieldwork at intervals in Chikhligam and Gandevigam, I conclude that the positive effect of a moderate rise in agricultural wages is largely negated by decreasing employment opportunities in agriculture for the local landless population. Low-caste women in particular were victims of this trend. Redundant village labour can only compensate for the local loss of income to a small extent by moving to other economic sectors, whether in the countryside or towns of south Gujarat.[1]

On a daily basis, seasonal non-agricultural work pays little more than agricultural work. The difference is that the workforce, consisting mostly of migrants, has to work almost continually throughout the period for

---

[1] For an analysis of the changes experienced by Halpati households in Gandevigam and Chikhligam during the past two or three decades, I refer to a separate study in which the dynamics of poverty conditions in these two villages of earlier fieldwork are extensively discussed (Breman 1993b).

Table 6.1. *Daily wages paid to rural and urban informal sector workers in south Gujarat, early 1991*

Kind of work	Amount
Agricultural labour in Gandevigam and Chikhligam	Rs 10–12
Seasonal work in rural industries (cane-cutting, stone quarries, roadwork, brickworks, saltpans)	Rs 10–15
Casual labour in and near small towns	Rs 15–20
'Helpers' on industrial estate within commuting distance from the village (Gundlav/Valsad, Chikhli Road/Bilimora)	Rs 16–20
Casual workers in Surat's urban labour markets	Rs 25–30
Semi-skilled workers, regular employees of urban workshops	Rs 35–45
Skilled powerloom operators	Rs 50–60
All-round diamond cutters	Rs 55–70

which they are recruited. During that time, family groups will often work together. For the households in question, this source of employment thus provides a disproportionately large part of their total annual income. Apart from the fact that non-agricultural daily workers are usually paid less than those in regular jobs, they are also less assured of employment than those who go daily to the same boss. The difference is undoubtedly due partly to the fact that more or less permanent workers are more skilled and experienced than casual workers who have to work with a variety of employers. As a result, skilled weavers and qualified diamond cutters can earn a daily wage that is five or six times higher than that of agricultural labourers. The margin is less for Oriya workers who report earnings in Surat which are 2.5 to 3.5 times higher than back home (Pathy 1993: 14). However, even before they made the move these migrants were better off than the landless mass surviving on low wages at the bottom of the village economy. The class of agricultural labourers in Orissa, just like the Halpatis in the countryside of south Gujarat, are hindered by their intense poverty from reaching the powerloom workshops in Surat. The heterogeneity in labour conditions which characterize the informal sector in Surat has its origins in socio-economic differences in the villages of recruitment. According to a conventional school of thought work migration is basically a reaction to new and better opportunities created elsewhere. However, a study summing up the impact of migration from rural areas, with particular reference to India, shows how inequalities which already existed before departure became sharpened (Connell et al. 1975.) The question who goes out, where and for what is predetermined by the hierarchical caste and class structure in the rural hinterland. The high variation in income between segments of the informal sector workforce is widened and made more complicated by the lack of standardized conditions of employment commonly found in the formal sector circuit. People standing in the early morning labour markets in Surat, but also powerloom operators or diamond cutters, are far from uniform categories all doing the same amount of work and, to the extent they do, are not necessarily paid the same wage.

The difference between rural and urban wage levels, illustrated in Table 6.1, is compensated to some extent by divergent costs of living. The commonly held notion that agricultural workers in the villages being nearer to food production can obtain it more easily and cheaply than industrial workers needs to be corrected, however. The landless of Chikhligam and Gandevigam have to depend for their daily needs on small local shops that charge more for rice, flour, etc. than urban consumers have to pay. The price level is affected by many factors, such as the weight and amount of commodities bought, i.e. the bigger the purchase the lower the price, and whether or not there is a 'fair price' shop in the vicinity. The high cost of living in Surat, reputed to be one of the most expensive cities in India, is closely linked to the alien origins of much of the population. Labour migrants, particularly single persons, have to pay more than local workers for food, shelter and other consumption needs.

Apart from the wage rate, the income of various sorts of labour is determined by the total number of days worked per year. In this respect, too, the informal sector shows great variation, not only among different types of activity but even within the same branch of industry or occupational specialization. That diversity makes it even more difficult to estimate the annual income of workers and the households to which they belong.

My estimate is that Halpatis earning their living in Chikhligam and Gandevigam as agricultural labourers work from 150 to 240 days respectively per annum. Seasonal work, for which migrants leave or enter the villages *en masse* after the rainy season, lasts from three to six working months. Casual work away from agriculture and the village, calculated on a yearly basis, provides a number of landless in my fieldwork villages with three to four months of employment. 'Helpers' taken on by employers on the industrial estates of Valsad and Bilimora can count on five to eight months of employment per year. The urban employment arena is not only larger but also busier. The early morning markets provide job-seekers with short-term employment totalling 60 to 150 days per year. In Surat, street or home-work can be expected to provide an income for seven to ten months of the year. A regular job in a small enterprise assumes employment that will pay a wage for 150 to 270 days per annum. Full-time weavers will work for at most 270 days in a year. The majority of diamond cutters have to be content with working 150 to 240 days. The cyclical nature of activities that is said to be characteristic of agriculture also applies to a large part of the informal sector. In the monsoon, for example, work in the open air has to cease completely or is drastically reduced. Such peaks and falls in production occur not only in agriculture and the countryside, but also on industrial sites and in urban workshops operating under a roof. This may be due to temporary shortage of raw materials, fall or rise in turnover, etc. As pointed out earlier informal sector employers use such fluctuations to motivate their decision for not increasing the capital-intensity of their firms and for maintaining a 'flexible' workforce, that is to say no permanent employment. In fact, the capricious and often unpredictable alternation between work and idleness typifies the existence of labour in the informal sector. *Akashi roji*, what work the day will bring is as unpredictable as the weather, is how casual workers speak about their daily struggle for existence. One woman has described her anxiety about the variable outcome of trips to the morning market as follows:

When we leave home for the casual labour market, we only hope that we can find some work opportunity. But as the time passes, and the group of contractors and *mukadams* begin leaving the market along with their just selected labourers, we realize that there is hardly one out of hundred chances that we would get any work here. So we begin to worry. What do we do now? What shall we cook at home? How to feed our children? Such questions begin to haunt us. (Punalekar and Patel 1990: 124)

The apparently obvious solution of combining various sorts of employment is feasible only to a limited extent. Rather than contrasting with one another, the peaks and falls in various sectors of rural and urban industry show a parallel pattern of inclusion and exclusion. Agricultural work in the village can to some extent be alternated with unskilled work as day-labourer elsewhere. However, any more skilled specialization providing a higher income almost excludes the possibility of temporarily seeking another source of livelihood. The various work spheres that provide more or less permanent jobs are almost shut to one another. Families who leave after the monsoon to undertake seasonal work elsewhere and stay away for some months, cannot immediately be fitted into the local economy on their return. After a period of more or less forced unemployment, they leave again in the following season. With the exception of irregular mobile workers at the bottom of the rural economy who move individually or in groups in search of work, the informal sector is broken down into various circuits of labour which, notwithstanding the low degree of skill required, have little linkage with one another. As a result, a temporary shortage of work in one sector cannot immediately be overcome by a switch to another. The travel costs involved, the lack of contacts, inexperience, and barriers thrown up by people already working in other sectors, all play an important role. This segmentation caused me to determine in the course of my fieldwork that the lowest paid informal sector workers could not survive unless they earned an income for at least 120 to 150 days per year. The majority manage in one way or another to work for 150 to 240 days, as much as possible in their own domain of employment. The proportion that can count on work for 270 or more days per year is much smaller. The more skilled among them who, even in the eyes of their employer, rank as regular employees, represent an elite among the informal sector proletariat.

The combination of wage level and total work days only theoretically yields the gross amount that is paid to labour in a certain branch of industry. Numerous disruptive factors affect the final calculation. For instance, there is a linkage between the greater or lesser availability of work and the size of the wage. Not infrequently, an employer will send his workers home with a lower wage during the off-season. A variation on this is evinced by price fluctuations on urban labour markets. As time progresses, the remaining workers have no choice but to accept the lower rate that is offered them.

In the early morning hours, the wage rate may be at some higher level, say about Rs 20 or Rs 25. But one or two hours later, the wage rate may go down by Rs 2, 3, or 5. (Punalekar and Patel 1990: 127)

Finally, there are all kinds of wage variations, not only among enterprises in the same branch of industry, but even among workers who are taken on by an employer for the same work. These are sometimes due to seniority or skills. However, an informal sector employer may also pay a slightly higher wage to workers who have gained his favour, for whatever reason, than to the rest of the workforce, without giving any explanation for such discriminatory treatment. Not arbitrary but structural is the discrimination suffered by women in all labour markets which belong to the informal sector. To give just one example, there are no female powerloom operators. They are only employed in these workshops for non-mechanized jobs which do not require any skill. Consequently, sharp gender differentiation is a major feature of the wage pattern also when male and female workers perform the same tasks (Agrawal 1992: 209–14).

Due to these sharp fluctuations in income, even among those with regular jobs, any estimate of the annual amount on which households of wage workers in the informal sector exist, can only be speculative. According to calculations by the Government of Gujarat, at the start of the Eighth Five-Year Plan (1991) in order not to be below the poverty line a household consisting of two adults and three children needed Rs 40 per day. It is clear that the majority of workers who form the subject of my study, lead a miserable existence much below this level of expenditure. Even if two adult members of an agricultural labourer's family in Chikhligam or Gandevigam should work every day, which is out of the question, their combined earnings would still be less than the income minimally needed for a reasonable existence. Not having two square meals a day throughout the year, as reported by half of the agricultural labour households surveyed in Valsad district (Basant 1993: 384), must be a powerful motive for going outside in search of work. The armies of seasonal migrants and the growing number of almost or totally landless people who, for varying periods, seek casual employment of any sort in the open air in countryside or town, live in equally miserable circumstances. Together, these categories, which I estimate to form half the labour force in the informal sector of south Gujarat, live far below the poverty line. Slightly better off are those in villages and towns who work for one employer in all kinds of workplaces as low-paid employees with little security, and also the low-skilled workers who find employment on a fairly regular basis. I estimate that this category, closer to the poverty line but still below it, includes one-sixth of all informal sector workers. The remaining one-third consists of relatively more skilled and better paid workers in steady employment, such as powerloom operators and diamond cutters. On the basis of their wage (Rs 50–70 per day) and the number of days worked (more than twenty per month), this elite segment of the informal sector manages to earn an income that lifts many of them above the poverty line. The better financial standing enables such workers to send part of their income to the family back home. This is primarily to ensure the upkeep of those who remain behind and also, if anything should be left over, to pay off debts, to improve the house or to buy a plot of land for when the migrant is going to return to Orissa. The split householding – productive male(s) staying in Surat while the less productive females and children make do with whatever income they get from the land in the native place – is a heavy burden on the shared budget. For powerloom operators the amounts remitted to the villages range from Rs 400 to more than Rs 2,000 per year, according to a report dating back to the middle of the 1980s (Mehta and Gandhi: 130). The more substantial remittances belong to the aristocracy among these migrants, i.e. labour contractors and weaving masters. They are also the ones – not more than 10 to 12 per cent of the army of alien workers coming from

Orissa – who manage to purchase in the village more agricultural property or to release land from mortgage. It also happens that such better-off migrants use their savings to buy or build sheds in Surat slums for providing shelter to workers recruited by them. These investments naturally strengthen the control of work bosses over newcomers to the city who are often also dependent on their benefactors for finding employment. Not all young men who have come to Surat to work as powerloom operators or diamond cutters share their earnings with household members left behind. Pathy reports on the Oriya migrants:

> One fourth of the workers have failed to save money to send money home. But in most cases that was due to their recent immigration, ill health and long period of unemployment. Of course, in some cases it is due to wasteful expenditure in food, drink, dress, entertainment, drugs and gambling. (Pathy 1993: 15)

Diamond cutters from Saurashtra in particular have quite a reputation for indulging in the comforts and vices of big city life. On the other hand, money which is sent home does not always consist of savings. Not infrequently workers ask their employers for an advance on labour to be performed in order to meet urgent consumption needs of family members back in the village. How to remit money is a technique with which fresh migrants who have just landed in the informal sector are usually not familiar.

> I asked my employer to give me my money so that I could send some by money order. He gave me rupees 300 and the address of post-office near Zampabazar. I was illiterate and did not know anything about post or how to send a money order. I went to the post-office. There was too much of crowd and one police-man was standing. I just stood there for two hours not knowing what to do. Then one man from the post-office asked me why I was standing there for such a long time. I explained him. He helped me in sending my money order. I kept Rs 100 for myself and sent Rs 200 for my mother. (Lobo 1994: 47)

The amount spent by the workers themselves for their requirements in Surat is often inadequate for a life free of poverty. Sources of credit – i.e. jobbers, workmates, neighbours and bosses – had to be constantly tapped, not only to cover the daily cost of subsistence during periods of unemployment, but also to send money to the dependent household members who had to be left behind. To conclude from these remittances that labour migrants by and large succeed in improving their economic condition outside the village is shortsighted. What they send home are often not savings but advance payment for labour still to be performed when required by moneylending employers or their agents.

My analysis is based on a number of considerations whose plausibility I have tried to demonstrate. Definite corroborative data are not available, largely because the exercise undertaken here has a fairly weak empirical basis in the fluidity of relations between most employers and employees in the informal sector. Apart from the lack of any regularity in employment, a noticeable characteristic of this largest sector of the economy is that wages are seldom determined and paid with any punctuality. In discussions with informal sector workers they rarely convert the yield of their labour into a specified daily wage. To them, such a calculation would be largely fictional.

Payment

The simplest method is that of payment of casual workers who have to scrape a living by doing all sorts of jobs outside and inside agriculture in the close vicinity of the village. Their earnings are paid out at the end of their work time: a day, part of a day, or a number of consecutive days. Sometimes an employer will make an arrangement with them for work some time later; in that case, the agreement for work to be done in the near future is sealed with a small advance on wages. Their earnings are based mostly on piece-rate rather than on a fixed rate for a day's work. The work may be individual or may be carried out by teaming up for the occasion with a few mates. In the latter case the person who arranged the job is paid by the employer, and he divides the amount among members of the group in proportion to the work done. Female labourers are not excluded from such group work, but the initiative is seldom taken by a woman. Nor is it customary that payment should be made direct to young females. In fact, this occurs only if a household does not include adult males. This is different, of course, if a gang is wholly composed of women as happens to be the case, for example, at the time of transplanting paddy. The female leader of the gang is in overall charge of the operation, decides who to contract for the work and takes care of negotiations, if any, with employers. Such brokers are regular members of their gang and share in all the work to be done. Still, they have a greater say and to that extent come close to the figure of the *mukadam* discussed in chapter 5. In her study of caste, class and gender in rural South India, Kapadia has given us the profile of such a female gang leader:

the recruiter did benefit greatly from being the one who constituted the group because she had a greater say than anyone else on who became part of it. Since she distributed jobs, her powers of patronage were considerable, and if, like the redoubtable Sarusu, she regularly recruited laborers, then her influence was great. This was because a recruiter like Sarusu was perceived to have the ability to offer almost continuous employment, and so the women she recruited did not question her actions. (Kapadia 1995: 225)

The amount of the wage and the mode of payment for casual work vary little in or out of agriculture. Labourers from Gandevigam and Chikhligam who have found employment on an industrial estate work mostly on piece-rate and are paid wages weekly or fortnightly. It is seldom that they are taken on as permanent workers with all the rights that entail according to the Factory Act: bonus, dearness allowance, providence fund, sick leave, vacation, etc.

In view of the superficial contacts characteristic of the urban casual labour markets, it might be thought that job-seekers return home at the end of the day with the money earned. This is by no means always the case. Although the contractor or jobber will agree to pay everything and at once, these work providers regularly default on their promises:

Paliben Dahyabhai Rathod of Navsari Bazar narrated how the behaviour of the contractors changes after the work is completed. When the work is about to be finished, the contractor begins making false complaints. He would say that they have not done the work properly. They have spoiled the work, etc. and then he would withhold part of their wages. 'That is their usual trick and we know this too well', she said. (Punalekar and Patel 1990: 132)

Employers also resort to such methods to ensure themselves of sufficient casual workers for the following days or just to signal their hold over the workforce.

Workers in the textile mills and diamond cutting ateliers are among the best-paid employees in south Gujarat's informal sector. Diamond workers are paid per stone cut and polished, an amount that fluctuates with the degree of difficulty involved in processing the stone. Their wage is dependent on the quantum of uncut stones received by the patron from traders, the hardness of the stone, and the particular processing phase entrusted to the worker. However, payments also vary greatly among cutters. The atelier owner favours the best workers by giving them the most profitable processing phases and by giving the hardest stones to newcomers or to less favoured hands who are not indispensable and from whom he would not hesitate to dock wages if they ruined a stone. As a consequence, in a fairly small workplace some workers will earn a much higher wage even than is paid in the formal sector, while workmates sitting at the same *ghanti* may earn less than half that amount. Payment is irregular and frequently has to wait until the boss receives money owing to him by his suppliers. The *karkhanedar* has varying degrees of success in persuading the traders to pay an advance when complying with their orders. On the other hand, the cutters are often unable to wait so long for their earnings, and they ask the patron for an advance, called *baki*. This is not only done to get hold of their wage arrears, but also to meet some items of major expenditure that have to be made at various times of the year. This custom is so large-scale that most experienced diamond cutters need to continue working to pay off the loans that they have taken from their employer, who thus keeps the workers tied to him. According to one source, the capital that workshop owners invest in their labour force is twice or thrice the value of their machines (Pathak 1984: 155). The tariff rate for diamond cutting is more or less standardized throughout the industry. Workers who change their workplace do so, or threaten to do so, in order to bargain for a higher cash advance and the promise of more work. The new employer will then repay the claims of his predecessor. Only cutters who are known as skilled craftsmen are able to do this. Quitting or dismissal is often due to conflicts that are not only caused by the tricky settlement of loans. Workers threaten their patrons (and patrons in turn their suppliers) by stealthily exchanging stones given them to cut for inferior stones already polished. The theft of stones is common. Major traders often have a couple of toughs in their regular employ to find the thieves and use brute force in coercing them to repent. It is important for cutters, in turn, to find a workplace whose owner has a good reputation among the traders who consequently regularly supply him with stones. These diamond workers naturally receive the highest *baki*. On the other hand, they have least reason to betray their patron's confidence, particularly not if both parties belong to the same community. They then have an intimate friendly relationship, known as *bhai-chara*, which largely cancels out the inequality between employer and employee. This is not the case with young men from landless households in rural areas who have entered the cutting profession at the height of the boom period and are the first to be discharged in a recession. They have more difficulty in finding regular employment and the cash advance that goes with it. They are also less likely to build up a relationship of trust with the patron. Only the best workers among them are able to overcome the social handicaps that hinder their careers as diamond cutters. The crisis suffered by the diamond industry in the early 1980s, and still more vehemently at the end of that decade, resulted not only in a considerable drop in wages but also in such long-term unemployment for cutters of low caste that many of them had no choice but to leave the industry (Koelen 1985: 89–96).

The inflow of migrants into Surat's textile industry has continued unabated for many years. Wages paid to powerloom operators depend on the number of metres that they weave during a twelve-hour work day or night. In this sector, too, wages vary from month to month, fluctuating as much as twenty-five per cent above or below the average level (*Working and Living Conditions*, 1984: 32–3). Considerable differences are found among workers who operate the same machines in a workshop, variations that are principally due to the number of days worked and to increasing the work effort beyond the twelve-hour standard. It also happens, however, that the employer pays some of his workers a slightly higher rate per metre than others. These are the more experienced hands who are thus discouraged from going over to a competitor willing to pay the same rate. These industrialists also prefer to maintain a small core of trusted workers, both to ensure regular production and recruit new hands who function as a continually changing reserve workforce. Employers also make discreet use of another discriminatory method which can lead to considerable wage differences, namely, the arbitrary deduction from wages of an amount for 'damage'. This practice came to light during the large-scale investigation of labour relations in the textile industries of Surat:

Deductions are made in the workers' take-home pay on account of damages in cloth. According to workers, the low-quality material, mechanical defects, etc. are also responsible for the poor working results. But the blame is squarely placed on the workers and their wages deducted, the workers complained. (*Working and Living Conditions* 1984: 66)

Women home-workers in the *jari* industry are subjected to the same practices, as one of them reported: 'When we go to the trader with our finished products, they do not allow us to speak. They weigh the material, go through our embroidered cloth pieces one by one, and finally work out our dues. They alone know the mechanism of calculating or rather miscalculating our wages. They will deliberately change their facial expression to show us that we have committed some mistakes somewhere. And in the end, they will pay us less than we had expected. We have by now got used to this practice of theirs.' (S. P. Punalekar 1988: 123)

Some weavers are allowed to engage an apprentice and, after a couple of days, are given more looms to operate for the duration of the 'apprenticeship'. In this way they can increase their production above that of other weavers. Fewer workers are granted the privilege of an advance on wages, a custom that is still rare in this branch of industry.

Wages are usually paid once a fortnight. The difference in treatment described above between the small group of weavers who belong to the 'permanent' core and the rest who constitute the marginalized majority in the industry, leads to considerable wage variations. According to the investigation held in 1984 among 1,635 textile workers, the bottom 25 per cent earn only one-third the wage of the top 10 per cent, while this 'aristocracy' earn approximately double the take-home pay of half their workmates. The bottom category in this branch of industry is formed by male 'trainees' and 'helpers' and also of women and children. The inferior plight of female as compared to male workers has been discussed before.

Young children, whatever their age and experience, belong to the lowest paid.

Wages for the army of workers who hire out their labour power far from home for an entire season are determined and paid on another basis than those of day workers or of workers in semi-permanent employment. A cash advance is the key for binding labour going out at a later period. The size of the down-payment is decided by negotiation. The worker wants as much and as early as possible. As the employer's agent, the *mukadam* is required to bargain for a minimum amount preferably as close as possible to the date of departure. All sorts of subsidiary factors are of influence, such as previous work experience and the number of accompanying family members. Seasonal workers are explicitly told not to take anyone with them who is unproductive, such as very young children or old men or women too old. The presence of such non-working dependants is said to be detrimental to daily output. External circumstances also play a role. In my report on initial research into the employment of cane-cutters in the plain of south Gujarat I suggested that harvest failure in the recruitment area due to continual drought stimulated the exodus. The usual army of marginal and landless peasants desirous of joining the trek to south Gujarat, threatened to become larger than had been the case in previous years. The sugar factories reacted to this acute crisis in the hinterland by reducing the recruitment premium to far below the normal amount (Breman 1978/79: 53). The course of events involved in payment of a cash advance has been discussed in an earlier chapter. The inevitable result is that these temporary migrants leave home with a debt burden which they have to repay in the coming months with their labour power. To check on the daily average received by cane-cutters is not really relevant in their case. Throughout the season employers do not give workers more than a small allowance, barely sufficient to cover the cost of their food, rather than setting the wage bill on a regular basis. The managements of the co-operative sugar mills even manage to economize on this maintenance allowance by stocking large quantities of sorghum which is then issued once a fortnight in rations that are sufficient only for the cane-cutter and his wife. This is also a way by which the factories discourage the accompaniment of non-productive members of the household.

The small cash allowance and grain ration doled out to the gangs are insufficient for their subsistence. The grain ration of two kilos per day is based on the needs of two workers, as is the payment of two rupees per day; when small children accompany their parents, however, this is quite inadequate for all their daily requirements. Some workers from Saurasthra who in 1987–88 came to the south Gujarat plain for the first time in the harvesting campaign, told me that they spent at least five or six rupees per day on food; they were clearly indignant about the absurdly low allowance which the factory considered to be adequate for their consumption. (Breman 1990: 579)

Ten years earlier, the factories still paid fortnightly wages, deducting in installments the amount that had been advanced during the monsoon. Why was that interim payment stopped? In my report on the renewed fieldwork I gave three reasons: administrative convenience, bank interest gained on non-paid wages and, quite the most important, strengthening the hold over the workforce during the campaign (Breman 1990: 578). The employers give other reasons for introducing the new rule which amounts to deferring wage payments until the end of the season: to counteract the deceit practised by most *mukadams* in the periodic settlements and to combat the after-work vices of gambling and drinking in the cane-cutters' camps.

A short time later, I discussed such practices with a gang of road workers and they knew exactly what I meant. The road contractor who employed them had suggested the same arrangement at the start of the season, arguing that they would have more left over at the end. The Kathiawadis, who have the reputation of great militancy, decisively refused the suggestion. They have agreed only to the phased deduction from their fortnightly wage of the outstanding debt.

In the brickworks, on the other hand, it has been customary from time immemorial to pay workers only a living allowance during the season, just as is now done in cane-cutting. This occurs sometimes once every eight days, but sometimes at longer intervals. Owners of small businesses are particularly negligent in this respect, postponing payment, to be made in cash, as long as possible. The brick-makers, of course, want just the contrary, i.e. to collect as much as possible. The norm is fixed, however, and amounts to the fact that the *karchi* (or *khavati*, literally, an eating allowance) is never more than half the production of the preceding week or fortnight. *Karchi* is divided among gang members according to a fixed ratio reflecting the value attributed to the labour provided. The largest amount is paid to the brick-maker, the *patavala*. He is followed by the workers who knead the clay in the pits with arms and feet, then by the men and women who bring the mixture to the side and give it with both hands full to the brick-maker. A lesser amount is paid to the one who lays out the wet bricks, an older boy or girl. Least of all is given to the children who carry the bricks away from the place where they are formed. And even they have different rates, according to their ability to carry one or two bricks at a time.

A similar differentiation forms the basis for the periodic allowance paid to other categories of labour in the brickworks. The *mukadam* registers the number of bricks produced by a gang each day and, for example, the number of times that a *chapavali* carries a headload of bricks to or from the kiln. Each time that the latter walks up or down a wobbly plank or improvised ladder she is given a small tin token; when she has twenty-five of these she exchanges them for a larger one. At the end of the day, these tokens determine her total earnings, which the gang boss notes in a little workbook that she carries with her. This also occurs with regard to the bricks formed by the *patavala*. The record is intended partly to dispel any impression among the workers that they are being deceived. The illiteracy of the majority means that this becomes a symbolic ritual which they have to seal with their thumbprint. The owner and the *mukadam* use these daily jottings as evidence with which to convince the migrants that they have earned no more, or even less, than is consonant with the quota for their production set in advance. Payment of a disproportionately large allowance would affect the debt repayment.

As observed, the principal gang in the brickworks can claim a living allowance of at most half the tariff payable per 1,000 bricks. An interesting factor, however, is that the tariff is determined at the end of the season only. When asked, the brick-makers gave me to understand that they would only be told the new rate at the time of departure. Until that moment, the previous year's piece-rate applied. This retrospective price fixing is done by brickworks owners in mutual consultation with the intention of preventing labour costs from increasing to more than their usual share of the market price, as a number of employers patiently explained to me. The *mukadams* told me that the regional Union of Brick Manufacturers sent an informer to the various works to check that its members did not pay more than the agreed rate. Any employer who was found paying more than the minimum tariff was fined.

At the end of the season the labour nomads are all dismissed. In the days before that, the employers will have settled accounts with their *mukadam(s)*. In the agro-industry this is a large-scale operation in which within a few days tens of thousands of cane-cutters receive the balance of their wages for many months' labour. In 1987 an observer appointed by the High Court of Gujarat was present when this happened and described the rough treatment to which the workers were subjected. The management of one factory, for example, even refused to provide drinking water for the migrants who had to queue for hours in the burning sun, awaiting their turn.

The way in which the management through its security staff tried to enforce the discipline on the workers, the inhuman way in which the management tried to organise workers in certain groups to receive payment, and the way in which the workers were directed to form a queue, was really painful. The workers were given treatment as if herds of animals are being organized in certain groups to be carried away from one place to another. The security staff used to move with sticks in their hands and always used insulting, and sort of abusive language whenever they had to deal with harvesting workers. (quoted in Breman 1990: 580–1)

Agro-industrial managers defended their *modus operandi* with the argument that by settling the wage bill directly with the workforce at the crucial payment time they were able to prevent the *mukadams* from appropriating part of the earnings of their gangs. This is a fallacy which ignores the informal settlement that follows in the migrant camps before the sign is given to depart for home. During the season, the gang bosses have entered into all sorts of petty transactions with their gang members: to supplement the scanty living allowance, money with which to buy alcohol or to pay a gambling debt. With the aid of his own administration, the *mukadam* also has to account for the varying output of the *koytas*. As the only semi-literate in the company, the *mukadam* is quite able to manipulate the figures to his own advantage and the end of the season is his appropriate opportunity (Bremen 1990: 579–80).

In other branches of seasonal industry, the employers even make no pretence of protecting the migrants against their gang bosses, and prefer to settle the final payment through these middlemen since this considerably facilitates their accounts. Workers not yet hardened in the life of a migrant are no proof against the machinations with which the *mukadam* extorts part of their earnings.

In the course of the season, the balance of power shifts between temporary employers and employees. The former suffer loss if the migrants stay away when the season starts or soon desert once it has begun. They need not fear this later on when the debt of the contracted workers has been turned into a credit balance and they have become dependent on the good faith of the patrons. The already authoritative behaviour of the latter worsens until reaching its nadir at the final settlement. When the time comes for the labour migrants to leave, it sometimes happens that they are sent away without payment, being told that the employer will bring the money to their village. Complaints in this respect were heard by a government committee which, many years ago, inquired into working conditions in the saltpans of Bombay.

The accounts of earnings of salt pan workers are usually settled at the end of the season. During the season advances of different types are given to the workers to meet any of their requirements, but the final settlement of the wage agreed upon is made at the conclusion of the season usually in May. Complaints were received at some centres that the final settlement of accounts is in many cases delayed; thus causing hardship to the workers especially those coming from outside the centre. (Report Salt Pan Industry 1950: 14)

Seasonal migrants in Chikhligam told me similar stories about their experiences in the brickworks. Sometimes the final settlement was simply not made. The owner claimed that he had given the whole amount to the *mukadam* who, in turn, insisted stubbornly that he had not been paid a single *paisa*.

All these uncertainties entail that the last and the only real pay day is a very tense affair. The size of the *biyanum*, the credit balance built up by the migrants, varies greatly. The net amount fluctuates with the size of the original debt, the number of working family members who have accompanied the contracted labourer, loans that have been advanced between times, and finally, the total days worked. It is no exception for a seasonal worker to hear that he has nothing left or even that he has to return home in debt. Variation is the rule, and this hinders any systematic comparison of wages among the migrant workers. But they all appear conscious of the fact that life consists of a never-ending cycle of working to repay a debt and then, in order to acquire fresh credit, the advance selling of one's labour power.

This vulnerability entails that casual workers right from the start are basically defenceless against the deception practised by employers or their agents.

When the labourers were asked as to why they do not protest against such malpractice, they replied that they were not able to speak anything against the *mukadams* or contractors. They can only express their anger or agony to fellow workers and keep silent before others. They say: 'If we are not given our dues and if they take work from us without paying, we will curse them that they would die miserable. They will not be in a position to enjoy their ill-gotten wealth.' (Punalekar and Patel 1990: 131)

On the other hand, there are signs that workers in the lowest ranks of the economy are becoming more assertive, even in a situation of surplus labour. Rural workers who report to the early morning labour markets are now less willing to agree immediately with what employers offer them.

'Earlier, it was easier for us to persuade them. They never questioned, nor did they hesitate a bit to climb into our tractors. Hardly did they haggle for wages or other things like food or transport facility back to Anand after day's work was over. But now they have become clever and smarter,' said one well-off farmer from Uttarsanda village who often took casual labour market labourers to his fields. (Punalekar and Patel 1990: 47)

To the providers of work who have always taken it for granted that the amount they wished to pay would not be questioned, the need to have to negotiate terms of employment is a revolutionary change.

The principle of contracting and sub-contracting

Piece-work is a manner of contracting under which the employer persuades, or in effect forces, the labourers to determine their own input and to vary it in length and intensity according to their working ability. In Gandevigam and Chikhligam, casual labour on a piece-work basis or for carrying out a particular job has become the dominant form of employment during the last few decades. This applies to a broad range of activities within the rural economy. I have drawn attention to this trend in agriculture in an earlier publication (Breman 1985b: 275–81; see also Kapadia 1995: 218–32). Day labourers not only work in the fields under an *udhad* arrangement, such as cutting grass or harvesting a paddy field for an agrarian wage previously agreed upon. Similar contracts determine their input in other rural economic activities as navvy, worker in a sand quarry, loader-unloader on a lorry, and so forth. To a certain degree this practice makes them comparable to village craftsmen who work on their own account and at their own risk. Contracting-out is the guiding principle in the diamond industry. The workshop owner in reality acts as middleman between the trader on the one hand, whose property the stones remain, and on the other hand the cutters and grinders who work for him on a more or less regular basis.

The reason which seems to be very strong for payment of *baki* is that many a time the unit owners do not receive regular payment of *majdoori* [note: labour cost] – from those who offer job work. This is the payment by the agent who brings rough diamonds and passes the polished diamonds to the traders-cum-exporters. The genesis of *baki*, at any rate a part of it, can therefore be placed in a proper perspective when, on a wider view, we take into account the connections between industry, trade, working of the financial intermediates, including banks, and eventual export of diamonds. (Pathak 1993: 252–3)

In the powerloom sector, contracting-out is also commonly used by employers, frequently fledgling producers who do not yet dare to set up as independent owners, in order to restrict their operating risks. Job work is the name given to the agreement whereby the owner of capital bears all production costs other than labour, i.e. thread, workplace, machines, electricity. Labour is supplied by the contractor, who commits himself to provide the woven goods at a previously fixed rate per metre. If the market price then rises his profits do not increase, but on the other hand he does not lose if prices fall. The role of the actual producer is nothing more than that of labour contractor. Without any capital of his own, his profit consists of the margin between his own labour costs and the price that he has agreed with his principal. The data on this industrial process compiled during my fieldwork in 1986–87 show that, as against the wage paid to a weaver for operating one loom for twelve hours, the contractor who hires him rakes in the same amount for his role as manager. If the latter is also the owner of the loom and the workshop, the net yield for the employer rises to three to four times the price received by the labourer. Similar arrangements exist in the *jari* business in Surat which is monopolized by a small group of big traders.

This class of traders purchases the raw materials and also owns the factory premises and machines but does not come into the direct contact of the workers. These traders give their own factory and machines to others on rent and get their own goods processed. They pay the labour charges and retain the finished goods. The persons who take the factory and machines on rent, hire labourers from outside and make finished goods, and, thus, these persons come into direct contact with the workers. The traders do not have to worry about wage rate, working hours, casual leave etc., of the workers. (Soni 1990: 125–6)

In the textile dyeing and printing works the entire labour process is divided up into units that are completely contracted out to gangs led by a *mukadam* and on previously determined terms. It is an organization of the labour process which frees capital owners from the bother of managing production and from any possible claim by workers on their responsibility as employers. According to one researcher, the avoidance of such responsibility is even a prime motivation for entrepreneurs to contract out.

The main reason behind the prevalence of contract labour system in the processing industry is that the owners prefer not to be bothered with the problems of dealing with the labour which, according to the employers is becoming increasingly unmanageable. (Desai 1981: 30; see also Mehta and Gandhi: 108–9)

The various modes of employment that I came across during my field-work show that wages form an important and usually the largest factor of total operating costs in all sectors of production examined. This conclusion is incomplete, however, unless we also note that added value is siphoned off at all the various intermediary levels. The sum of money paid to the labour contractors in the dyeing-and-printing mills is only partially converted into wages and passed on to their gang members. In the powerloom workshops the weaving master asks a commission from the fresh hands recruited and the employer may also decide to give him something extra for his good services. One might argue that these costs of supervision are part and parcel of the total wage bill. However, not only supervision is included in the total labour charge but also the cost of control which employers are willing to pay in order to keep the workforce in a docile state. As a result, the wage which the actual worker receives is quite small, certainly in proportion to the market price of the product, but even as a share of the total amount registered as labour costs in the financial books which employers keep for their own eyes only. The unequal distribution illustrates the high degree of exploitation that occurs in the context of capitalist accumulation which has a strong mercantile character.

Mercantile in this connection refers to the way capital is organized for industrial production. So far I have explained the hire-and-fire operations which dominate the informal sector work regime by mainly referring to the abundant supply of cheap labour. However, while discussing in an earlier section the low capital-intensity of business practices in this milieu, it became clear that the persistence of backward technology is conditioned by structural constraints that oppose management practices aiming at an increase in productivity and, more generally, by a long chain of dependency relations which do not make it very attractive for industrial employers in the informal sector to replace loose labour by fixed capital. Only focusing on the employer–worker nexus, however, would not do justice to the more encompassing setting in which capital and labour are brought together over the boundaries of segmented economic circuits. Un- or low-skilled workers kept mobile at the bottom of the informal sector are tied via jobbers, foremen and other labour agents to industrialists who, in their turn, remain bound, but precariously so, to traders and other capital owners connected to or even firmly established in the formal sector of the economy. This whole set of relationships constitutes the essence of mercantile capitalism which, while severely restricting the bargaining power of labour, provides capital with maximal freedom for manoeuvre.

As noticed already in the introductory chapter, contracting out of work helps in creating the illusion that labour is performed under conditions of self-employment, a circumstance which further strengthens its label as part and parcel of the informal sector of the economy. Frequently, however, own-account work is a misleading term insofar that it conceals the wage dependency of the mass of the workers who are forced into extreme self-exploitation. As earlier noted it is by no means exceptional for weavers to work even longer than the obligatory twelve hours. It is expected of them if a member of the next shift does not turn up to take his place at the loom. One workshop owner whom I met defended this custom by insisting that it was not compulsory. According to him, many weavers were all too willing to serve the loom for thrice twelve hours at a stretch if the occasion should arise. They consider it a windfall, a chance that gives them the opportunity to earn more money. Such an appraisal, however, is based on an interpretation of freedom of choice which ignores the harshness of the fight for existence that gives rise to such behaviour.

The conversion from wage labour to work for one's own account and risk are terms that may be used by the researcher but never by those thus engaged. To them, such a transition in no way signifies any drastic change in the uncertainty that marks their daily existence. For example, women who have journeyed in vain to the morning market and are unable to find work will try to make their labour power productive in other ways. In their study of the operations of these casual labour markets, Punalekar and Patel summarize the alternative sources of income to which women will then turn:

collecting rags, waste papers, plastic bags, bottles, etc.; making baskets and winnowing baskets; making plastic toys, balloons, etc.; making photo-frames; making eatables or food items for the *lariwallas*; selling old clothes; making tin boxes; making brooms; carry loads in the market; working as coolie in vegetable yards or at bus or railway station; providing help in handcart pulling; selling old containers, bottles, tins, etc. . . . charcoal collection, wood work, collecting twigs of *babul* or *limda* trees, and selling them [as tooth brushes]. (Punalekar and Patel 1990: 139)

Contracting out the production process, whether in parts or in its entirety, to a middleman who is prepared to mobilize and supervise the necessary workforce, is also very common practice in all branches of seasonal industry. It occurs least in cane-cutting. Cane harvesters are certainly paid in proportion to the amount cut and their gang bosses are paid commission on the gang's total, but they operate as the lowest link of management and have no scope to manoeuvre when concluding a standard contract for the duration of the campaign (see Breman 1978/79: 52-4).

The gang bosses in brickworks and saltpans have greater latitude in dividing up the wages than in cane-cutting. The following passage taken from a report on the manner of employment in saltpans on the coast near Bombay during the 1947-48 season, is still relevant:

The *Patel* or the *Khatedar* – who, in effect is a sort of recruiting agent – undertakes the responsibility of securing the requisite number of workers for individual pan owners. He advertises the jobs in the villages concerned and enters into contracts with the workers in regard to wages. He brings the required batch to the salt-pan centre and binds himself to the owner for the good behaviour and efficiency of his gang. Wage distribution, consequently, is to the individual *Khatedar* or *Patel*, who in turn settles with the workers under him. Though wages may have been fixed on a uniform scale, the *Khatedar* may not usually make corresponding distribution. Two or three new-comers in the gang do not receive full wages. The cook or *Bhandari*, usually a relative of the *Khatedar*, is paid much less. In the case of a few more skilled and experienced workers in the gang, however, contracts regarding wages do exist. (Report Salt Pan Industry 1950: 9)

In a number of quarries and also in road construction I came across a more advanced form of contracting out. A *mukadam* who was asphalting a stretch of the road between Maroli and Sachin with a gang from the Panch Mahals proved actually to be a sub-contractor. The road builder paid him per ton of processed asphalt. The *mukadam* transposed this amount into a daily rate which varied considerably for the fifty men, women and children in his gang, and the total of which remained far below the amount paid to him. In another version, the manager of a quarry close to Chikhligam drastically limited his contact with the workers by delegating all work tasks to an experienced employee. He took the day's production for a fixed price per weight according to the size of the rocks. However, he charged his sub-contractor for use of the compressor and dynamite, and for the experienced workers who worked with the dynamite. He kept out of the arrangements made between sub-contractor and quarrymen, but was well aware that these were at a far lower level. Finally, the modality of sub-contracting is very common usage in brickworks, a seasonal industry in which the *mukadam* figures as a typical employer of labour. Experienced jobbers-cum-gang bosses meet all the characteristics that give these middlemen their widely varying reputation among employers and employees respectively. One of these characteristics has not yet been examined, namely, the *mukadam*'s activity as someone who undertakes to supply his patron with bricks at a fixed price and who makes all his own arrangements with the workforce, i.e. their coming, manner of employment, and payment. His independence is far less if he does all this under orders and is paid for his effort, usually with a commission for each 1,000 bricks made under his supervision. In comparison, it is far more advantageous for the *mukadam* to work on contract.

The *mukadam* does not form the last and lowest link in the multi-tier system of contracting and sub-contracting. The head of a team of cane-cutters or of a group of brick-makers who bring along their own helpers, enters into a contract with them. The head of a *koyta* does not only commit himself when he accepts earnest money. Dependent on the amount involved, he also has to take his wife and possibly a child with him to help in harvesting. This also applies to the *patavala*, the brick-maker who is the key figure of his gang. If the size of his family is not sufficient, he leaves it to the *mukadam* to supplement his group. Sometimes, however, the *patavala* will complete his own gang by entering into agreement with members of other landless households to work the whole season for a fixed amount, which he hands over on their return to the village.

This procedure forces the male seasonal migrant to turn those who accompany him into a commodity and to treat them accordingly. The work regime to which they are subjected necessitates that affection between adults and the parental protection of children be set aside.

In the brickworks I watched as a young woman impatiently took her baby off her breast because she urgently had to resume hauling bricks; young girls who at first are weighed down under a headload of six or eight dry bricks, are congratulated when their arms become sufficiently long to enable their promotion to carrying ten bricks; their smaller brothers or sisters also acquire added value as soon as they are able to run with two wet bricks instead of one; just 14 days after the birth of her baby, a woman takes up her work of passing the clay to her husband, and thus relieves her daughter of about 15, for whom this work is far too heavy. And early in the morning the mother of an infant of less than three sets him on a heap of clinkers where his tiny fingers pick up pieces of coal to put in a basket. For all this the *mukadam* pays a premium. The Halpati from Chikhligam with whom I watched the little boy explained its significance: 'Everyone who comes has to work, and only those who can work may come along.' (Fieldwork notes)

The principle of contracting and sub-contracting and the piece-work that usually accompanies this employment modality not only conveys the contractual ruthlessness inherent in hiring labour but also provokes tendencies of alienation which affect primary relationships and extend even into the household sphere. One author relates the instance of a married woman who was made to work in her father's *jari* factory in order to repay the loan taken by her in-laws (Soni 1990: 144). Debt bondage is indeed an important mechanism of exploitation in a rural and urban economy dominated by petty commodity production.

Bondage

There can be no doubt that the cash advance with which a recruiting agent forces many of the migrant mass to leave their homes is also used at the worksite to bind them for as long as their presence is needed.

I have already pointed out the similarity between the worker who thus loses his freedom and the former *hali*, the farm servant who spent all his life in bondage. Workers who get into debt know that, in exchange, they, whether singly or with family members, are expected to provide labour power and accept the obligation to do so whenever it is demanded by the employer or his agent.

In a brickworks just past Surat I encountered a young Halpati who had left home for the first time as seasonal migrant. He found the work very heavy and feared that he did not have sufficient physical strength to keep it up for several months. But it is impossible for him to leave because the *mukadam* has given him the large amount of money needed for his marriage. Not only this year but next year too, he will have to go with the others to repay the advance with his labour. Before this he had worked in a factory, a job that he owed to the help of a friend. The wage that he had earned there was far higher than the weekly subsistence allowance from which he and his wife, who had accompanied him, had to live. Why hadn't he stayed in the factory? The owner did not know him very well and had refused to give him the advance he had asked for. He had no other choice than to turn to one of the jobbers in the village. (Fieldwork notes)

Notwithstanding the parallel with the debt bondage in which the *hali* also found himself, the agreement entered into by this seasonal migrant has another and more restrictive character. It is doubtful whether the length of the bonded employment indicates the real difference. In the past, the farm servant started with a debt that over time increased rather than decreased. Repayment with the intention of putting an end to the relationship was not the aim of either party. The bond between the households of servant and master was entered into for an indefinite time, often lasted a lifetime, and could even be extended into the next generation. This does not apply to present-day workers in or out of south Gujarat who work in order to repay a debt and who have the greatest difficulty in persuading their employer to provide more and longer credit. Nevertheless, to stress the contrast between then and now in terms of a long-term versus short-term debt bondage would be to ignore the variability that has always existed (see Rudra 1987: 158–9). A simple duality implies the need to identify a structural shift on the basis of a fairly arbitrary indicator. *Halis* did in fact leave their master formerly while, conversely, labour migrants in the contemporary setting sometimes commit themselves for more than one season.

Since he gives them work, they do not refuse to accept commission money. The labourers do not have much dissatisfaction about this. They feel that they get the work and protection from him. 'He saves us from hunger and starvation', some labourers said. Some consider him as 'guardian'. (Punalekar and Patel 1990: 149)

Others, however, express themselves much more critically about this middleman:

Their behaviour is atrocious to say the least. They have little feelings for the health, well being and safety of their workers. They are scrupulous in setting the work-targets but miserly when paying the dues of the workers. If anything, they are 'the heartless' employers. (Punalekar and Patel 1990: 145–6)

In my opinion, the present situation differs from the earlier one in that the present-day worker who enters into debt repays it with labour power without subjecting himself in any other respect and unconditionally to the will of the 'master'. In comparison with the servitude of former times, the present arrangement is more restricted in nature. The employer is primarily interested in attaching labour, no less but also not much more than that. Although traces of servitude are certainly present in cases of long-term employment, the lack of freedom that formerly existed in my fieldwork villages has lost its social legitimacy (Breman 1993b).

Labourers who fail to meet their obligation to work are exposed to sanctions of varying nature. The range of methods available to owners of seasonal industries was discussed in the section on the recruitment of labour migrants. The brutal behaviour by moneylending employers against those who are at the bottom of the labour hierarchy is seen as a matter of course, but even diamond cutters may be forcefully called to order, as the following example shows.

One morning I observed a stranger walk into the premises of a diamond factory and call out one of the workers. The stranger was talking most of the time and the worker did little more than mumble a few words. After a few minutes of this one-sided dialogue a small crowd gathered around the two. The spectators consisted mostly of the worker's colleagues who had come out of the factory. The stranger then started slapping the hapless worker. The worker did not resist; he only tried to protect his face with his hands. The worker's colleagues who had been following the dialogue did not disapprove of this assault. The stranger was a *karkhanedar*. The worker who had been in his employment had taken a loan from him, but had left the factory without repaying the loan, or even informing his creditor that he was changing his job. The *karkhanedar* had traced the missing debtor and demanded instant repayment. The worker and the *karkhanedar* worked out a compromise whereby the former agreed to return to his old employer and work for him till his debt was fully repaid. The workers and *karkhanedars* are agreed that a worker may leave his employment only after clearing his debt. (Kalathil 1978: 104–5)

The internalization of dependency suggested by the above passage would seem to give an employer the right to deprive an indebted labourer of his freedom of movement and, if found suitable, not to shrink from using physical violence. On the basis of my own fieldwork, however, I am inclined to refute that impression.

In the course of time I have certainly heard many tales of non-economic pressure with which dependent labourers were victimized. Occasionally such incidents occurred even in my presence. When I visited a number of brickworks near Bombay in 1972 from my base in south Gujarat I found watchmen who had to guard the terrain. Not only against trespassers it appeared, but above all to prevent the desertion of migrants from south Gujarat. At that time it was fairly common that the employer or otherwise the *mukadam* instilled discipline among the workforce by hitting and kicking 'unruly elements'. A Halpati from Chikhligam told me that he had watched horrified while some of his colleagues were beaten up for various transgressions. When he started work one morning too late the angry gang boss threatened him that now his turn had come to be beaten up. Thus frightened, he ran away on that same day. It must have happened many times that men and women are forced to migrate for the first time with the bait of an advance, without knowing what was waiting for them or even where they were going. Migrants from south Gujarat complained about this to members of a government committee which, in 1947–48, investigated modes of employment in the saltpans of Bombay:

complaints were lodged by workers coming from outside the centre that they were brought to the centre without their knowing their place of destination or the nature of the work which they were supposed to do. If these complaints are true, it is not surprising that the Kharwas, after working for a couple of months, might attempt to go back to their villages. (Report Salt Pan Industry 1950: 14)

In 1986 the son of a Bombay brickworks owner told me that in the past the name of his father in itself had been sufficient to scare the wits out of the landless in my fieldwork area. More reassuringly he added that only 'dishonest' workers had any reason to be worried. He regretted that the time had passed when such people could be thrashed without mercy. Perhaps even more ominous than the actual use of force were the proclamations that a worse fate awaited transgressors if they continued to arouse the wrath of their superiors.

The employers used such threats above all to prevent migrants from deserting. If they still persisted in doing so, not only could they expect corporal punishment when they were caught but also measures were taken against other members of the gang who were sometimes ordered to repay the deserter's outstanding debt. Such an attempt to recoup the damage was itself not without risk, however, since people confronted with such a demand could also decide to desert. It was more effective to deduct the money given as advance from the *mukadam*'s commission, thus increasing his diligence in finding the deserter and bringing him back. I noted in one case that an owner's son together with two gang bosses came all the way back to Chikhligam, when I was there at the time of my first fieldwork, to catch a Halpati deserter and to take him back to Bombay. There he was given a merciless beating and then disappeared, never to be heard of again. Beaten to death, surmised his family back in the village.

This last passage has been written in the past tense because it is my impression that such punishing practices are now rare. This applies not only to the work regime in the brickworks but also to cane-cutting in the fields, as I reported in my last research report:

Mukadams normally have little trouble in disciplining their workers and, even when this is done with the use of some force, they know that they can depend on the covert or even overt support of factory management. Intimidation can give rise to heated reaction, however, particularly when physical rather than verbal force is used. It would be quite inaccurate to picture the cane-cutting army as a docile mass of people whose spirit has been broken. *Mukadams* who handle their workers rather too drastically are likely to encounter some who are not afraid to show forcible resistance. In describing a number of such incidents, my informants among the lower ranks of factory managements stressed the impulsive behaviour of cane-cutters. I was given to understand that while the migrants seemed not to be offended by the grossest of curses, they would sometimes explode in anger at some futility and would then not hesitate to attack the offender with a cutting knife. The likelihood of such an eventuality helps to curb the unrestrained exercise of power. (Breman 1990: 576)

Has the proletariat of south Gujarat then at least been liberated from the use of extra-economic force? Such a claim would be too simplistic and would not do justice to the nakedness of the work regime in the lower echelons of the economy. That hopeful question needs to be qualified in two respects. Firstly, workers who are bound in debt still experience non-economic pressure. It is questionable whether that is any different in the case of temporary workers who retain complete freedom of movement. The textile workers in Surat, for example, whose ascribed lack of loyalty prevents them from being granted loans by their employer and who derive no surety at all from their employment, do not dare to protest against the treatment meted out to them.

A little questioning would mean immediate retrenchment, abuse and even physical assault in front of friends. Retrenchment, scolding and beatings are daily ongoing common phenomena in the textile units of Surat. (Barik 1987: 171)

Employers continue to instil discipline, that is to say in the way they see it, by resorting occasionally to violence. When in Gandevigam a labourer was caught in early summer 1994, allegedly in the act of stealing mangoes, he was tied to a tree and mercilessly beaten up by some Anavil boys. In a similar incident a few weeks later two Halpati men were given a similar treatment in a nearby village but more brutally so. After having been also roped to a tree their heads were half shaven and they were kicked and beaten so much that they fell unconscious. When one of them awoke and asked for water a Patidar, exclaiming that he did not mind giving in to that last wish, urinated in his mouth. The other Halpati never awoke and died some time later. By any definition this would fall in the category of extra-economic coercion which, according to Rudra, does not exist any longer. He may have been right for West Bengal where a political climate prevails that makes such practices wellnigh impossible. I am afraid, however, that in most parts of India this is not the case.

The second qualification concerns my observation that physical aggression is more than simply a means with which employers can control their employees. The forcible use of power by the strongest over the weakest also occurs in interrelationships among workers. One incident that has stuck in my memory was the way in which a truck driver at a brickworks beat and cursed a woman who had taken the liberty of splashing him with dye during the *holi* festivity. Customarily women are the target and the victim of men, both in symbolic and real encounters, and not *vice versa*. This applies also to the relationship between the two sexes in the cane-cutters camp and in the brick-makers gang. I have frequently had to stand by while men, perhaps due to their inability to resist their patron or his agent, have used more than curses against their wives.

The imposition of 'discipline' by coercive means is not a characteristic of unfree labour only, as is shown by Chakrabarty in his study of the work regime in the capitalist jute mills of colonial Calcutta. Authority was not only excessive but depended also on a certain use and demonstration of physical force. Managerial power had, therefore, a necessary extra-legal dimension to it.

Even more vicious, from the worker's point of view, was organized managerial terror (as distinct from sporadic physical assaults) that was unleashed on labour at moments of protest. In the flow of such excessive, organized managerial violence, the police, the *sardars*, and the *durwans* often acted as capillaries, aiding the flow. (Chakrabarty 1989: 175)

That the regimentation of the workforce by employers or their agents bears the mark of terror is true even today for most of the worksites where I have gone in the course of my research on labour in India's informalized economy.

Debt bondage is, and will continue to be, the method by which employers ensure themselves of a supply of cheap and unskilled labour. For reasons that will be discussed later, all sorts of seasonal industry prefer to bring in the needed workforce on a large scale from elsewhere. Their acute and continual poverty, however, means that such workers can only be detached from their home milieu with the aid of a cash advance. Even when that debt has been worked off, however, employers refuse to pay the earned wage. Instead, they credit it to the accounts of their workers. This is ostensibly done to encourage savings and to prevent the migrants from wasting their money on alcohol and gambling, say the employers. This pretext to protect the contracted workers against themselves, as it were, is based on numerous negative stereotype opinions regarding their behaviour, such as wastefulness, lack of discipline, and general economic improvidence. The real reason, of course, is to prevent the acquired labour force from leaving the workplace prematurely. The combination of advance and payment in arrears enables employers of seasonal industries to bring in workers, to immobilize them for the duration of their employment and, finally, to send them away again. The removal of migrants at the end of the season is also part of the assignment given to jobbers-cum-gang bosses. *Mukadams* who lead the cane-cutting army are required to sign a statement that obliges them not only to report with their gangs at a given date, but also to disappear again at the end of the campaign (Breman 1978/79: 190). Requirement is for attached labour, of a circulating type that comes and goes. In my opinion, it would be incorrect to explain debt bondage as continuation of a semi-feudal mode of production. To that extent I fully agree with the position taken by Rudra. However, to argue, as he has done, that members of landless castes contract themselves willingly into attachment and actually form a privileged category comparable to employees in the organized sector of the economy (Rudra 1990b: 260), completely overlooks the dependent, obsequious status inherent to such agrarian arrangements. My impression is that this political economist strongly resisted the idea that the bonding of labour is still practised through the debt mechanism, because in his own dictionary that could only be read as the persistence of (semi-)feudal production relations. However, that happens not to be my own conclusion. Notwithstanding the fact that the supply of labour seems to exceed demand, employers use force and oppression as tools with which to increase their hold on the workers. Such forms of neo-bondage result from the weak market position of the subordinated party, but are effected in a social framework based on capitalism. In other words, unfree labour may well and actually does go together with the drive towards capitalist accumulation dominating the economy of both rural and urban India. An anomalous necessity is how Miles has characterized such unfree labour arrangements under capitalist regimes in different parts of the world (Miles 1987).

Based on a short round of field investigations carried out in Haryana, Brass has argued that debt is the mechanism by which agricultural labourers, and farm servants in particular, continue to be attached to their employers (Brass 1990). He followed up this empirical paper with more analytical essays in which he clubbed together as revisionists a wide range of authors who, in one way or another, do not share his views presented as orthodox purity. As one of this targeted bunch of renegades I find myself castigated for presumably having tried to wish away the lack of freedom which is the essence of forms of labour attachment widely practised in India's agricultural economy up to today.

The revisionist project which structures much recent writing on unfreedom eliminates the element of coercion from most or all agrarian relationships, and subsequently reclassifies them as free wage labour. Hence revisionist contributions to debates about rural labour theorize what marxists term unfreedom as a form of equal exchange, or a benign (and thus tension-free) arrangement to the benefit of all parties to the relation. (Brass 1993: 36)

I hope that I have been more nuanced than reported by Brass. What I have basically tried to do, also in earlier publications, is to distinguish feudal from capitalist labour bondage. Debt is manipulated as an instrument of coercion in both cases but that similarity should not mislead us to conclude that nothing has really changed between past and present (see also Breman 1993b: 297–316). What I have called neo-bondage is less personalized, more contractual and monetized, while also the elements of patronage have gone which provided some protection and a subsistence guarantee, however meagrely defined, to bonded clients in the past (see Breman 1974, 1985b and 1993b). The process of change which I have observed in south Gujarat over a period of several decades seems to represent a wider trend which has also been documented for other parts of India. In a recent report on agrarian relations in Haryana, Jodhka has refuted the argumentation on which Brass built his deproletarianization thesis of agricultural labour, a misplaced term anyway, in that state. While confirming the existence of debt bondage, or practices of labour mortgage, Jodhka points out that the labourers themselves intensely dislike relationships of attachment which they try to avoid altogether or otherwise to end as soon as possible. The agrarian situation he describes, a decline in the number and proportion of attached labourers, is similar to the one I have found in my area of research.

There has not only been a formal change in the system of attached labour, substantially also the relationship has changed considerably. Development of capitalism in agriculture has been accompanied by a near total erosion of the ideology of patronage and loyalty. This has also eroded the unquestioned power of the dominant castes and landlords in the rural society. And the growing integration of rural society into the broader national economy has meant opening up of possibilities of employment outside agriculture and the village. (Jodhka 1994: A-106; see also the comments on this paper by Brass 1995 and Jodhka's subsequent rejoinder, 1995.)

As already mentioned, debt bondage, apart from being a recurrent feature of informal sector employment, is also a pervasive mercantile practice by which traders manage to keep control over industrialists through a variety of sub-contracting arrangements. Raw material is supplied to the industrialist which he has to process: e.g. cutting and polishing diamonds, manufacturing *jari* or making grey fabric out of yarn. The supplier-cum-creditor does not allow the employer, however, to set his own price for the value added or to sell the final product to another party. Thus, both capital and labour are constrained by debt bondage in an extensive and multivariate chain of dependency relationships characteristic for a configuration of mercantile capitalism.

Secondary terms of employment

In daily usage, the term 'secondary terms of employment' has acquired the meaning of all sorts of conditions and benefits to which the worker can lay claim in addition to his wage. Derived from regulations applicable to employment in the formal sector of the economy, it is not surprising that such provisions are lacking in the labour scene under discussion. That lack applies also to that section of the working masses in south Gujarat which is semi-permanently employed in the diamond and textile industries.

Cutters: Bonus, leave with pay and provident funds are not extended to diamond workers. The organization of *karkhanedars* called the Diamond Cutters Association has been resisting attempts by the government to extend factory laws to the industry by taking shelter under the Shops and Establishments Act and by harping on the smallness of the units. (Kalathil 1978: 101; see also Kashyap and Tiwari 1982: 124)

Textile Workers: Medical facility, weekly holiday and statutory leave, bonus, and other facilities are completely denied to these workers. Any minor complaint against these evils would invite scolding, physical assault and immediate retrenchment. They are not made permanent even though they continue to work for years in the same unit. (Barik 1987: 171–2)

In an unusual meaning, however, there are signs of secondary labour conditions. These concern not rights but duties to which the workers have to adhere in order to get employment and then keep it. This aggregate of unwritten rules lays down what the employer considers to be desirable work behaviour: to show maximum flexibility; to be satisfied with the wage; to work overtime when necessary and to accept any interruption in production without grumbling and without pay; to conciliate the boss or bosses by being obedient and subservient. The list of qualities is endless, but amounts to the fact that every worker is expected to learn and behave according to the informal code of 'proper behaviour'.

Workers who leave their villages for short periods of a few weeks usually have to manage without shelter in the district to which they go for harvesting or other agricultural work. In rural areas these short-term migrants will bivouac in a farmer's courtyard, in a barn, in a school porch, by a bus stop, or simply along the roadside (Breman 1985b: 243–9). Small groups or families who attend an urban casual labour market for a longer period will stay in a nearby field in a shelter improvised from waste material. Sometimes even that is not possible to construct, and many have to suffice with leaving their meagre belongings – cooking utensils, a few rags with which to cover themselves at night – in the open by the ashes of the fire on which they had cooked a meal the previous evening. Large numbers of street children who roam the towns without the care of any adult also lack any fixed abode:

Many of these loners are found engaged in such occupations as shoe-shining, begging, entertaining or selling trinkets, shoe-laces, ball-points, strings, combs, lottery tickets etc. on a mobile train. Their residence is often moving. If the train takes them to Baroda or Ahmedabad, they are found resting on a railway platform there. They return to Surat station next day by the first available train. Their life situation is indeed very unsteady and unsettles our conventional notion of home, security and safety. There is nothing like stability and permanence to their life-style . . . We have come across this group of floating or semi-settled population living on footpath, platform or under the railway bridge. It is likely that we may not meet them again on the same spot at the same time. (S. P. Punalekar 1993: 80–1)

Compared to these lowest categories, the established urban workers who at least have a roof over their heads are naturally in a better situation. Yet the majority of them have hardly any chance to enjoy any sort of privacy during the oft-interrupted or varying part of the twenty-four–hour period, that is their off time. This applies to the majority of diamond cutters and textile workers in Surat who, without losing the status of aliens, have settled semi-permanently in the city. I have visited a large number of diamond cutting and polishing ateliers that are altered each evening into a dormitory. Even those workers who find their own shelter live together with many others in dilapidated and crowded premises under abominable conditions (Kashyap and Tiwari 1982: 143–8). The housing of textile workers is just as miserable:

A large-scale inquiry held in this milieu brought to light that 60 per cent lived in huts made of dried mud, rags, bamboo and corrugated iron. It is impossible to stand upright and the lack of ventilation means that to stay there is to be choked by a combination of heat, dust and smoke. The majority of workers live in one room and have to share it with 6 to 15 others. This yields per person a surface area of less than 50 square feet. (*Working and Living Conditions* 1984: 83–4)

Nevertheless, even these dwellings are better than improvised shelters in which seasonal migrants have to live. Cane-cutters, road workers, brick-makers and saltpan workers set up their mobile or permanent bivouac literally on the edge of their workplace.

Soon after arrival, the brick-makers set to work to build their hut from rejected material left on the worksite at the end of last season. From the heaps of broken and incorrectly fired bricks they take the good ones and pile them into walls of a metre or more high. These loose structures are then roofed-in with any waste material available: branches, corrugated iron, plastic sheets, etc. In this 'house' they then deposit the belongings brought with them from the village. These are very few: a couple of pots, vessels, mugs and plates, and some extra clothes for those who have them. Men, women and children sleep on sacks spread on the ground. For protection against the cold of the winter night they cover their bodies with what I can only describe as rags. These shelters stand in rows next to one another, untidily distributed along the edges of the terrain. They are dark holes that have to be entered by crawling through the entrance. There is always someone sleeping because the inhabitants have varying work times. That is just as well since the space is insufficient for everyone to lie down together. Boys and girls thus often sleep outside. There is water nearby, but all sanitary provisions are lacking. Children as well as adults answer nature's call in a corner of the terrain, a neighbouring field, or along the road side. The brickworks' owner has to provide wood for the fires on which the women prepare meals and these provide some warmth in the cold nights. He also provides oil for the lamp needed to light the brick-maker's workplace during night. But the costs of these are charged to the brick-makers. For these provisions and depreciation due to breakages, i.e. badly-made bricks that crumble during the initial drying stage, each gang has to make another 5 and sometimes even 10 per cent above the daily quota without wage. I know of only one brickworks, on the periphery of Bombay, whose owner has had coolie sheds put up for his workers. He did so with the encouragement of a local government official who supplied him with the necessary cement at low price.

The cane-cutters' camps are still just as scandalously bad as they were at the time of my first fieldwork. No improvements at all have been made in the meantime. In my last report I noted their condition as follows:

When the cane-cutters reach the plain at the beginning of the season, they are equipped with a couple of mats (*palas*) and two bamboo poles. This is the material with which they have to build a shelter to be used as their bivouac for approximately seven months. 'Shelter' is actually too grand a word for these tent-like contraptions that are open on one side and in which the members of a cutting team cannot even sit together, let alone lie down. The *koytas* thus have to sleep in the open, around the embers of the wood-fire on which the evening meal has been prepared. Some rags provide their only protection against the cold and unseasonal rain during the winter months. Having survived these wretched conditions, they are then plagued by mosquitoes in the summer.

The camps consist of an untidy collection of this makeshift accommodation along the roadside or in an open field without drinking water, a washplace, toilets or any other sanitation necessary for giving basic decency to human group life. Some camps are fairly small, inhabited by a few dozen *koytas*; others may house some hundreds of cutting teams, packed together into a very small space. These then take on the appearance of improvised slums, providing outsiders with a shocking picture of the poverty and deprivation in which these migrant workers have to live. The tents are separated from one another only by cooking places.

Any carelessness with fire can cause the camp to burn to ashes within a very few minutes; a major disaster whenever this occurs, although most inhabitants have very few possessions that need saving. Together with the inadequate shelter, the lack of even the most elementary facilities indicates that seasonal migrants are basically adrift during their stay in the plain. When the canefields in the neighbourhood of the camp have been harvested, the *koytas* move on to another spot and set up a new bivouac. (Breman 1990: 581)

In view of the miserable circumstances in which they have to live and work, it is hardly surprising that migrant workers frequently become ill. Among respondents interviewed in the large-scale inquiry held among textile workers in Surat, almost all of them young men in the prime of life, 35 per cent had been forced to absent themselves from work for longer than a fortnight in the current year due to illness. Another 28 per cent had not worked for shorter periods due to reasons of health. Apart from the fact that medical costs are not paid, the workers are not compensated for loss of income (*Working and Living Conditions* 1984: 96)

Chronic illnesses and deaths are regular occurrences in the cane-cutters' camps, partly as a result of poor hygienic conditions. Each day, 10 per cent of the workforce is too ill to work, which does not mean that the others enjoy good health. In the orthodox but authoritative opinion of the *mukadam*, however, fever, diarrhoea, sore throat, sores and other wounds on legs and arms are not adequate reasons to stay away from work (Breman 1990: 583). A similar regime rules in the brickworks. In this desolate habitat I have on various occasions witnessed the death of a man, woman or child. When I visited a large brickworks near Navsari in 1982 I experienced how panic broke out among the workers when it was rumoured that two members of a gang who had become sick shortly after one another were suffering from cholera. Notwithstanding the orders shouted by *mukadams* that they must keep on working, the labourers took flight. Within a couple of hours the worksite was deserted. The high absenteeism due to illness is undoubtedly influenced by the poor quality of food and water. Seasonal migrants in particular often live far from the inhabited world and lack the time in which to buy basic necessities. The amount that they have to pay for their daily requirements is often higher than in the village. Consumption is minimal and consists chiefly of carbohydrates. Food that includes vitamins, proteins and other elements with a disease-resistant effect is too expensive for their budget. Brick-makers are given prior assurance that, when necessary, the patron will provide medical care and accept the costs of that care. From long experience, however, contracted labourers know that such a promise has no value.

When I visited a brickfield in Bombay in 1972 the owner, whom I had come to know ten years earlier, took the trouble of going around with me to show that nothing had changed in the meantime. An older woman made use of my presence to ask the *sheth* humbly for a favour. Her son had lain in the hut for a couple of days with high fever and could not work. Might he go to the doctor? The implication was that the owner would pay for the consultation and for the medicine. At first he snarled that she had to arrange it through the *mukadam*. But the mother persisted and followed us around the worksite. At last, in view of my company, the patron could do nothing other than to give bad-tempered permission. To me he said that there was one sort of medicine that almost always had effect in such cases: stopping the living allowance. 'Then they soon go back to work.' (Fieldwork notes)

The final aspect that I wish to discuss is the loneliness of most labour migrants. This needs some clarification, especially in the case of diamond and textile workers of whom I have just reported that they are forced to live crowded together in one-room shelters. This is mostly done in the absence of their family or nearest relatives with whom contact is difficult at such long distances. These migrants live in an environment made up almost entirely of males of the same age group. Diamond workers in particular are mainly young and unmarried males between the ages of 16 and 25 who, in the urban jungle of Surat, seek an outlet for their lack of familiar and affectionate relationships in voluntary but sometimes forced homosexuality. Textile workers live under similar conditions:

About one third of the respondents lived by themselves in Surat. Even when other family members lived with the respondents they were more likely to be male relatives than spouses. As a result most workers can be said to lack a sustaining domestic atmosphere which again is known to provide protection against loneliness and proneness to disease. (*Working and Living Conditions* 1984: 93–4)

The owner of a large factory with whom I discussed this matter denied that the deficiency in the workforce from the material and emotional viewpoint had any harmful effect on productivity. In his opinion, the spartan lifestyle did not hinder a high labour input to such a degree as to justify the costs of all sorts of social provisions. Wastage was high he admitted, but workers who were worn out after a few years could easily be replaced by the induction of fresh blood.

The solitary existence of urban street children who lack any parental care is harrowing in the extreme. Satish, a 15-year-old boy who lives in Surat's railway station, is a good example:

At present he does the job of cleaning train compartments and begging along with singing songs in the train. He lives a vagabond life . . . The railway platform is his home. He takes bath there, sleeps there and uses the railway toilet. At times he sits alone on a platform bench and passes time . . . He has one short and one pant which he uses daily. He puts on a dirty coat over his shirt, which he purchased for Rs. 10 from a rag-dealer in Zampa Bazar. He does not have footwear. He moves around with bare feet. He spends four days out of a week on literally empty stomach. Even at the time of interview at late noon, he said that he had not eaten since morning. So we gave him Rs 5 for food. He takes food from a *lari* [hand-cart] whenever he has money . . . He knows nobody, even in his community. At each place he has some friends who are like him, i.e. wandering type. He does not get much help from them. He does not spend much time with them either. He prefers to stay and move alone. (S. P. Punalekar 1993: B-65)

Although the majority of seasonal migrants set off together with their families, which is not always a question of choice, their togetherness on or near the worksite is far from being what is usually understood as normal family life. When man, woman and child are allotted different tasks they sometimes see little of each other and do not always spend the nights together. Owners or *mukadams* repeatedly exercise their authority by demanding sexual services from unmarried and sometimes from married women. Illegally distilled alcohol is drunk in large quantities and quarrels and fights break out about trifles. The hard and raw atmosphere offers little opportunity to show one another the affection that is needed by both children and adults. Women have a lot to endure in this milieu because they have to cope with all sorts of household chores in addition to the heavy work. The situation in the cane-cutters' camps is described below.

Densely packed together in the camps, the cane-cutters lack any social domain of their own into which they can retreat. There is no closed space, however small, into which husbands and wives or adults with their children are able to meet in intimacy, to work off their frustrations, to cope with their pain and misery, and to comfort one another. The *koytas* live in each other's shadow, perhaps one square metre apart from one another. Any private deed thus immediately gains public attention, and they are only too conscious of the assault such an environment makes on their human dignity. (Breman 1990: 582)

Unavoidably, an outsider is appalled at the abject poverty. Among seasonal workers it is worse. The awfulness of their lives can be seen from a comparison with the much higher standard of living enjoyed by semi-permanent industrial workers. On the basis of calculations in which the earnings of diamond workers are set off against the high cost of urban living, 19 per cent of these workers nevertheless lived below the poverty line (Kashyap and Tiwari 1982: 154). Another investigation, also directed towards compiling quantitative data, showed that the incomes of almost 43 per cent of textile workers in Surat are below the level at which, according to government criteria, a life of human dignity can begin (*Working and Living Conditions* 1984: 63–4). My own more qualitative observations concur with this variation in range between the two categories. In connection with these results, however, I must also state that an enormous gap divides this industrial class of semi-permanent workers from the state of extreme and chronic deprivation in which the floating mass at the bottom of the labour hierarchy has to exist. Based on research into the non-agricultural employment of farmers and labourers in a tribal village on the eastern edge of the south Gujarat plain, Koelen describes the difference between the lifestyle of the most successful diamond workers (sons of larger farmers) and that of the average brick-makers (marginal landowners and landless labourers) in a way that concurs with my own findings:

the brick-makers can be identified by their khaki 'shorts', traditional sleeveless shirts, but particularly by their battered shins and feet, the cutters are recognisable by their bicycles, transistor radios and their urban-type clothing: bell bottoms, colourful shirts, shoes with platform soles, and watches that are worn so loose around the wrist that they hang down to the middle of the hand, well visible to all. The cutters are the fancy boys of the village. (Koelen 1985: 77)

Rural workers originating in the landless milieu are unable to do more than survive with seasonal work. The wage which they are paid does not enable their reproduction. In the majority of cases, participation in the annual trek to remote places of employment is inescapable for both men and women and even children. Their labour power is needed to guarantee continuation of the household in the economic sense. The season comes to an end when the climate changes. But were it possible for work to continue during the monsoon, the exhaustion suffered by the workers after just a few months would drive them back to the village. Some time is needed before they can recoup their working capacity. When they arrive home the migrants are able to do little, if anything at all. The Halpatis who return to Chikhligam spend their time sleeping and lazing, and also drinking. I found some in their huts, dead drunk even before midday. One informant told me that he often resolves not to assign himself for a new season. Labour in the brickworks is too heavy and the wage too low. But from whom other than the *mukadam* can he obtain credit with which to meet his daily necessities in this period of unemployment? When work is stopped during the monsoon, the jobber goes through the villages like a rat-catcher, a welcome but at the same time a cursed figure.

7 State care for unregulated labour

Slow and differential access to formal sector employment

Government intervention in the labour system is concerned primarily with what is known as the formal sector of the non-agricultural economy. Under that common denominator fall the skilled and relatively well-paid part of the working population in wage-jobs, based on regular employment and represented in bargaining rituals by trade unions who seek their membership primarily or exclusively among such workers. They are white- and blue-collar workers, employed in factories and offices, workplaces which produce commodities but which also operate in trade, transport and other branches of the service sector, employees of both private and public enterprises, located in large and small cities or in the countryside. The majority are involved in large-scale industries, under working conditions that are protected by a great many legal provisions. Those regulations concern not only the amount of wages and the procedure to be followed in fixing that amount, but also establish numerous other collective rights, sub-divided according to rank and grade, which may be claimed by the employees involved. The proportion of the working population in wage-employment that is protected in this way is far surpassed in size by the mass of workers who depend largely or entirely for their livelihood on wage-employment outside the formal sector of the urban or rural economy. Because of the lack of reliable quantitative data I have to suffice with a rough estimate of the ratio between the two categories into which the working population outside agriculture is divided. For south Gujarat as a whole, I assume that of all non-agrarian wage workers, no more than 20 per cent (a percentage that varies according to whether the location is more rural or more urban) is in regular employment in the formal sector of the economy, as described above. Only they are able to claim the rights that are connected to such a permanent job. At this high level of aggregation, sufficient and adequate statistical data are not available; for more definite figures, there was thus no choice than to take as point of departure the situation in the countryside which has been the area of my fieldwork during the last thirty years.

The notable position traditionally occupied by the Anavil Brahmins has been based on their lifestyle as big landowners. According to the 1921 Census this was the main source of income for 785 of every 1,000 members of this caste. In the late colonial era they showed a growing interest in the more urbanized professions, for which they gained educational qualifications. From their midst came the station masters and post-masters, functions which formed the regional basis for the modernization process led by the British. After Independence this trend away from agriculture accelerated. I. P. Desai, who came from this milieu, wrote in his study of the village in south Gujarat in which he was born and bred:

They are now convinced that not agriculture but salaried employment or occupations . . . are the means of livelihood. In their evaluation of occupation, 'service' comes first and probably agriculture has no place. Education is, for the Anavils, the suitable preparation for life in the city. Now it is fixed from the day the boy goes to school that he has to be a salaried employee and they think of what he has to be and think of what they call the 'line' for the boy. (Desai 1966: 81; see also Breman 1974: 160, 221)

In their case, the step outwards was also a step up the new social ladder. Employment outside agriculture and the village could mean nothing other than to gain a foothold in the formal sector of the economy. In the following generation, this urban orientation extended to employment in the free professions, such as doctor, lawyer or accountant, although not at the expense of the Anavils' interest in 'service' jobs, preferably in government employment. Implied in the latter orientation is a wage-dependent status, though ideally in a position of leadership or management. Finally, more and more Anavil Brahmins have accepted technical or administrative staff postings in private business. In my two fieldwork villages, many younger members of this caste are employed in such a supervisory capacity on the industrial estates of neighbouring towns.

The Kolis from Gandevigam, as members of an intermediate caste, combine their lives as small farmers with low-grade technical or industrial work away from agriculture for which some skill is required. It is a pattern of occupational diversification that is confirmed by their increasing interest in some form of technical training. Many factory workers in permanent employment are Kolis. This applies to a far lesser degree to the large numbers of clerical workers who man government offices in the region. The public sector in general is in fact an arena of employment in which Kolis are under-represented. This is due partly to their classification as Other Backward Community (OBC), entailing that they are not given preference in the positive discrimination policy from which members of scheduled castes and tribes have profited. One element of this programme is the reservation of jobs in the public sector in order to help the target group to make up for their social backwardness. During the last few decades the series of measures taken in the framework of this attempt at positive discrimination have enabled younger Dhodhiyas from Chikhligam in particular to become upwardly mobile. Their advance has invariably been preceded by some years of education. Equipped with school-leaving certificates they have been able to penetrate into the lower ranks of the government bureaucracy and the teaching profession, to become bank clerks or to work for the railways or post office. Education has also helped the Dhodhiyas to qualify for permanent employment in the large-scale industries which have sprung up in the region (see also Veen 1979: 58–61; Lal 1982: 37; Breman 1993b: 322–3). Nevertheless, this route upwards has remained closed to the majority of Dhodhiyas from households that own little if any land. They are inspired by the success gained by the vanguard of their caste but see no chance of following that example.

Employment in the formal sector is an even more distant dream for the Halpatis in the two fieldwork villages. The policy of positive discrimination ought to favour them more than any other. That this hardly occurs in practice is due above all to the fact that landless households do not meet the preconditions that seem to be set to even making a claim to the facilities reserved by government. The biggest handicap is that landless households do not have the necessary surplus to be able to send children to school and then launch them in the direction of protected employment. The handful of Halpatis that have managed to become eligible for such jobs belong to the category of marginal landowners, or are the fortunate few who thank their access to a protected livelihood to goodwill shown to them combined with mediation by someone from a higher social class. Even then, these exceptional cases of advancement seldom get any further than the lowest positions in the formal sector circuit: watchmen, peons and cleaners in government offices, for example. Nevertheless, in their own milieu they are seen as people who have made it.

This overview shows clearly that one's position in the agrarian order, i.e. ownership or non-ownership of means of production expressed in amount of land, is determinant for access to employment and to the monetary yield that it offers in other sectors of the economy. For those at the bottom of the rural system, the formal sector is an almost impregnable fortress whose walls are strongly protected and can only be climbed with help from within. To outsiders, those who receive *pagar* enjoy a form of property that makes them comparable to landowners in the agricultural hierarchy. A steady wage on the basis of regular work implies security of existence and also gives social dignity to the person who is employed on such conditions. Those who work in the formal sector of the economy, not necessarily in the lowest and least paid ranks, may find this an exaggerated notion. Nevertheless, in more than one respect, as owners of capital they usually enjoy a different lifestyle and have far better life chances than do the much larger mass of totally landless who have to survive with the aid of casual work. The discrimination felt by the latter is further fostered by the extremely sluggish expansion of the formal sector.

Notwithstanding the strong growth of the government machinery in particular which, during the last quarter-century, has come closer to the local level, absorption into the protected segment of the labour system over the whole line has only been able with difficulty to keep pace with the increase of the working population. The consequence of this relative stagnation has been that, simultaneously with the drop in illiteracy or semi-literacy, educational requirements are now made for jobs that earlier needed little if any formal training. This is a phenomenon to which I have earlier drawn attention (Breman 1980: 45).

Crossing the sharply drawn frontier to economic zones marked by formal labour arrangements is entering a circuit characterized by the coming into effect of numerous legal regulations from which, theoretically at least, such employment derives its security. In addition to the Minimum Wages Act (1948) under which wage scales are established, all sorts of secondary conditions form part of the work contract and augment the bargaining position of the employee as against the employer. These include the Factories Act (1948) containing directions about working hours, vacations and leave, safety and facilities at work, restrictions on the use of female and child labour, as well as rules concerning government control in those spheres; the Payment of Wages Act (1936) which regulates manner of payment, penalty clauses and wage deductions; the Workmen's Compensation Act (1926) covering the risk of industrial accidents and occupational diseases which temporarily or permanently impair the health of the employee; the Industrial Disputes Act (1947) with regulations concerning the settlement of disputes; the Provident Fund Act which lays down the gratuity due to the employee on reaching retirement; the Employees' State Insurance Act which regulates health insurance; and the Payment of Bonus Act (1965) which indicates the percentage of wages to be paid to employees as an extra annual allowance. This packet as a whole makes it understandable why wage workers who can claim these benefits represent a privileged section far above the much larger part of the working population who lead a shadowy existence in the informal sector of the economy.

Only thirty or so years ago, the conventional wisdom was that the informal sector would decrease in size as the capitalist mode of production grew. That type of wishful thinking has faded away. The transformation towards capitalism has indeed accelerated in most sectors of the economy but without causing any considerable expansion of employment in the formal sector. Various economic analysts close to the world of national and international policy-makers, have suggested that this stagnation was caused by extending and upgrading industrial labour legislation, under strong trade union pressure, during the last few decades:

The major culprit is seen in the job security regulations introduced during the late 1970s and strengthened during early 1980s through changes in law. Specifically, the reference here is to the change in the Industrial Disputes Act making it necessary for enterprises employing 300 or more workers to seek government permission to effect lay-offs, retrenchments and closures, in 1976 and making it applicable to establishments employing 100 or more workers in 1982. (Papola 1994: 12);

In India, the growing power of trade unions plus minimum wage legislation have no doubt confounded any downward pressures on wages that might otherwise have arisen. (Kannan 1994: 19)

The lesson drawn from such notions is that government should grant permission to management in formalized public and private business for an 'exit policy' in order to get rid of redundant and inefficient labour. Both authors quoted above have challenged the view that formal sector employment in India is stagnating due to what is nebulously called policy-induced rigidities in the labour market. Papola, for instance, has pointed out that real wage increases in industry during the 1970s and 1980s were accompanied by rapid productivity growth (Papola 1994: 11).

If this is indeed a more general trend one should then raise the question why not more instead of less labour has managed to find employment in formal job conditions. In my analysis of the reasons why informal sector employers continue to prefer prolonged hiring-and-firing to stabilizing their workforce, I have argued that many industrialists are sub-contractors who lack control over input and output factors. They operate in markets which are kept in a state of flux, under circumstances which make them highly dependent on traders. Casualization of labour is one of the strategies favoured by petty commodity entrepreneurs in order to shift both risk and cost of production to a party with even less bargaining power than they themselves have. Following up on the line of argumentation started in the last chapter the conclusion now seems to be that employment practices based on constant recruitment and dismissal are typically associated with mercantile capitalism. However, informalized labour arrangements do not remain limited to that specific mode of production only but are also characteristic for corporate capitalist business as exemplified by the agro-industries in the countryside of south Gujarat. The sugar mills in the countryside of south Gujarat are owned and run along co-operative lines by peasant producers. Although at the start liberally endowed with state capital, these large-scale rural enterprises do not tolerate official intervention in their management. The emerging Green Front is to a large extent in control of market conditions and has increasingly been able to dictate the terms of the trade, both prices of input and output, to the government. Cultivating and processing sugarcane is very profitable business for peasant producers, but the huge army of harvesters annually recruited for the duration of the campaign suffer from labour conditions which do not distinguish them from the workforce engaged in petty commodity production. Still, I hesitate to conclude that the persistence and even expansion of informalized employment modalities in a wide range of rural and urban economic settings can simply be explained as expressing the basic incompatibility between capital and labour. What I have observed in the course of my fieldwork is that the reluctance shown by employers to give a better deal to the workforce they need has to do with their resistance to formalize production out of fear that their sharp business practices would become subject to increasing state surveillance. Regulating organization of work by accepting protected terms of employment is objectionable not only because it raises costs of production. It should also be resisted in order to avoid control by government as much as possible. Rejection of public interference in what they consider to be their private domain is an article of faith to informal sector employers and for that reason they also insist that dealing with labour is nobody's concern but their own. Keeping books according to legal prescriptions and opening them for official inspection is considered to be an intolerable intrusion to which industrialists and other entrepreneurs react with undiluted aggression. This attitude is not just a matter of principle but is inspired by downright unwillingness to balance individual profit maximization with transferring and utilizing part of the accumulated surplus for the commonweal. The relationship between capital circulating in the informal sector economy and the state is quite antagonistic. The idea that capital accumulation is exclusively a formal sector phenomenon while subsistence in a culture of poverty would be characteristic for the informal sector (Kruyt 1993: 4) is much too simple. Surplus value is squeezed out of labour and converted into capital in the economic echelons on which I have concentrated in my research. However, exploitation of the workforce is not the only way to make profit. Shah has made pertinent comments on the kind of business climate dominating the industrial landscape of Surat:

Textile: . . . a part of production is not reported for the simple reason of tax evasion (to be precise, excise duty). Margin of profit in the units is so high that they increased their profits several times within ten years. Reported under-production is also linked with illegal use of electricity, non-payment of excise duty and blatant violation of labour laws. It is widely known in the city that these entrepreneurs, the underworld, police and excise as well as octroi departments are hand-in-glove. The factory owners pay *supari*, i.e. brokerage to the gang leaders who manage to get yarn in the city without paying octroi, and smuggle fabrics outside the factory without paying excise duty. These gangsters are used against labourers whenever they demand legal rights. Weaving, dyeing and processing units generate huge black money in the city. (G. Shah 1994: 3–4);

Diamond: Like powerloom, a majority of diamond units (64 per cent) are small, employing less than ten workers. There is also *bhagla* system, i.e. divisions to avoid implementation of Factory Act. Concealed employment in the industry is widespread 'to economise on labour cost', to circumvent the labour laws or to avoid giving workforce statutory benefits and to keep them submissive. (6)

The government of India is in an acute state of crisis because at various levels of public action there seems to be very limited scope for widening and deepening the base of taxation in society. Instead of promoting exit policies for formal sector labour, state intervention should redress the deplorable lack of control over informal sector capital. The latter option points to the need to change the policy trend from deregularizing to regularizing modes of employment.

Dynamics in real life, of course, are just the reverse. The dismantling of factorized textile production in Bombay and Ahmedabad, to which I have referred earlier, is illustrative of this shift which is very disquieting from the viewpoint of more humane labour relations. Various studies report on industrial closures or cutbacks and on the exodus of hitherto protected workers into the informal sector. In the registered manufacturing sector cotton textiles experienced a decline of about 3.6 per cent per annum in employment, reducing the number of workers by 3 *lakhs* between 1980–81 and 1988–89 (Papola 1994: 13). In Gujarat alone, the closure of textile mills caused 50,000 workers to lose their permanent jobs. While this happened dismantled powerlooms from Bombay were reinstalled in informal sector workshops in Surat which did thriving business. In Ahmedabad, an enquiry into the consequences of mass dismissals early in the 1980s has shown that of the tens of thousands of victims in this city alone, rather more than half had to depend on self-employment while almost as many existed on their casual labour (B. B. Patel 1988: 60–3). According to another research report some of the labourers who became redundant in textile mills had joined powerloom workshops in the city where they were paid less than half of what they used to get previously for the same type of work as formal sector employees (Joshi 1985: 4). Others who were laid off are to be found as job-seekers in the early morning casual labour markets, a fall in economic and social status that is difficult to accept.

It was reported that when the textile mill in Bilimora closed, a few workers migrated to Surat to seek work in art-silk mills. A few of them were lucky enough to get similar jobs. Those who could not secure any such help started visiting the casual labour market at Chowk Bazar and Station Area. 'Unless you are friendly with them and develop sufficient confidence, they would not reveal that once upon a time they were the regular workers of that closed mill,' said one informant of Bilimora town. (Punalekar and Patel 1990: 46)

Punalekar adds that the time has passed when these morning markets were attended only by temporary migrants from the countryside who were trying their luck in town for the first time. Nowadays they have become catchment reservoirs for workers 'who are retrenched, laid off or dismissed from the organised sector' (45–6).

Wage labour in the informal sector of south Gujarat, even with the restriction that I have made, i.e. ignoring own-account workers (self-employment), is a term used for want of any better for an enormous diversity of workers; these vary from the almost or completely landless who earn their living all the year round in the immediate vicinity of Gandevigam and Chikhligam in all sorts of activities in and out of agriculture, to seasonal migrants in all branches of agricultural and non-agricultural work who leave or enter the area of my fieldwork periodically, to the floating stock of workers who, without any prospect of permanency, commute to the small and large workplaces on which the non-agrarian economy of town and countryside in south Gujarat is so prominently based.

What these workers have in common is no more and no less than that they are excluded from formal conditions of employment and all the legal conditions with which that is accompanied. Employment based on formal sector conditions ought to provide protection to a far greater part of the working population than the one-fifth which is able to claim some degree of protection. That this segment remains so small is due to the explicit refusal by employers to stabilize their workforce. One could understand why it is difficult to regularize and organize street workers or other segments of the working population floating around in the urban and rural economy. However, there is also a large grey zone in-between, consisting of labour which in principle goes daily to the same worksite and employer. These categories of more continuously employed casual labour are also deprived of elementary rights which would comfort them with a modicum of security and dignity. Characteristic of their plight is the situation in the booming powerloom workshops of Surat:

although the majority of the workers are aware of one or the other labour law, no complaints are registered for fear of losing the job. Powerful unions do not exist as there is no unity amongst the workers who come from all parts of India. Moreover, the majority of them are either new in the industry or probably still not adequately trained and, as a result, do not complain for their rights such as reinstatement in job or for protection of wages and leave or for compensation for injury while on work. The vast majority of these workers, in fact, are not members of labour unions as the artsilk industry, by and large, is unorganized and most units are registered under the Shops and Establishment Act. (Mehta and Gandhi: 133)

It cannot be a coincidence that trade unions are by and large non-existent in the informal sector landscape. There was no organized activity whatsoever at the workplace in the case of 91 per cent of all textile labourers in Surat interviewed by Agarwal. But also among the remaining small category which acknowledged the presence of a union only a handful confessed to being members (Agrawal 1992: 192).

In order to avoid compliance with labour laws a large majority of textile industrialists in the city have registered themselves under the Shops and Establishment Act. This applied in mid-1980s to a total of 12,600 units. Only 700 units in this sector operated on the basis of the Factories Act (Mehta and Gandhi: 126). The legal status of the diamond ateliers is similar in character. All these nearly 10,000 units are covered also by the Shops and Establishment Act (1948). Under pressure from associations of owners and employers the government has agreed that factory legislation should not be applicable to these branches of industry. The two Acts have the same objective, but the Shops and Establishment Act regulates labour relations in small firms employing less than ten workers. These industrialists have the advantage that control over their workshops is not assigned to labour inspectors but to the local authorities. In practice, that delegation of power means that little if any control is exercised. Has the government remained totally non-active to reach out to the various segments into which the large masses of informal sector labour are sub-divided? Certainly not.

Regulations covering employment in the unprotected sector

The principal characteristic of dependence on wage labour in the informal sector is that there are no rules to restrict the authority of capital over labour. The significance attached to this aspect is so great that, rather than the informal sector, it could well be called the unregulated sector, the sector of the economy with its own rules and dynamics which largely or entirely are beyond state interference. It is tempting to describe the labour system in this arena in terms of a jungle in which only the right of the mighty prevails. Such a presentation is basically unjust, however. To be more precise, it ignores the efforts made by government during the last quarter-century to extend its reach to workers who lead their threatened existence in the shadow of the formal economy. In fact, that effort has been taken on behalf of all categories of industry that have been discussed in the previous chapters.

Restricting myself to the state of Gujarat, it can be seen that government concern for this unorganized and heterogeneous mass of workers is directed in the first place to the bottom class in what has remained to the present day the largest economic sector, that is, agriculture. Soon after Independence, in 1948, the central government directed the federal states to introduce a minimum wage for agricultural labour. In the majority of states that directive was without effect for a long time. In the 1960s, however, the course of the Green Revolution made it clear that the landless part of the rural population profited hardly at all from the agricultural growth that had been achieved or from the gradual increase in prices received by producers. Policy-makers became sensitized to the argument that the increasing class polarization in the countryside could affect social stability. Their fear of radicalization was plainly worded in the report of the committee set up by the government of Gujarat in 1964 to make recommendations for the announcement of a minimum wage for agricultural workers:

The implications of a lack of policy for agrarian labour to the political and social stability would be easily appreciated. The developments in Asia and Africa are an eye-opener. The working class in general and the agrarian labour in particular in our country has retained their moorings to our basic philosophy of our life and living. They might have grown restless and frustrated now and again, but by and large they have shown great patience in the otherwise discouraging situation around them. This is extremely healthy for the country and for all its citizens. This, however, should not make us complacent. It should be treated as a favourable factor to do something quickly to improve the lot of those on whose face we read signs of discontent and disparagement. The forces of extremism are waiting to take over the situation once these indications intensify a little. (Report Minimum Wages Employment in Agriculture 1966: 78–9)

This passage suggests that emphasis was placed more on the countering of a social revolution than on raising the landless mass to a life of human dignity. The committee, which included spokesmen of both employers and employees, was chaired by an independent expert while a high-ranking government official acted as its secretary. An inquiry held among what were known as 'progressive' farmers, i.e. substantial landowners who were interested in modernizing their business, social workers, extension officers and other professionals, workers' representatives or at any rate what passed as such, provided the necessary data on which to make an assessment of the state-of-the-art in the agricultural economy. Subsequently, the committee undertook a lengthy tour and held local hearings. Its members spoke with representatives of 133 institutions and 191 individuals, visited 100 villages, and covered a distance of 12,000 km. Field visits were also made, to my own research region among others. The remarks made in the committee's final report clearly showed that it had become aware of the high degree of deprivation suffered by agricultural labourers in south Gujarat:

Visits to *Halpati* colonies presented a picture of unhealthy and unhygienic conditions of accommodation with meagre household effects for less than a bare living. The surroundings were filthy and neglected. Vices, particularly of illicit drinking were the rule. The *halis* [serfs] and their families were under-nourished and in poor health. Large families with many children doing nothing or little and living a purposeless or directionless life were other tragic features. (Report Minimum Wages Employment in Agriculture 1966: 39)

One of the committee's findings was that expenditure on food demanded no less than 80 per cent of the household budget of agricultural labourers. The committee completed its work two years after its appointment. What were the recommendations that it submitted to government?

The committee rejected the idea of attuning the wage to the minimum cost of living for an agricultural labourer's household. It was impossible to give an unambiguous answer to the question of quality and quantity of the most essential goods, restricted to food, clothing and shelter. Moreover, it would be incorrect to fix a reasonable amount without making allowance for the agricultural situation and the paying power of the farmers. This weighing of pros and cons led to the pragmatic proposal that government should do no more than slightly raise the existing wages, maintaining the variation between men and women. However regrettable these might be, they had developed in practice over a period of time. While recognizing the desirability of social reform, the rapporteurs did not neglect to point out that a rapid and drastic rise in the price of labour would provoke agricultural employers to anti-social behaviour. Finally, a subsidiary consideration with which the committee sought to justify its conservative position was that the wages of agricultural workers must in any case remain below the rate paid to labour in other economic sectors. Otherwise, the members argued, there would be no incentive to leave agriculture. One committee member, an old social worker of Gandhian persuasion, found the amount suggested for south Gujarat to be unacceptably low, too low even to cover the most essential needs of existence. But even he was persuaded to endorse the recommendations by an assurance that the tariff for this zone of fertile land and prosperous agriculture would be increased in the near future. That assurance has never been met.

It was not until 1972 that the government of Gujarat introduced the first Minimum Wage Act for Agricultural Labour. The wage level was fixed only a fraction above the amount recommended by the committee six years earlier. In subsequent years, rises in the cost of living made a number of adjustments necessary, lastly in 1990. This usually occurred in the months immediately preceding elections for the state's assembly. Following up on this legislation regulating the wages to which casual day labourers and annual farm servants had a right, the first social security provisions intended especially for these categories were introduced. Since 1983, on payment of a nominal annual contribution, the workers are covered by a life insurance which gives them or their surviving relatives the right to monetary compensation in case of disablement or death respectively. At approximately the same time, another law was enacted giving female agricultural workers a sum of money on the birth of a child, equal to six weeks' wages for the first child and four weeks' wages for the second. Another benefit which also originated in an election campaign is the government pension for aged agricultural workers who have no means of their own and no adult children. Agricultural labour falls outside the scope of this study, and I therefore refer for more particulars to a number of earlier publications in which I have discussed this budding state-backed protection and its lack of effectiveness (Breman 1985a: 1051; 1985b: 299, 349; 1993: 334–51).

The trend towards decreasing employment in agriculture of marginal landowners and landless in my fieldwork villages gives rise to the question of whether government concern has not been directed towards workers who have been pushed on a large scale into other sectors of the economy. The affirmative answer that I have already given to this question can be elucidated further by referring to the Report of the National Commission on Labour issued in 1969. That study mentions a sizeable category called unorganized workers. This aggregate term refers to a great diversity of non-agricultural wage labourers with the common characteristic that they had remained unorganized. This situation, which amounted to an inability to look after their interests collectively, was said to be caused by the following factors: (*a*) casual nature of employment; (*b*) ignorance and illiteracy; (*c*) small size of establishments with low capital investment per person employed; (*d*) scattered nature of establishments; and (*e*) superior strength of the employer operating singly or in combination (Report NCL 1969: 417). Even before the informal sector concept, introduced in the early 1970s, became common usage in international literature, the presence, nature and significance of this sector of labour in India's economy had thus been remarked upon.

The NCL report is an important source of information regarding conditions of labour at the bottom of the economy in post-colonial India. There can be little doubt that its findings inspired the government of Gujarat to institute in 1971 a commission whose task was to investigate employment and working conditions in various branches of industry within the state that made use of unprotected and unorganized manual workers. The order was that the investigation should be concluded with recommendations on the introduction of legal measures with which to improve the situation of such labour. The committee drew up an ambitious plan of study which included a scrutiny of the available literature on the subject. The members also visited Bombay where, after a number of strikes by head loaders in 1965, the government of Maharashtra had introduced a scheme to regulate the employment of these casual, unskilled and ambulant workers to be found in market places and other congestion points of economic activity. The committee suggested that the field of study in the state of Gujarat should be mapped on the basis of three questionnaires: the first directed towards trade unions and social workers, the second to employers and their organizations, and the third to jobbers and their sponsors. Out of the 1,240 questionnaires distributed, however, no more than thirty-nine were filled in and returned. Field investigators employed by the Office of the Commissioner of Labour in Ahmedabad went out to gather more information. Finally, the committee toured around the state to collect factual data. In ten localities in Gujarat they examined 89 persons, whose evidence was recorded (Report Committee Unprotected and Unorganized Labour 1972). Ultimately, the whole exercise had little result. It is my impression that the complexity of the task was a major obstacle in producing a satisfactory outcome, even more than the limited time at the committee's disposal. To begin with, no conclusive definition was reached of what should be understood under 'unprotected' and 'unorganized' labour. Apart from terminological vagueness, attempts to estimate the volume involved were stranded in the absence of statistical and other data.

The primary source of information on the subject is almost non-existent. The facts on these categories do not flow as a by-product of administration. Even the Census data carry classifications which do not give us the information on unprotected and unorganized labour in the forms and classifications that we need. For, our purpose is not merely to have data on them but to have them in such a way that they could be fitted in an operational frame of policy. We, therefore, went out into the field to collect data on these categories and with the assistance of the primary guidelines and the co-operation and help of the various government and non-government agencies attempted to collect statistics on these forms of labour. It is needless to mention that the information that we could collect is very rough. (Report Committee Unprotected and Unorganized Labour 1972: 11)

The final report warned government not to depend on the mentioned, very incomplete, figures. Whatever action should be taken should be preceded by the compilation of more and better data. One of the principal recommendations was in fact the establishment of a research cell within the Office of the Labour Commissioner to fill this gap. That advice has led to the institution of a small cell which keeps itself busy by collecting statistics that are incomplete and rather dated.

In its attempts to formulate a policy concerning unprotected labour, the government of Gujarat seems to have followed the example given by Maharashtra. In the latter state legislation was introduced regarding the payment of head loaders (*hamalis*) in Bombay who, early in the 1960s, had stopped their work on a number of occasions to force public authorities to intervene in the spiralling conflict with their employers. The result of that arbitration amounted to a formalization of the working conditions of this loosely structured occupational group under a law that was enacted in 1968. This legal *mantra* is a milestone in the jurisprudence on informal sector labour in west India and has been incorporated in the Report of the National Commission on Labour (1969: 436–7). Government was represented in the council that was set up to keep an eye on implementation of the agreement reached. In practice, the regulation of head loaders' labour was probably fated to be short, undoubtedly linked to the absence of a strong trade union movement. It is, of course, not so easy to organize the casual workforce that can be found in the early morning labour markets. Bombay has eighty such *nakas* in different parts of the city which attract on average 200,000 labourers in the post-monsoon months. The Labour Office has conveniently classified them as 'self-employed', a term which suggests that these people do not need the help of government in their search for work and getting a reasonable price for their labour. New efforts made by social activists belonging to non-government organizations to regularize modes of employment for *naka* workers in Bombay have again failed miserably (Pandya 1993). That concerted action is not in principle out of the question for such categories is proven by the comparative effectiveness with which such heterogeneous and footloose occupations, without even a permanent and fixed workplace, have long managed to protect and harmonize their interests collectively in Kerala (see Kannan 1988).

The formalization of labour relations is shown not only by ratification of employment conditions by government. Following from that fact, and clearly modelled on industrial legislation in Kerala, qualified government officials take part in the regular consultations between employers and employees. The permanent presence of these officials means that implementation of the legislation is also institutionalized on the basis of a tripartite representation.

Legislation regarding Bombay *hamals* and other casual workers taken on for heavy physical labour, represented the first of a series of initiatives with which the government of Maharashtra showed its intention to improve the situation of irregular workers outside the factories and other large-scale enterprises. The way was opened in 1965 by setting up a committee whose task it was to examine this problem. The working group concluded as follows:

> that the persons engaged in avocations like *mathadis*, *hamals*, casual workers employed in docks, *lokhandi jatha* workers, salt-pan workers and other manual workers mostly worked outside fixed premises in the open and were mostly engaged on piece-rate system. In a number of cases they were not employed directly, but were either engaged through *mukadams* or *toliwalas* or gangs as and when there was work. They also worked for different employers on one and the same day. The volume of work was not always constant. In view of the peculiar nature of the work, its variety, the system of employment and the system of payment, and the vulnerability to exploitation of this class of labour, the Committee came to the conclusion that the application of the various labour laws to such workers was impracticable. It recommended that the working and employment conditions of unprotected workers should be regulated by a special enactment and gave an outline of the scheme and the act. (Report Committee Unprotected and Unorganized Labour 1972: 33)

This was the start of the Scheduled Employment Act which regulated conditions of employment for wage workers in far more branches of industry in Maharashtra's informal sector than had formerly been the case. The numerous committees set up for a wide variety of industries concentrated their much wider mandate on establishing a minimum wage. In some cases this had already been done when labour unrest gave rise to government arbitration. For example, strikes that broke out in 1946–47 in the saltpans along the coast near Bombay were settled in this way. Many of the workers in this seasonal industry came from south Gujarat. These migrants, among whom Halpatis from Valsad district were mentioned specifically, took part in the strike but only played a fairly passive role (Report Salt Pan Industry 1950: 29). In different parts of the country the centrally designed Minimum Wage Act of 1948 also led to special measures for wage workers in what was much later to become known as the informal sector. The increasing interest which the government of Maharashtra again showed in 'unprotected' labour from the mid-1960s onwards caused the existing list of scheduled employment to be adjusted. Added were the workers in brickfields and roofworks tile manufactures, on which a committee reported in 1969 (Minimum Wage Committee Employment in Bricks and Roof Tiles Manufactory 1969). In 1976, a new committee charged with the revision of wages in this latter branch of industry reported that a large proportion of workers engaged in northern Bombay each year were recruited in south Gujarat. When the committee suggested that local labour should be used, in line with Maharashtra's official policy, the employers' representative replied that productivity of Gujarati workers was much higher (Report Minimum Wages (Revision) Committee in Bricks or Roof Tiles Manufactory 1976: 6).

As these examples show, many seasonal migrants from my fieldwork region ended up in Bombay in workplaces for which the state government started at least a quarter-century ago to promulgate regulations concerning the wages that should be paid. At about the same time, similar measures were enacted in Gujarat. The committee on unprotected and unorganized labour that was set up in 1972 was able to refer to a Minimum Wage Act that had been promulgated many years previously concerning nineteen scheduled employments, whilst a similar Act was in preparation for another five such categories of wage labour. At that time these did not include road workers and brick-makers, but that was changed a few years later. One criterion for government action was that the branch of industry in question should employ minimally a thousand workers within the state's borders. That was no problem in the case of these two industries (road construction and brick-making), whose combined labour force was calculated by the committees involved to be more than 100,000.

In all cases the procedure prior to the promulgation of a Minimum Wage Act was the same. Government appointed a small committee chaired by an independent outsider and with a membership of representatives of employers and workers in the industry concerned. The secretariat of the committee was invariably entrusted to an Assistant Labour Commissioner, an official who served many such task groups in that capacity. If it was a new initiative, the Office of the Labour Commissioner sometimes held a brief preliminary survey of the number and size of enterprises, their distribution throughout the state, their management, the composition of their workforce, and so on. The committee always attempted to gain additional information. The questionnaire that was especially designed for the purpose was sent to employers, their organizations, social workers and other persons or institutions considered able to speak on behalf of the workers. The final report inevitably included the comment that response to the questionnaire had been lamentably low and that it was therefore impossible to draw any representative conclusions.

The report on labour in quarries and stone crushers (1974) mentioned that only 10 questionnaires were returned out of the 240 that had been sent out. The panel charged with making proposals regarding salt-pan workers distributed 192 questionnaires and received six back. The committee which tried to gain information in this manner on conditions in brickworks (1975) received replies from no more than 18 of the 426 addresses on the mailing list. These figures show that the average response was no higher than 4 per cent. (Fieldwork notes)

Equipped therefore with very little prior knowledge, committee members then journeyed to the various sites of the investigated industries in Gujarat in order to acquaint themselves with the current situation, particularly as regards wages and how they were paid. Their visits were announced in advance in the local press, with an open invitation to all interested parties to appear before the committee on the announced date. Sometimes no one came to these hearings. The committee members occasionally visited a work site or tried in some other way to gain information. For example, the committee whose task it was to advise on roadworkers reported:

If during its travel the committee came across workers carrying on road construction work, its members got down from the motor and made detailed inquiries by asking questions to the workers as well as the owners. (Report on Workers Employed in Road Construction 1975: ch. 3)

The assignment ended with consultations among the members of the panel concerned on concrete proposals drawn up on the basis of their findings. Invariably the advice was restricted to the wage level. Only on rare occasions did a working group venture to pronounce on any other desideratum. For example, the committee on brickworks recommended that child labour should no longer be used in this industry and also requested government to take responsibility for educational facilities at sites of employment.

One question extensively discussed by almost all committees was the yardstick that should be used in establishing a minimum wage. In answering that question the various committees also adopted a standard argumentation. They inevitably started by referring to the standpoint taken by the Committee on Fair Wages set up by the central government in 1948. In that committee's opinion, a minimum wage should encompass not only what the industrial worker needed for mere survival but also allow for expenditure on education and health, for example, in order to ensure an adequate labour performance.

We believe that the minimum wages should be such as to ensure that the worker can not only maintain himself, but can secure enough to enable him to keep up his efficiency. For this purpose minimum wages should satisfy to some extent the need for education, medical aid and other conveniences. (Report of the Committee on Fair Wages 1948: para. 10)

If payment should remain below the level at which labour's physical health is threatened, then the industry in question should lose its right to exist, according to this committee. On the other hand, it added to its advice the remark that to fix the minimum wage at too high a level would defeat its purpose if it should result in decreased employment.

Some time later, an attempt was made to quantify the subsistence minimum to which workers had a right. After all, 'to some extent', mentioned in the advice just quoted, is a flexible concept. It was made more specific during the fifteenth annual meeting of the Indian Labour Conference in 1957. The recommendation accepted on that occasion states that a working family consisting on average of husband, wife and two children, should have the right to a packet of consumption articles made up of: (a) a quantity of food based on 2,700 calories per (adult) person per day; (b) a total of 72 yards of clothing per year; (c) for shelter the amount that government charged its own employees in the lowest income brackets for rent; and finally (d) a 20 per cent latitude in the budget for expenditure on fuel, lighting and other items. Without commenting on this specific packet, the National Commission on Labour subsequently accepted the correctness of an approach that took as its point of departure the provision of the workers' minimum needs. In its 1969 report, however, it added the proviso that in establishing such a level of minimum needs, the economic capability of the industry in question should be taken into account.

All these considerations were included with little comment in the series of Minimum Wage Reports submitted to the government of Gujarat in subsequent years. It is clear from all of them, however, that the last remark by the National Wage Board played a decisive role, although in most cases no serious attempt was made to subject the paying capacity of employers to any thorough scrutiny. The committee entrusted with making proposals on road workers' wages straightforwardly rejected any approach based on minimum needs, referring in doing so to the pronouncements made by many other committees. All committees were agreed, however, that it was necessary to adjust the amount of wages to increases in the cost of living. The formula thought of was the introduction of a special allowance, according to which workers would have the right to a monthly compensation in addition to their wages if the price index for primary necessities should rise by a certain number of points. By linking expenditure and earnings in this manner, so the formula ran, real wages would not fall. Revision in a following wage round would automatically mean that the special allowance paid so far would be included in the new basic rate.

In all the committees that were set up, the viewpoint of the employers was expressed more emphatically and frequently than that of the workers. The former was articulated both in writing and orally, presenting arguments that did not fail to impress committee members, as reports on their consultations clearly show. Employers argued among other things that wage increases would damage their competitive position with regard to similar industries in surrounding states where wages and other production expenses were much lower. Brick manufacturers threatened that if labour costs were increased they would mechanize their industry, with the inevitable result of a fall in employment (Report Minimum Wage Advisory Committee for Workers Making Bricks 1975: 34). In one location of quarries and stone-crushers in south Gujarat, that I have also visited myself in the course of my fieldwork, the owners acknowledged that the wages then paid were less than the level needed for the reproduction of labour, but claimed that it was simply impracticable to pay more. If that was enforced, they told the committee, they would have no alternative but to close the quarries (Report Minimum Wages Stone Breaking and Stone Crushing 1974: 16).

The committee on wage fixation in brick manufacture was one of the few to make any effort to gather quantitative data on the profit made by the industrialists. According to these calculations, production costs per 1,000 bricks fluctuated in the mid-1970s between Rs 48.50 and Rs 95.25. The share of wages therein varied between Rs 16 and Rs 35, or 33 to 37 per cent. The sales price amounted to Rs 80 to Rs 120. According to these figures, submitted to the committee by the owners, this meant a profit margin ranging from 20–40 per cent. Other conclusions can be derived from the data that I have compiled. Raw materials and government taxes form a more modest part of production costs than is suggested by the manufacturers. The share of labour costs, on the other hand, is higher, in particular because they should include the commission paid to *mukadams*. Total expenses are nevertheless lower, while the actual sales price is higher than reported. This points to a considerably higher profit margin, which I estimate at 40–60 per cent. Even on the basis of the figures supplied by the employers, the committee members would have had good reason to advise a higher wage rate than they did in fact suggest. The information they accepted indicated, namely, that no less than 84 per cent of the budget at the disposal of a brick-making family was expended on food. And even at that level the wages paid were not sufficient to purchase the minimally required quantity and quality of food, as expert witnesses testified, with the result that the workforce suffered acute malnutrition. One retired collector spoke in this connection of a flourishing industry in which the workforce was exposed to a form of super-exploitation. A spokesman for a trade union voiced his opinion as: 'We have to labour in their factory like animals' (Report Minimum Wage Advisory Committee for Workers Making Bricks 1975: 38).

The state of affairs in Gujarat corresponded with the conclusions drawn by Kannan with regard to the situation in Kerala (Kannan 1990: 8). In Kerala, too, state intervention was based on the principle that the satisfaction of minimum needs on a level of human dignity had to be the point of departure in paying unprotected workers. Instead, wages were fixed on the basis of a combination of pragmatic considerations, of which the going wage rate was the most important. A role was also played by the increased price of vital necessities and, finally, by the wages granted by government to workers in similar occupations in the same or a neighbouring state.

There is an interesting remark, casually made in the Gujarat report of the Committee on workers in saltpans, to the effect that employers only increased wages after government had first determined the minimum level (Report Minimum Wages Advisory Committee for Salt Producing Industries 1974: 31). I have found confirmation of this *modus operandi* in the rising trend of earnings of agricultural workers (Breman 1985b: 348–50). Such a sequence naturally does not signify that labour's market price is immediately raised to the legally prescribed minimum. Why that does not happen will be discussed below. It may be assumed that the committees were familiar with this phenomenon. The chairman of the working group looking into the terms of employment for road workers mentioned in the report that, in the same capacity as chairman of the committee for brickworkers, he had shortly before ascertained that the wages actually paid to those workers were far less than the bottom rate that had been laid down earlier (Report on Workers Employed in Road Construction 1975: 11). Nevertheless, he did not find this shortcoming a sufficient justification for more than a marginal wage increase or to press that the promulgated orders should be complied with more effectively.

The legislation has not brought about any real change. I am inclined to ascribe the lack of actual improvement to the limited affinity felt by responsible policy-makers with the world of workers. The instructions given to the successive committees and the results of their assignments imply a sanctioning of existing industrial practices, although the workers subjected to those practices would have benefited from their discontinuation. The committees noted several abuses, but without referring to them in their conclusions and recommendations. For example, it was established that brick-makers had to work 14–15 hours each day for their wage. Rather than recommending a labour agreement arrangement along individual lines – a type of contract prescribed by the established legal code – the committee was satisfied with the employers' explanation that in this branch it was customary to engage labour on a family basis. Perhaps the most important decision taken by all these committees was not to give in to the wish repeatedly expressed by workers' representatives for the introduction of a time-based wage; instead, it agreed with payment on a piece-work basis. The principle of sub-contracting thus continued to be tilted in favour of employers. The committee that had to advise on more general lines of policy regarding unprotected workers even suggested that, for that reason, they probably should not be qualified as wage workers:

Another important feature of the unprotected and unorganized worker is that quite a few of them tend to take the colour of self-employed particularly from those categories which do loading and unloading and without stable employer-employee relations and who are paid on piece-rate. It might be equally true that it is these categories which offer scope for conversion to self-employment over a period . . . It is on account of these features that the Committee feel that care should be exercised to avoid these from disappearing through too much of legislation and statutory strait-jacketing. (Report Unprotected and Unorganized Labour 1972: 52)

This remark fits with the dominant tendency to see the informal sector as a reservoir of self-employed. According to this stereotype, the heterogeneous mass of energetic and inventive mini-entrepreneurs inhabiting the lower echelons of the economy are quite able to look after themselves and are in fact better off without state intervention.

In drawing up the balance, it is my conclusion that what at first sight seems to have been a formalization of wage labour in the informal sector of the economy, in fact was little more than legislation that tolerated current practices. By dealing with each branch of industry separately the compartmentalization of the workforce was reinforced with the result that their joining of hands in organizations that were not trade specific became more difficult. The segmentation which characterized the vast and uncontrolled arena of work was not overcome by the introduction of a new set of policy directives, giving some minimal protection to labour, but got more or less sanctioned by codification. The streamlined conversion into a number of manageable rules only ostensibly caused government's grasp over the informal sector to be strengthened. Even in the initial phases, the announced cleaning-up of inhuman conditions of employment in the shadow economy became bogged-down in legal formalism. There are some immediate explanations for this disappointing outcome; namely, the weak bargaining power of discriminated labour, the rigid opposition by employers against all regulative measures, and the social identity of policy-makers at all levels of the political-bureaucratic system.

For a start, the voice of the labourers themselves was hardly heard. This becomes clear on reading the reports submitted by the committees whose task it was to suggest ways in which the position of the workers could be improved. The employers' viewpoint was put across more powerfully and clearly, expressed by themselves and by spokesmen of their orchestrated lobby. On the opposite side, the designation 'unorganized workers' in itself indicates that there was little if any evidence of collective promotion of interests. Trade unions did not exist at all in most branches of industry. Spokesmen on behalf of these unprotected workers were often caretakers who acted with sympathy but at a distance, and could not count such workers among their own adherents when appearing before the committees. The inability of the wage-dependent class in the informal sector to fight on a united front will be discussed in the last chapter of this study.

Another important element was the considerable social gap that divided those who made the rules from a clientele that for so long had remained invisible to policy-makers and which led an incomprehensible existence at the bottom of society. The condescension with which entrepreneurs discussed their workers, often in front of the committee, was in fact not very different from the denigration which imbued the attitude of many committee members towards these socially down-and-outs. This is shown by the tolerance and sympathy that can be read between the lines of the reports when employers complained about deficient labour morality in general and the lack of diligence among their workforce in particular. 'It is simpleton, illiterate and ignorant', was the terse comment of one committee regarding the social identity of saltpan workers in Gujarat (Report Salt Works Labour Enquiry Committee 1955: 21).

One aspect of the licentiousness said to characterize the life and work of such labourers and which was much discussed by committee members, was the impulsive and spendthrift behaviour attributed to them. This explains why a committee in Maharashtra, set up to improve the minimum wage of brick and rooftile makers, praised the initiative of one employer in retaining part of the workers' wages. This was put into savings banks and he kept the deposit books. Workers who wanted to withdraw money could only do so with his permission. An excellent method by which to stimulate thrift, thus the committee members opined enthusiastically (Report Minimum Wages (Revision) Committee in Bricks or Roof Tiles Manufactory 1976: 6).

An important omission in all minimum wage reports mentioned here is that the role of the jobber is not discussed or regulated. This attests to such a defective understanding of the organization of the work process in these branches of industry that the proposals for protection were doomed to fail for that reason alone. But the central government did not omit to fill this gap, after being exhorted in 1969 by the National Commission of Labour to put an end to the exploitation of workers by middlemen who seemed to be present in a growing number of economic transfer points and on an ever-increasing scale. The Contract Labour (Regulation and Abolition) Act 1970 was meant to cover the country as a whole, and was accompanied by directives to the state governments to take appropriate measures. The intention of this Act is to check the authority of jobbers and sub-contractors of labour over the gangs that they lead. The employment of such labour on a permanent basis is not allowed, but this applies only to firms employing more than twenty workers. Employers have to register if they use contract labour, while the jobbers who supply and lead such gangs have to be licensed. The effect of this measure is considerably restricted by the rule that it is not applicable in situations where employment is incidental or intermittent. This exclusion is dropped, however, in the case of work which had continued for more than 120 days in the preceding year and of seasonal work lasting at least 60 days. Labour contracted on this basis has the right to numerous facilities in the workplace: a canteen, a rest room, drinking water, a latrine and first aid. Wages have to be paid in the presence of an agent of the ultimate employer who is also liable for paying the wages if the labour contractor should shirk that obligation.

All categories of seasonal migrants to which I have devoted my attention, i.e. cane-cutters, brick-makers, road workers, saltpan workers and quarrymen, ought to be able to profit from the protection offered by this legislation. This has not been the case. One would also need to be singularly naive to assume that temporary workers would be given treatment such that is all too often withheld from formal sector workers as well. A number of publications have pointed out the over-ambitious nature of a number of clauses in the Act, combined with an imprecise and inadequate description of various facets of those clauses. The result is that the jobber-gang boss and the actual employer are left much scope to evade their responsibilities. Not all policy-makers are unhappy about this situation. They raise the question of whether it is advisable to restrict and eventually to do away with the middlemen between demand and supply. Surely such figures contribute to a greater flexibility of the labour market, which is in the interests of all concerned. This opinion can be seen, for example, in the contribution to a conference on labour migration held in 1985 by the then Director of the Gandhi Labour Institute in Ahmedabad:

The idea that the services of contractors for recruitment of labour can be dispensed with presupposes either that one can do without migrant workers or that the labour market for migrant workers is so well organized that one can get them when required without the intermediaries. Neither of those assumptions seems to be correct. It is said that even in mature economies the availability of migrant workers at the right time and place could be crucial. The labour market for migrant workers is so notoriously disorderly or disorganized that the employers do not know where the labour is available and the workers do not know where jobs are available. Exchanges do not usually register the migrant workers and there is no other systematic means of disseminating labour market information. (Subrahmanya 1985: 5)

This opinion assumes that self-regulating mechanisms are useful and necessary in order to solve the imperfections of the labour market. The logic on which it is based typically expresses the knowledge and point of view of a formal sector expert. Its presentation lacks any affinity with workers in the informal sector, whose underpayment is also due to exploitative practices on the part of those who mobilize their labour power.

Similar statements were made when, in 1979, the central government introduced the Interstate Migrant Workmen (Regulation of Employment and Conditions of Service) Act. This became law in 1980 on the anniversary of Mahatma Gandhi's birth, in reaction to the abuses caused by large-scale annual labour migration within north India in particular. In this Act, too, the jobber-gang boss plays a central role. In his absence, long-distance migrants are unable to seek protection that is provided by the law. The middleman has to supply his recruits with a workbook which includes, in addition to a photograph of its owner, details of the nature of work, wage rate, mode of payment, deductions and compensation for travel costs. Even more costly than this compulsory registration is the relocation allowance amounting to no less than 50 per cent of the monthly wage to which gangs of migrant workers have a right. For the rest, the legal conditions for contract workers apply.

The conditions mentioned are so far distant from reality that the majority of state governments have not made the least effort to enforce compliance with these regulations imposed under the Act. The Act itself makes this possible:

No court shall take cognizance of any offence under this Act except on a complaint made by, or with the previous sanction in writing of, an inspector or authorized person and no court inferior to that of a Metropolitan Magistrate or Judicial Magistrate of the first class shall try any offence punishable under this Act.

By simply not charging any official body with control over compliance with the law, contract workers who migrate to other states are left just as unprotected as they were earlier. The lack of follow-up was due not only to practical reasons. Whenever I tried to discuss this subject at a high bureaucratic or political level, I was told that the Indian Constitution expressly permits the free movement of persons and thus also of labour within the country. That principle of freedom of movement must under no circumstances be circumscribed. Sometimes I was told that labour migration was not only inevitable given regional imbalances between supply and demand, but that it also was a sign of progress on the path to economic development. To block this trend, I was told, would not be in the general public interest. The logic of such reasoning cannot be denied, but that applies only to thinking in formal sector terms. To suggest that the Khandeshi cane-cutters put to work for the season in the fields of south Gujarat, the Oriya textile workers employed for an indefinite period in Surat, or the landless Halpatis who trek each year to brickworks far distant from their village, are migrants who leave home because of their own free choice and who resort to this option out of well-considered self-interest to act as a vanguard in marking the route towards modern civilization, in my view testifies to a grotesque distortion of social reality.

In the same manner I could criticize three other laws that have been promulgated: the Bonded Labour System (Abolition) Act (1976), the Equal Remuneration Act (1976) and the Child Labour (Regulation and Abolition) Act (1986). In all these cases the legislations seem at best to have arisen from good intentions, but these have been formulated too hastily and carelessly and therefore lack efficacy. According to another less favourable opinion, the legislations were merely a façade of formalism and legalism with which, for political reasons of national and international legitimacy, government tried to give the impression that it cared for the interests of unprotected workers. Whether bonded labour has indeed disappeared as a result of action undertaken by government will be discussed later in this chapter. First, however, we shall examine in which way and with what results legislation regarding unprotected labour has been implemented. As we shall see, the operation of the machinery put up for this purpose has strengthened my scepticism regarding the achieved formalization of employment conditions in that massive underzone of the economy in which the majority of Indian men, women and even many children earn a meagre living with toil and sweat.

Implementation

In 1982, as one of the first states in India, Gujarat introduced a separate Inspectorate for Rural Labour, headed by a Rural Labour Commissioner seated in Gandhinagar. In areas such as south Gujarat with a high percentage of landless, divisions have been established from which officials primarily exercise control over the payment of minimum wages to rural labour. For further information I would refer to the essay that I wrote in 1985 on the daily routine of this rural labour inspectorate in Surat district (Breman 1985a). The conclusion that I reached at the time, namely, that this agency was deficient in all respects, is still valid in the light of data that I have compiled in the intervening years. My strongly critical appraisal seems to be vindicated by the recent report of the National Commission on Rural Labour:

the organization has not been effective. The officials are not adequately informed on their subject. They are not sufficiently motivated. The quality of the inspections is poor. In its totality also, the organization has not done well. There does not seem to be adequate understanding of and identification with the objectives of the organization. In the four years ending in 1988, the performance has been particularly poor in some respects. The number of inspections and consequent detection of violations and defaults are expected to go up following the revision of the minimum wage. In Gujarat the experience following the 1986 wage revision is in the reverse. The morale of the inspecting officers is low. (Report NCRL, vol.1, 1991: 208)

In earlier publications I have mentioned that officials of the Rural Labour Commission are also entrusted with enforcing the government of Gujarat's decree regarding a number of non-agricultural scheduled employments. In addition, there are separate offices at state and district levels whose staff primarily monitor the legislation for industrial labour in the formal sector of the economy. The distribution of tasks between the two Inspectorates is complicated and difficult for outsiders to understand. Employers become extremely irritated at having to cope with officers of different government agencies who come to check on their activities regarding constantly changing sections of labour legislation.

I should add immediately that inspection visits are not frequent because far too few officials are available to allow any accurate and regular control on that sector of the economy over which their powers extend. The overload about which the heads of these agencies rightly complain is augmented by the practice of leaving vacancies unfilled for a long time. The labour inspector is equipped with knowledge and power which make him a person of influence in the eyes of his clientele. This applies particularly to the official entrusted with control over formal sector employment, regarding whom on an earlier occasion I wrote the following:

The government labour officer, during an interview in his office, rattles off the various labour laws, stating the year and number, the jurisprudence and on further enquiry even the clauses giving exemption, all as if he were reciting holy passages from the *Mahabharata*. He could be rightly called the Brahman of the labour system and, indeed, his behaviour is commensurate with this. He is a Brahman also in the sense that he caters only for a small section of the population, namely those permanently employed in the formal sector, the top of work hierarchy. He is mostly concerned with the larger enterprises. He considers labour relations in the small industries, the workshops and other small establishments, to be outside his competence, as a domain that is difficult to survey and to control. (Breman 1980: 70)

His colleague, who operates in the shadow of the formal sector, has that aura of magnificence to a far lesser degree. It seems as though something of the defilement that radiates from the miserable existence led by the surging mass of casual workers at the bottom of the economy also reduces the status of the government agent who has the unenviable task of operating in their vicinity in order to provide the meagre degree of legal protection that is due to them.

The fairly rare appearances of the labour inspector in this milieu usually have an additional purpose than that for which he is sent. Breaches of the law are not identified in order to declare the employer in default and to force him to rectify the matter through sanctions. Far more frequently, the official will use his knowledge of the rules and regulations to demand hush money for covering up the transgression. This is easily done because not one employer pays the special allowances granted to wage labourers in scheduled employments by way of price compensation. Capitalizing on the discrepancy between practice and law provides the inspector with an income that is many times higher than his salary. It also explains why candidates for such a post are only considered if they are prepared to 'buy' it. This is done by paying cash to their superior or a local politician in compensation for the income that will subsequently flow so steadily and substantially. The actual payment for not taking any action was naturally not made during the tours of inspection on which I accompanied officials from the district offices in Valsad and Surat on a number of occasions between 1986 and 1989. These trips gave me the opportunity, however, to observe the behaviour of labour inspectors during their visits to quarries and brickworks from close quarters.

The man with whom I went to a brickwork near Navsari had been told by his superior to show me how such an industry operated. Assuming that this would be my first encounter he had chosen a large undertaking. Attempts to warn the owner by telephone of our coming had failed, and my appearance together with the official on a motorbike marked Government Labour Office caused a sensation. The head *mukadam* stopped us by the entrance to the terrain and hastened to warn the *sheth*, who nervously led us along the various gangs of brick-makers, diggers and donkey drivers who were hard at work. The labour inspector clearly avoided speaking to the workers themselves and directed his questions to the owner. The latter or the *mukadam* answered those questions, as non-committal as possible. Within hearing distance of the migrants, who silently continued to work as though we were not there, their origins and social background were discussed, their tendency to break their contract by accepting an advance but then not reporting for work, the continual necessity to exhort them to work harder, and in general the lack of discipline and mediocrity that was endemic to lower caste behaviour. But however equivocal the discussion on specific conditions of employment, it was clear that the workers did not receive that to which they had a right. When I said this aloud, to the embarrassment of my companion, the owner asked if we could not come to some 'arrangement'. The labour inspector quickly put away the notebook that he had taken from his bag in order to make notes. Our visit had only been intended to show me the works. He would soon return to explain his statutory obligations to the owner. There was no time to do that now because he had more to inspect that day. We departed without having spoken even to one worker. My visit to a quarry together with a government official posted to my fieldwork area was very similar. At the entrance to the isolated workplace hung a board with the announcement, in English, that the workers could obtain information on wages, payment, working hours, etc., from the district office. When I asked if this ever occurred, the reply was negative. My honest companion said that the board had to hang there. He added in the first place that the workers were totally illiterate, even in their own language, secondly that the district office was too far away, and thirdly that they would not take it into their heads to ask about their rights. Instant dismissal was the least that would result if they should do so. Nevertheless, he seemed to trust blindly in the information provided by the works owner. He did not even think of checking its accuracy by talking to some of the workers. When I enquired further during a later visit, the owner took me into his confidence and said laughingly that there was little truth in what he had said earlier during out first meeting. According to him, the government official who had introduced me also knew better. In prior consultation on how to handle my visit, however, the two had decided that it would be advisable to keep up the pretence of an official inspection and thus brazenly to maintain that the rules were properly being applied. (Fieldwork notes)

Indeed, the inspectors know more than is laid down in their reports. At the government office in Valsad in 1985 only nine brickworks were registered, although in reality more than 100 were established in the district. The man charged with control over this branch of industry, though favoured would be a more appropriate term, did not even take the trouble to visit the worksites. The chairman of the district branch of brick manufacturers paid him a sum of money every year to safeguard his members from inspection.

Wage workers in the informal sector remain invisible to government representatives, even to the handful whose task it is to defend them. There is nothing in the behaviour of the majority of these officials which could give men and women in the lowest echelons of the economy the idea that they are genuine and benevolent protectors of their clientele. Workers are mainly heard or questioned with the intention not of applying legal regulations, but of converting the latter to private profit. Instead of gaining any advantage from the transactions, the deceived workers were victimized. I have reported this fact in an earlier publication:

Even the labourers know quite well that the statements they make are often used for the purpose of extorting a bribe. Some of them were able to tell me exactly how much their employers had paid in hush money, sometimes only an hour or two after they had been obliged to set their thumbprints on paper. It is one more reason why labourers, when approached by GLOs, are not very forthcoming with information. (Breman 1985a: 1049)

My own observations in this respect agree with Streefkerk's remarks on the reputation of a factory inspector charged with control over employment in small-scale industries in a town close to my fieldwork villages:

It was said that he would inform employers of his visits beforehand so that they could keep ready the 'official' books and 'superfluous' workers could be sent home for the day or afternoon. He too did not concern himself with workers during his visits. However, it has become doubtful whether any worker is easily willing to talk to government officials about working conditions. As one textile worker from Bulsar [i.e. Valsad] said, he knew of only one case where an inspector asked a worker about his current wage level. The worker gave an honest answer and was promptly dismissed the next day. (Streefkerk 1985: 200)

On the side of the employers, more than distrust is at stake. Naturally, no employer is prepared voluntarily to increase the market price for labour to the legal minimum or in any other way improve the wretched working conditions. But many are even unfamiliar with the regulations that they are supposed to comply with, and also lack the knowledge necessary for the bookkeeping demanded by government. This applies particularly to the small brickyard owners who have opened-up one or two *bhatas*, self-made men who have worked their way up to become independent entrepreneurs from an artisanal background and without having had any education. These include, for example, the Prajapatis, constituting a caste of potters; the Khatris who own small textile workshops in Surat belong to the same category. Government officials who visit their workplaces equipped with their book of rules are given bribes simply to avoid the fuss and bother. A number of informers from this milieu showed some understanding for what they called reasonable desires on the part of their workers: permanent employment and all its accompanying advantages. This would naturally cause a substantial increase in the price of labour, but they were willing to make such a sacrifice in order to improve the abominable existence suffered by their subordinates. The problem, however, was that such a formalization of the labour system would enable the authorities to find out the real size of their production and, on that basis, to impose higher taxes, both on the raw materials used and on the added value of the finished product. Such drastic siphoning off of their ample incomes was intolerable to the textile barons. It would also put them into great financial difficulty since not only their incomes but also their payments were largely illicit, i.e. received as well as paid in black money.

The *homines novi* who usually originate in the social middle classes are more aggressive in their reaction when outsiders trespass on their domain. This is particularly so in the case of the Kanbi Patidars, members of a dominant peasant farming caste in rural south Gujarat, who during the last few decades have manifested themselves increasingly as entrepreneurs in many non-agricultural branches of industry (see also Rutten 1994). In the countryside and cities of Gujarat, such business-men have become the backbone of the political system. They are accustomed to buying what they need, including government support or abstinence. Their attitude towards government is marked by rancour, a sentiment that they are blocked in their economic freedom of action, and moreover that their social value is not respected. They feel that the officials have nothing to seek in their industries and they are not interested in the rules of formal sector economics. The real bookkeeping ledgers of such entrepreneurs, called *number be* (no. 2) or *kalum* (black), are for their eyes only. The 'white' bookkeeping that is shown to official busybodies is a façade, kept with no other intention than to pretend a semblance of legality. Researchers repeatedly encounter the phenomenon of systematic under-registration of the workforce. Streefkerk diagnosed it in small-scale industry in the main town of Valsad district (Streefkerk 1985: 661), while a study of the labour process in the diamond ateliers of Surat led to the same conclusion (Kashyap and Tiwari 1982: 20–1). Not more than 8 per cent of the workers in Surat's textile mills received a pay-slip. Only this small minority had identity cards such as are issued to permanent employees. The majority of the workers were not included, or were given false names, in the registers that management is obliged to keep (*Working and Living Conditions* 1984: 66). This was why it was impossible to identify some of the victims buried under the debris when a factory in which they worked collapsed in 1981. One of the state's highest bureaucrats, with whom I discussed this incident, commented that a state of total illegality rules in Surat. On the other hand, industrialists are highly indignant if they are not left alone after having paid large sums of money for the silence of officials about their illegal practices.

There was great excitement in 1985 when a group of officials from Ahmedabad 'raided' the offices of industrialists and traders in Surat in order to inspect the books. Local government officials had not been informed in advance of this visit, neither were they involved. This was done to prevent their warning their clients and thus nullifying the expected effect of the expedition. The captains of industry informed one another by telephone of the presence of the 'intruders'. The hostility with which the squad was received made it necessary to call in the help of the local police. The officer in charge reacted to the alarm call by saying that he could not make any manpower available. The mounting agitation can be illustrated by the attempt made in one workplace to throw some of the official inspectors into the factory's red-hot boiler. This could be prevented just in time, but not the physical violence that preceded it. (Fieldwork notes)

In such a climate it cannot be expected that workers will submit complaints to the labour inspectors on their own initiative and without restraint. From the talks I had with workers in many different places of employment and beyond the control of their superiors, I realized that the workforce in most branches of industry quite well realize the existence of rules and regulations designed to improve their situation. Perhaps they are not aware of the precise details and elaboration into all sorts of clauses, but this does not alter the fact that there is widespread knowledge among employees of minimum wage rates, for example. However, only exceptionally does an official seek direct, face-to-face contact with them. The survey among 1,635 textile workers in Surat mentioned earlier showed that this had happened to only 2 per cent. In the view of workers, the employer and the inspector are hand-in-glove. The agent of the state only comes to meet the boss and to have an intimate talk with him. The official is separated from his real clients by a great social rift. He has little if any understanding of their way of life, nor is he really interested in their plight. On the rare occasions that an employee dares to protest about employment conditions, it is questionable whether that complaint will be officially reported. Workers are helpless witnesses in transactions that largely occur outside their field of sight and which are not subjected to any form of control. Any recalcitrance they might show is running a risk that most cannot and will not afford.

In our study, 6 workers said that they were penalized for approaching the labour court; 7 workers stated that they were removed from the job for filing a case in the labour court. As stated earlier, the workers who feel that they are unduly penalized by the owners or management do not get the support of other workers because of job insecurity and harassment. (*Working and Living Conditions* 1984: 71)

This also happens to the more vulnerable Halpatis in Gandevigam and Chikhligam whenever they show any signs of militancy. Long before the stage of formal action is likely to be reached, the landowner for whom they have worked until that moment says that he no longer sets any store on their services. And that is not all, because other employers in the village will refuse to employ such a troublemaker (Breman 1993: 307). In small-scale locations in rural areas, such a boycott gains potency that is lacking in the anonymity of a big city.

Compliance with more recent legislation is hardly any better. And this notwithstanding the fact that the regulation of both contract labour and of long-distance migration has come about by way of concession to public outcries regarding excesses reported in various parts of the country. While a former Minister of Labour expressed himself pessimistically regarding implementation of the Interstate Migrant Workmen Act at a conference held in Ahmedabad in 1985, the diligence and progressive action of the government of Gujarat were praised by central-level bureaucrats at the same meeting and held up to other states as an example. The measures taken included, in addition to the obligation for labour inspectors to make a prescribed monthly number of inspections and to report immediately on their findings, the setting-up of a special squad to carry out surprise raids each month in all districts and to report thereon to the minister in person. The need for continual vigilance was also discussed in one of the conference papers. The military sounding jargon suggests maximum decisiveness. The announcement of the action to be undertaken is in itself sufficient for the self-satisfied statement at the end of the analysis that everything is being done to ensure success (Sheth

1987: 252–5). Since then, nothing has been heard of the vigilant commandos and their hunting expeditions.

Attempts to restrain the labour contractor have met the same fate. The jobber-gang boss whom I see as a key figure in the landscape of labour, is noticeably absent in inspectors' reports. These middlemen have been very successful in blocking the formalization of informal conditions of employment. The dual role fulfilled by the middlemen is well illustrated by the way in which *mukadams* in the saltpans along the coast near Bombay have managed to prevent any extension of the Minimum Wage Act to saltpan workers and also to turn it to their own profit. As I have mentioned earlier, the labour unrest which broke out in the mid-1940s was the reason why these workers were included in the first list of scheduled employments in Maharashtra. The strikes were led by trade unions, a rare phenomenon in the informal sector as a whole but certainly in seasonal industries. At the time of my fieldwork in the mid-1980s some of these organizations proved still to exist. I took up contact with some of their leaders in Bombay, and our talks brought me to the conclusion that, among migrant workers, only the *mukadams* had applied for membership of the unions. They receive the formalized wage which employers now pay to middlemen, thanks to relentless trade union activity. They also receive the amount stipulated for piece-work by their gangs. The trade union is not concerned with the conversion that then takes place into informal sector prices with which the *mukadam* fobs off the members of his gang.

The number of *mukadams* who have gained their licence or who have even applied for it, is only an insignificant fraction of the total who ought to do so according to the law on contract labour. The registration lists kept by the district offices in Surat and Valsad principally report the names of middlemen who act as sub-contractors of work in the formal sector of the economy. The jobbers-gang bosses of whom hundreds operate in the branches of industry on which I focused my research have stayed out of bureaucratic view, even when they carry out work on the orders of government itself. The committee that was set up to provide road workers protection under a Minimum Wage Act reported that three-quarters of all orders originated with Public Works Departments, but without that fact having any noticeable influence on compliance with the rules.

By way of excuse for the ineffectiveness of existing labour legislation, the bureaucrats frequently complain that the mass of workers who form the target group played only a passive role in the efforts made to improve their situation. According to this line of thinking the workers' low level of knowledge caused by illiteracy keeps them ignorant of the protection available. More generally, fatalism, a principal characteristic of their attitude to life, is said to hinder the victims in taking action to demand their rightful claim. Such a definition of the problem in terms of a culture of poverty caused the government of Gujarat to launch a plan for stimulating the social consciousness of the rural proletariat. Since 1982, in a number of villages in districts with a high concentration of landless, Rural Workers' Welfare Centres (*Gram Majur Kalyan Kendra*) have been opened, where a rural organizer informs the workers about what government is doing for them. This social activist also has the task of strengthening the workers' resistance. Unemployed educated youths from lower castes are employed for such promotional action. They are given a modest monthly allowance that is roughly equal to the amount earned by an agricultural labourer in the same period. On an earlier occasion I have described the ineffectiveness of this scheme in practice and made some critical remarks regarding the preconceived ideas on which it is based (Breman 1985a: 1050–2). I omitted on that occasion to spell out the inner contradictions that characterize government's social programmes of this sort. How genuine is the appeal to this vulnerable bottom class to achieve greater solidarity and defiance if, whenever this is manifested, the authorities immediately and often hard-handedly take action to de-escalate it on the pretext of maintaining law and order? An appeal to the need to maintain public safety is standard procedure in putting an end to agitations of labour unrest which occur regularly and spontaneously in the informal sector of the economy, but which are mostly of short duration and restricted to a few locations. The cane-cutters who, at the end of the 1981 campaign, protested against payment of too small an amount in back pay for which they had worked during the preceding months, were forcefully evicted from the factory premises by the strong arm of the state and hurriedly transported back to their home villages (Breman 1990: 591–2). In the brickworks around Vadodara a strike broke out in 1983 among the workforce that was brought there each year at the start of the season from Uttar Pradesh and Rajasthan. In despair at the employers' refusal to increase their wages and at the lack of support shown by government agencies in their attempts to insist on what was their legal right, a few thousand brick-makers marched to the city to draw public attention to their plight.

From many kilns only the men came as the women and children were prevented from leaving the kilns. On the complaints of the owners, police beat up some workers at the Nandesari cross-roads, on their way to Baroda for the meeting . . . Without food, water and any other facilities this sit-down demonstration turned into an enforced hunger-strike; the Municipal authorities refused the use of even a water connection. Two babies were born in the course of the week in the Badami garden near Dandia bazar. The pathetic condition of the workers generated no sympathy in the city. What did arouse a reaction was that Baroda's beautiful gardens had been converted into slums by these workers. (Randeria and Yagnik 1990: 85)

The conflict ended in a compromise that employers subsequently refused to fulfil. They were not in a hurry because the season came to an end and the migrants had to return home without achieving anything. The brick manufacturers were determined, however, that any continuation of the protest in the following season must be thwarted. In the middle of the rainy season they asked government to revoke all labour laws that were applicable to their branch of industry. The list of demands that they submitted to the state's Chief Minister was accompanied by a purse of Rs 1.1 *lakh* for a disaster fund that he had initiated. On the basis of similar incidents encountered during my fieldwork, I have concluded in a recent publication that the façade of harmony put up by government in fact hides actual unwillingness to shift the extremely distorted social balance towards the poor and defenceless with anything more than empty promises. Even those caretakers who quite legitimately concern themselves with the fate of the underdogs, are told sooner or later that they may be accused of subversive activities (Breman 1990: 282).

It has been emphasized that compliance with the Minimum Wage Act is hindered by the small-scale character of informal sector activities. How would it be possible, for instance, to control every farmer who now and then or even regularly employs agricultural workers? This is a debatable excuse which certainly does not apply to employment in large-scale agro-industry. The administrative capability at the disposal of co-operative sugar enterprises in south Gujarat is quite adequate to allow compliance with labour legislation. That this is not done has nothing to do with serious logistical problems and everything to do with political opposition. In that connection I reported the existence of a secret memorandum in the Surat office of the Rural Labour Inspectorate. That remarkable ukase forbade the inspectors 'until further order' to undertake any action against the management of the powerful agro-industrial lobby because of non-payment of the prescribed agricultural wage to the army of cane-cutters. The first time when this absurdly low minimum was established, the committee recommended that these harvest workers be granted an allowance of 20–25 per cent over the daily wage. According to my calculations, a cane-cutter's earnings until today remains substantially below the basic rate to which local landless have a right. A prominent politician in Gujarat explained why the multitude of migrant workers are deprived of the provisions granted to them by law. This army of migrant men and women, he said, have neither the vote in the place where they live nor where they work. This statement was not meant to be cynical and indifferent. But the chilly explanation of non-action on the part of those invested with administrative power does give cause for such an opinion, as I wrote earlier:

Not long ago, the Collector of Surat acknowledged in an interview that the *koytas* indeed lead a miserable life, but, he added, the government is simply not in a position to antagonize the sugar lobby. On the same occasion the Chief Minister of Gujarat went likewise on record to the effect that there would be no question of implementing the existing labour laws. (Breman 1990: 281)

In a separate essay, written at the end of a study into the work and lives of textile workers in Surat, Baxi, then Vice-Chancellor of the University of south Gujarat, drew attention to a report issued by the Second Labour Law Review Committee (Government of Gujarat 1983–84). He supported the distinction made therein between transgression and subversion of the law. While transgression might be corrected through legal action, that is not possible in the case of subversion of the law. Because, the committee stated:

subversion means planned systematic disregard of labour legislation involving an organized anticipation of immunity from any kind of credible law enforcement process. In other words, subversion of labour law is a public conduct which denies the relevance and reality of the law as providing norms for social action. It, therefore, implies a trend towards collective lawlessness which involves on the side of organized capital and organized labour an assertion of superior political power over the state and the law and on the side of the state a public admission of its inability to impose social justice. For the workers who are the victims of subversion of labour law, subversion prevents the growth of social consciousness and organization which alone could provide sources and stimuli for a more vigorous and just administration of the law, and constant redefinition. (*Working and Living Conditions* 1984: 105)

Concurring with Baxi, I regard this passage as adequately summing up the situation in which the people at the bottom of society find themselves. While on the one hand propaganda of the state apparatus rigidly maintains that it wishes to improve the lot of unprotected workers, on the other hand it makes great effort to portray Gujarat as a capitalist's paradise. Advertisements in the national media entice industrialists to Gujarat with the message that its people are of a peaceable nature and that labour relations are harmonious. The least that can be concluded from this imagery is that government, as third party, has little interest in the 'untouchables' under the capitalist mode of production. I am inclined to go a step further and suggest that informal conditions of employment dominate the economy, not despite but thanks to state intervention. It is after all no coincidence that diamond cutters and powerloom workers are covered by the innocuous Shops and Establishment Act, or that dismantling of the textile mills that for many decades dominated the formal sector of Bombay and Ahmedabad kept equal pace with the installation of tens of thousands of powerlooms in small-scale workshops in new and rapidly growing industrial centres such as Surat in south Gujarat. Loom operators are included in the long list of scheduled employments, a classification which seems to assist in non-compliance with the labour laws. Without being able to insist on the formalization of conditions of employment, large segments of the working population have even lost the feudal-type protection that formerly accompanied their life and work. Against this background it is easy to understand the complaint in a recent report, commissioned by the government and containing the results of a comprehensive inquiry into the employment of rural labour in India:

> The conspicuous co-existence of mushrooming high-wage islands in the organized sector on the one hand and miserable conditions of labour in informal urban and rural sector (both farm and non-farm) on the other and the corresponding dualism in capital/labour intensities and associated levels of productivity are the result of our inability or even unwillingness to implement a sound and firm wage policy. (Report NCRL, vol.1, 1991: 23)

Nevertheless, it would be incorrect to think that men, women or children who are too vulnerable to complain to the government as a third actor about their treatment at work, are not covered by any regulations. To them apply the unwritten rules of the employers, who also have at their disposal a rich arsenal of informal methods with which to enforce compliance. In the final chapter we shall discuss how unprotected workers defend themselves against this authoritarianism of the employers' will.

Unbinding labour

The promulgation of the Bonded Labour (Abolition) Act in 1976 was in reaction to critical press reports over the continuation of forms of bonded labour in various parts of India. It is interesting to note that during the Emergency which curbed political freedom in the country from 1974 until early 1977 and also curtailed various rights of organized labour including the right to strike, the central government determined that an end should be put to the traditional servitude which kept landless workers of low castes captive to landowners who belonged to higher castes. The redemption of these farm servants from a situation of bondage even became one of the action points added to the programme of social reform launched by

Indira Gandhi and her son Sanjay. At the initiative of a number of prominent bureaucrats, the National Labour Institute (NLI) (a research and
documentation centre in New Delhi sponsored by the government) held
conscientization and rehabilitation camps in various places throughout
the country. Bonded labourers identified in the region invited to these
camps were told during meetings lasting one or two days how they could
extract themselves from control of their masters, and which means of
support they could claim during their transition to a free and independent
life. The NLI's bulletin repeatedly reported on these activities. The orga-
nizers undoubtedly had the best of intentions, but it is doubtful whether
their efforts had any lasting effect. This also applies to the instruction with
which the central government charged the state authorities to exercise
careful supervision over compliance with the law by setting up Vigilance
Committees and by taking suitable measures to mitigate the dire straits in
which freed victims found themselves. Gujarat was one of the identified
regions and its authorities were directed to put an end to conditions of
bondage, particularly in the south of the state. A year later, Gandhian
social workers declared that no less than 171,000 agricultural workers
lived and worked there in bondage as *halis* (Marla 1981: 61).

This was not the first time that the *hali* system was abolished by legal
prohibition. In 1923 a similar instruction had been issued when the ruler
of Baroda (Vadodara) put an end to bonded labour. In practice, this had
little effect.

In July 1923 the Government of the State by proclamation declared this whole
system of forced indenture as illegal and allowed the *Raniparaj* [tribal] serf to
repudiate it if he chose to. But the intentions of the Government were not properly
interpreted by subordinate revenue officials and the operation of the Government's order is therefore not effective. (Census of India 1931 vol. XIX/1: 255)

In that part of south Gujarat which was under direct British rule,
bondage of agricultural workers to high caste landowning households was
not forbidden. Local government officials such as village heads and police
patels were told, however, that in future they might not co-operate in
retaining and returning attached servants who were on the run to the
masters they had deserted. In the late colonial era, and only partly
through these measures, *halipratha* gradually lost its legitimacy in the
agrarian order. My interpretation is that this occurred in such a way that
colonial authorities did not determine the course taken by social
processes but ratified it, did not set the trend by causing changes in
relationships between masters and servants but reacted to a more
immanent shift in social forces between those opposite parties (Breman
1974: 77–9).

The leaders of the Independence movement were equally unable to solve the problem of bonded labour. The manner in which they tried to do so, reluctant and wavering, differed little from the position taken by the colonial government on this matter. At the annual meeting of the National Congress held in 1938 near Bardoli in south Gujarat, Sardar Patel was forced by the pressure of agitation among thousands of Halpatis from the surrounding area to bring about a compromise between landowners and landless. A year later the agreement, which combined a wage increase with debt redemption, was pledged in the presence of Gandhi and Nehru. Gandhi took the opportunity on this occasion to announce a new caste name for these agricultural workers. They were in future to be known as Halpatis, i.e. workers with the plough, and no longer as Dublas, a nomenclature to which adhered the stigma of weaklings (Breman 1985b: 137–9). In 1947, when this informal accord also foundered due to the unwillingness of landowners to fulfil the agreement, the government of Bombay state to which Gujarat then belonged, set up a committee in order to make recommendations for 'rehabilitating this class of agricultural labourers and for enabling them to live a life consistent with human dignity and self-respect'. The committee's report confirmed that the *hali* system was based on bondage. Its advice to government that the system should be abolished was accompanied by suggestions as to how the material conditions of the landless population might be improved. No official action was taken. A few years later the authorities gave two reasons for this lack of response. Firstly, they argued, the system of bonded labour had never been legally enforced and thus there was no necessity to put a formal end to it. Secondly, the landowners and *halis* had already concluded in mutual consultation that to do away with the system would be in the interest of both parties. This statement referred to the intervention of Morarji Desai and Gulzarilal Nanda. In 1948, these two senior congress leaders, at that time ministers in the state of Bombay, had brought about an agreement that made any further government intervention unnecessary (P. G. Shah 1958: 209–11). Once again, agricultural employers proved in practice to take no notice of the compromise that had informally been agreed upon. Agricultural workers continued to suffer debt bondage as a direct result of the refusal to pay them a wage with which they could lead a life in freedom.

Nevertheless, various reports show that the *hali* system disintegrated in course of time (see Breman 1974). This conclusion can be clearly seen, for example, in the analysis of agrarian conditions made by a working group in 1964 which recommended introduction of a minimum wage rate for agricultural workers. According to that expert opinion, farmers in south Gujarat were increasingly reluctant to take on new *halis*; on the other hand, the farm servants considered themselves no longer obliged to remain attached to their master. They backed out of their contract by simply staying away, without bothering themselves about repaying their debt. The employers were powerless against this one-sided cancellation of the bondage. Legally, socially and morally, they lacked the means to persuade the workers to go back to work or force them to repay the loan that had been granted by way of advance on wages. What remained of this mode of bonded labour was on the point of disappearing, stated the committee. It is interesting that this report sought the reason for the persistence of remnants of bondage chiefly in the 'backward' behaviour of agricultural workers. Only in the second instance and in much more exonerating terms, was the traditional lifestyle of landowners mentioned as an additional reason:

It is good that the system is dying. Whatever is left of it is due to ignorance of the Dubla and his apathy to search for an alternative. In some measure the inertia and stiffened social sinews and the habit of indolent, undisciplined and disorganized village life to which the *hali* is accustomed inhibits a switch over either in the same occupation or in towns and cities in non-agricultural work. The termination of the system is most welcome as it is frustrating, degrading and exhausting to the labourer. It also kills the soul of the employer, deprives him of his nicer values and emotions and reduces him to a hard-hearted individual unable to move at the wretchedness and misery in front of them. The system through an excessive dependence on feudal living deprives the farmer of his faculties of thinking and initiative. It does not enable him to get toughened to fight the world before him on his own. (Report Minimum Wages Employment in Agriculture 1966: 48)

The import of the passage agrees with the customary explanation of the tenacity with which elements of bondage have continued in India's rural areas. This is also the stance taken by the National Commission which reported on the state of labour in India in 1969. The authors concluded that bonded labour was still a common agrarian practice in different parts of the country. Experience had shown, according to their opinion, that legislation in itself would not be sufficient to put an end to coercive practices of this nature. That would be possible only with an increasing commoditization of the agricultural economy and the greater availability of institutional credit (Report NCL 1969: 409). According to such opinions, there are signs of an inextricable linkage between bonded labour and a feudal lifestyle which still permeates the rural system in particular. That, however, is not my opinion. I have outlined the changes that have taken place over time in the relationship between agrarian master and serf against the background of the transition to a capitalist mode of production. The present-day farm servant in south Gujarat, even when in debt to his employer, is no longer burdened by the lack of freedom that characterized the former *hali* existence. Seen in that light, the government of Gujarat was right in stating, in reaction to the new law in 1976, that there were no more bonded labourers in the state. Investigations in the Surat and Valsad districts, however, came to widely varying conclusions. That difference of opinion is due above all to the answer to the question of whether indebtedness is sufficient reason to speak of bonded labour. I am inclined to associate myself with those who answer in the negative, principally because the behaviour of the present generation of landless illustrates their determined refusal to behave as bonded workers (see also Jodhka 1994, 1995). As I have also argued in another publication, extra-economic pressure is still exercised but less than in the past. The lack of any alternative to meet their acute subsistence needs, leaves many landless with no choice but to sell their labour power in advance: for a shorter or longer term, to farmers or other employers, in or out of the village. The moneylender in this way attaches the labour power of the person who receives the credit. The dependency that results from the transaction is quite compatible with a labour relationship along capitalist lines. The pressure is of an economic nature and results from an extreme form of exploitation. As explained in another publication, this bondage, other than the earlier *halipratha*, is not coupled with personal subjugation to the will of the employer (Breman 1993b: 297–316). Incidents, however, do still occur. In an earlier chapter I made mention of brutalities committed on some Halpatis in the area of my fieldwork as late as the summer of 1994. While old-aged men and women among the rural proletariat have an endless repertoire of such horror stories relating to the past, an indication of the changing times is that nowadays such events are not only more rare but also give rise to massive and violent counter-reactions. In this instance as well. The news spread like wildfire throughout the *taluka*. From all directions Halpatis came to Khadsupa, where the heinous deeds on their caste mates were committed, and closed off all village roads in order to pressurize the police to take action against the high-caste perpetrators. These angry demonstrations signalling the mobilization of subaltern power were widely covered in the regional press (see *Gujarat Samachar*, 16 May 1994, and subsequent reports which appeared in the same and other newspapers published from Surat).

Ending the exploitative relationship demands other and more powerful action than the government apparatus has been prepared to take. Unjustifiably, government intervention has principally been extended to labour in the agricultural sphere. As has been amply shown, the situation in which Halpatis find themselves outside the villages of my fieldwork as brick-makers, the recruitment of cane-cutters for the campaign in the fields of south Gujarat and of saltpan workers, road workers and other seasonal migrants encountered during my fieldwork, differs little from the fate of members of this underclass who are employed as farm servants. Certainly, there are differences between these categories of labour. Permanent workers in agriculture bind themselves for an indefinite period to local landowners, while migrants only enter into a contract for the coming season. Whether or not labour is unfree, however, cannot be deduced by making a distinction according to length of employment, as Rudra has justly remarked (1987: 301). The Commission entrusted with investigating the conditions of rural labour has rightly concluded that the various coercive practices to which informal sector workers are still subjected should be given more attention by government. One of the principal recommendations in the final report advocates the setting up of a National Authority on Bonded Labour to evaluate the various legal prohibitions as well as the measures towards social rehabilitation which should follow emancipation (Report NCRL, vol. 1, 1991: xlv).

Bondage through debt is a characteristic that seems to be common to seasonal migrants, in and outside Gujarat. Work migration is sometimes accompanied with a drastic curtailing of freedom of movement through the use of extra-economic pressure, including physical force. Such cases were reported in various parts of India only a few years ago (e.g. Devi 1981; Mishra 1984; Chopra 1985; Singh and Iyer 1985; Shah et al. 1990; Das 1990). Such abuses could perhaps have been combated within the framework of recent legislation which regulates contract labour and long-distance migration. Invariably, however, the official apparatus is willing to take action only very slowly, if at all. When it does occur, notwithstanding all opposition, this sort of state intervention has hardly any positive effect. The press now and then publishes sensational reports on the liberation of men, women and children from a quarry or other form of excavation, usually by social activists. These are mostly migrant workers, brought there from far distant places by agents of the employer and subjected to a harsh work regime. They are not allowed to leave the workplace and are deprived even of the most elementary facilities necessary for even a low-level human existence. Without outside help it would have been impossible to put an end to the conditions of detention and deprivation in which these people are made to live. What happens after their liberation remains unclear. The obvious procedure would be to return the people to whence they came. From the viewpoint of legal terminology, however, they have rarely been forced to leave their homes and have usually had some knowledge of what awaited them. If the migrants had not been earlier to the same locations, then they would have heard sufficient about them in their immediate surroundings to know that it would be better to stay away. The lack of any alternative sources of employment and income, at home or elsewhere, means that they are unable to make that choice. The only real solution is what government programmes are apt to call rehabilitation: to meet the economic needs of the victims in a manner that increases their freedom of choice and puts an end to the structural dependency in which they exist. But this element is absent in the policy that is implemented. The scarce documentation that is available shows that the rehabilitation of bonded labour has been so inadequate that often these people are bound to fall back into the former situation of bondage. It seems that the social underclass has to fight for its emancipation without being able to insist on adequate state protection.

The authorities have made little effort to remove the causes that keep workers tied in debt to employers or their agents. That neglect is aggravated by the tendency of many bureaucrats not to consider labour bondage, particularly if it is a temporary phenomenon, as a serious problem (see Srivastava 1987: 14). The whitewashing of such practices, with which owners of means of production ensure themselves of sufficient workers at the right time and for the lowest possible price, goes hand-in-hand with the argument that the agreement has not been entered into with the use of extra-economic pressure and in most cases will last for less than one year. Seen in that light, freedom of action is curbed but not unconditionally.

Apart from such 'nuances', spokesmen for vested interests also seem to have the impression that the lowest ranks of the labour system lack the discipline that is essential if production and productivity are to be increased further. We have already seen that government officials are very receptive to employers' complaints that the mass of unskilled labourers from low social milieux do not work in such a way that would justify a higher wage and better treatment. In 1964, the Committee entrusted with introducing a minimum wage for agricultural workers in Gujarat had this to say:

We have frequently heard a more or less universal complaint about the inefficiency of agricultural labour. The labourers, it is argued, are inclined to work for fewer and fewer hours and put in inferior and slipshod output. The farmer-employer probably rightly feels that their employment even at the existing level of wages is a losing proposition. We are inclined to put a good deal of weight on this complaint not so much because the farmers make it or that the committee wants to escape the decision on the fixation of minimum wage but because the minimum of the latter when determined could be only on the basis of a certain minimum number of hours and the quality and quantum of output during that period. If such a correlationship is not maintained while working it out and deciding on the level of wages, agriculture will come in for an additional dose of inefficiency. It will have a deleterious effect on the labourers who will learn to emphasize reward to the relative neglect of a corresponding responsibility associated with it. This is happening with the industrial labourer and other urban workers in some measure. (Report Minimum Wages Employment in Agriculture 1966: 69)

On the very next page of the report, the Committee warns that a rise in wages must not encourage the vices of agricultural workers, such as alcoholism.

This social denigration has a dual significance. Firstly, such notions suggest that members of the underclass in the informal sector lack the physical and mental equipment required for minimal standards of efficiency. The first post-colonial ethnographer wrote about members of the largest landless caste in south Gujarat, the Halpatis whom I came to know in Chikhligam and Gandevigam, that through their degradation to servitude in the past they had developed a slavish mentality that deprived them of the vitality which gave rise to dynamism in life (P. G. Shah 1958: 25). Apathy, inertia, docility, passivity and many other terms of similar import describe the incapability attributed to the Halpatis to lead a life that is motivated by energy, diligence, sobriety, regularity and responsibility. Over the years during my fieldwork I have had to listen on countless occasions as landlords, industrialists and government officials listed the negative qualities that determine their view of the bottom layer in society. In brief, it amounts to saying that the pauperization found in that milieu was due to the Halpatis' own licentiousness:

a Dubla hamlet at night was but a battleground, crowded with drunkards. Heavily drunk men and women were found making rows, using abusive language and lying sometimes unconscious in a most hideous state. (P. G. Shah 1958: 218)

The moral is clear. Shortly after Independence, the prohibition of alcohol in Gujarat brought about under pressure from Gandhian social workers, heralded the upliftment of a tribal caste to the social level of the mainstream population. Led by reformers who had the best of intentions for them, they learnt to take the first step on the way to a better future. Since then that promise of progress has not been fulfilled, but that fiasco has not changed the persistent urge of higher social strata to stigmatize the inferior behaviour of the landless. In the eyes of policy-makers, this rearguard forms a troublesome impediment in the transition to a modern and developed society.

Condemnation of the deviant behaviour of the new untouchables has yet a second objective, namely, to arouse understanding for the idea that harsh treatment is perhaps unavoidable to prevent breach of contract and to impart the necessary work discipline and other virtues. If such regimentation is accompanied by some temporary restriction on freedom of movement, is that not in the long term in the interests of those who undergo the regimentation? Such a resolute approach should naturally not deteriorate into the use of force. On the other hand, however, this raw workforce is much less bothered about the harnessing of their undisciplined behaviour by employers or their agents than critical outsiders are inclined to assume. It is an approach in which the labour brokers excel. Rooted in the same milieu as the workers, are they not the best to know how to get a grip on their disorderly clients? Referring to long practical experience, that argumentation conceals a whitewashing of cases of labour bondage like those I encountered during my fieldwork. These are arguments with which government officials, who deal with informal sector labour in their professional capacity, are very familiar. And more than that. On the basis of their own elevated social status, they are all too often inclined to subscribe to such elite opinions. This also explains my conclusion that, under government surveillance, unfree labour and capitalist production relations are quite compatible.

8   Proletarian life and social consciousness

Adrift?

For rural workers in the central plain of south Gujarat, the home village is no longer the only or even the most important arena of employment. The moral economy which formerly kept the landpoor and the landless proletariat tied to the village and, conversely, obliged the owners of land or of other means of existence to rely exclusively on labour from the village or, at least, to give priority to 'our people' whenever help had to be hired, is now only a memory. Even in the past tense, it is an idealized construction that is exaggerated, by both parties in opposite directions, in order to show up the contrast with the present situation more sharply. This does not alter the fact that mutual involvement which was so natural in the past has made way for an external orientation which has strengthened internal lines of division. In this respect I would note that the breaking-up of local patron–client relationships preceded the outflow/inflow of labour in the countryside and did not result from it. It is certainly a fact that, once this trend had started, the moral economy continued irreversibly and more quickly to decline under the influence of large-scale labour circulation. In the modern economy, wage hunters and gatherers circulate along a wide variety of workplaces in differing branches of industry, whether or not in agriculture, or in the home village. The occupational multiplicity that characterizes the annual cycle of the rural proletariat is not only affected by seasonal fluctuations but is connected to the peaks and dips that also continue to determine the pattern of non-agricultural production. The succession of short-term activities, coupled with changes of worksite and frequently also of work sphere, gives this sizeable and loosely structured reservoir the same character which, in the urban economy, has lately become known as the informal sector.

It would be incorrect to give the impression that a drastic turn-around in the structure of economic production occurred recently or more or less overnight. The social history of Chikhligam, situated further into the

NCL
Migration: rural rural

interior, shows that for some generations now members of households with little if any land have been accustomed to migrate for part of the year in order to supplement their income from agricultural labour. This trend has accelerated during the past quarter-century. Development of physical infrastructure, i.e. construction of roads and subsequent building-up of a network of bus connections, has certainly played a part in this. In course of time distance has become easier to bridge. Widening of horizon is also expressed in greater familiarity with the outside world. This varies greatly, of course, but even the social space in which the rural underclass moves around has undergone scale enlargement. Orientation towards situations and events away from the village is contrasted by penetration of external influences into that habitat. One aspect of this two-way traffic in terms of employment is that the growing number of inhabitants who leave home for a shorter or longer period in order to seek a living elsewhere is countered by a variable stream of migrants coming into the village. Conventional modernization studies tend to praise labour migration as a step forward in the development process. This is based on the unsubstantiated assumption, that migrants leave their homes because work is not available locally, while elsewhere their presence is needed to meet the lack of labour power. According to this fairly naive interpretation, wage differences form the principal if not the only motivation for mobility. Members of the National Commission on Rural Labour also seem to have succumbed to this actor-biased explanation based on rational choice which, in my opinion, underestimates the extra-economic forces that operate both on the departure and arrival side.

The prevailing big differential in wages between different regions has induced the migration of labour from the poorer regions to the areas of Green Revolution. Large-scale migration of labour from Bihar to Punjab is a classic case in point. There are now more than 10 million rural migrant labourers in the country. Inter-regional migration of labour in the process of development is inevitable and also desirable from the point of view of raising agricultural productivity as well as improving the income of labour. (Report NCRL, vol.1, 1991: vi–vii)

This point of view is difficult to harmonize with the synchronic in- and out-flow of massive armies of workers to and from south Gujarat.

What seems at first sight to be a turbulent spectacle of ebb and flow, an amorphous mass which flows back and forth without much sense of direction, proves on further examination to consist of workers who leave, stay away or return with a definite objective in mind. Their nomadism varies according to length of time and distance, is not restricted to a single sector of the economy, involves both old and young people, individuals and households. The step outward is not a step in the dark. The mobilized workers follow existing routes and make use of earlier experience and contacts along the way or at the place of destination. Primordial loyalties, i.e. the intervention or recommendation of fellow residents of village or *taluka*, members of the same caste or kin group, play a very important role and determine the access to or exclusion from the various migration circuits. Foremen and jobbers act as professional intermediaries, the latter particularly in mobilizing gangs of workers for all sorts of seasonal industry.

The majority of men and women who leave the village to do unskilled work return there again after a varying period of time. The nomads from elsewhere who flow in large numbers into the countryside of south Gujarat particularly during the dry season, usually disappear when the monsoon approaches. In the same period, many workers in the textile mills and other industries of Surat and other urban centres, return home on leave for one or two months. In their case, 'home' is in villages far away in other states of the country. The disruption of employment has been explained by suggesting that long and irregulars hours of work together with bad living conditions create a state of physical and mental agony from which the army of migrants can only recover by retreating every now and then to their place of origin. According to another type of interpretation it is not the need for recuperation but on-going involvement in agricultural operations of these alien workers that is a major reason for going home and coming back again after some time in a never-ending cycle. In line with debates which already started during colonial rule, an underlying argument of the latter view is to blame migrants for refusing to commit themselves unconditionally to an urban-industrial way of life (see Thompson 1993: 398).

A common factor among the heterogeneous mass of migrant workers rotating around this area is the lack of permanent jobs with protective employment conditions such as those that apply in the formal sector of the economy. The durability, regularity and security that mark working life in the dignified circuit of employment are given shape in the combination of at least some of the following contractual features: work which requires formal education; payment based on time; complete and standardized payment immediately or shortly after the actual performance; regular and not excessively long working hours; organized protection of the workers' interests; and institutionalized bargaining procedures for consolidation and expanding acknowledged rights. Informal sector employment is distinguished by low scores on all these points, individually and collectively. However, as I have stated elsewhere (Breman 1980) a sharp dichotomy does not exist. Holmstrøm has adopted the continuum that I outlined but has altered it into a sloping plane divided into various zones of different degrees of steepness. His

final/inferous
not dichotomy

typology, based primarily on an analysis of urban labour markets, those of Bombay and Ahmedabad in particular, describes a landscape which I also found in south Gujarat. In his richly documented social morphology of Indian labour, Holmstrøm retracts the sharp dichotomy that he had supported in an earlier publication:

> My image of the 'citadel' was too simple. The organized/unorganized boundary is not a wall but a steep slope. Indian society is like a mountain, with the very rich at the top, lush Alpine pastures where skilled workers in the biggest modern industries graze, a gradual slope down through smaller firms where pay and conditions are worse and the legal security of employment means less, a steep slope around the area where the Factories Act ceases to apply (where my wall stood), a plateau where custom and the market give poorly paid unorganized sector workers some minimal security, then a long slope through casual migrant labour and petty services to destitution. (Holmstrøm 1984: 319)

My own interest is directed principally towards the broad-based foot of the slope, the bottom zones in which a very large proportion of the total working population is to be found. From this milieu of a complete or almost complete lack of assets that I have taken as the starting point of my study, only a rather small portion succeeds in finding and climbing the path that leads straight to the top of the slope, to the protected citadel of employment. The massive underclass lacks the equipment necessary to undertake such an uphill march. But those who try to fight their way up even a small part of the slope encounter all sorts of obstacles that prevent them from reaching their target or ensure that they do so only temporarily. The larger proportion have to stay at the bottom and have no choice but to go out hunting and gathering a wage.

Instead of speaking about one long extended slope, as Holmstrøm does, I am inclined to argue that the landscape of labour has the appearance of a vast plain broken by many larger and smaller hills. These hills are zones of industrial activities whose top is made up of workplaces that are related to, or which even completely satisfy, the criteria just listed as characteristic of formal sector employment, while from lower down attempts are made to gain access to the secure but fenced-off positions. Seen from this point of view, the social complexity cannot be reduced to a unilinear labour hierarchy. The configuration that I have in mind is that employers in every branch of economic business encircle themselves with a fairly small core of permanent workers through whom a reserve of casual workers can be drawn in and dismissed, in accordance with the need of the moment. Great mobility and fluidity prevail at the foot of the hills. There are many candidates for whatever chance that is made available. Those who qualify in the first instance are then interested in prolonging their employment for an indefinite period in the hope of, finally, gaining access to the privileged corps that enjoys more permanent tenure with all the advantages that this entails. Such a nucleus–periphery configuration may also be found in the early morning casual labour markets, prime examples of clearing houses in the demand and supply of manual labour. Regular employers here, however, are surrounded by a crowd of favourites who are rewarded with privileges in terms of recurrent employment.

There are a few workers who due to sheer grit and good luck have been able to strike good relations with some *mukadams* and contractors. These few are able to get 'regular' work with one or two contractors throughout the year. They have slightly different status than others. They are called 'permanent' workers by the *mukadams* as well as fellow workers. To please them, alongside provision of regular work, the contractors give them 'bonus' during Diwali. (Punalekar and Patel 1990: 133)

The chance of occupational advancement, in the sense of changing from casual labour to owning a job is limited, with the result that such labour is forced to maintain its floating character in a horizontal direction. The strategy based on upward mobility within one branch of industry is thus under constant pressure from the necessity to seek or accept a temporary opening in an entirely different sector of the economy in the hope that it will lead to more durable employment.

Vertical mobility, and particularly promotion to employment in the formal sector of economy, is a rare phenomenon. Members of the bottom castes and classes in the rural hinterland also find it difficult to get access to informal sector jobs which are better paid, higher skilled and more regular. The large majority of diamond cutters and powerloom operators, who stand at the top of Surat's urban informal workforce, belong to low-to-intermediate castes in their place of origin and come from households owning at least some land. Existing socio-economic inequalities in the milieu of departure are thus perpetuated and further sharpened by differential incorporation on arrival in the informal sector arena.

Even more than men, women find it difficult to get access to more attractive job opportunities. Agrawal concluded in her study of textile workers in Surat that while males increasingly seek and find entry to traditionally female jobs, the reverse is out of the question (Agrawal 1992: 258). Would that trend imply a growing gender imbalance in the composition of the workforce, not only between the formal and informal sectors but ultimately also within the informal sector? This is what another researcher on the same subject seems to suggest in a long-term macro-analysis, showing how in various organized branches of industry which used to be dominated by women, their participation in the work process has declined drastically over the past thirty years due to rationalization, mechanization and automation. According to Patel, factory management in collusion with trade union leadership opted for a patriarchal ideology – arguing that women were 'supplementary workers', that they 'work for pin money', that their 'primary role is domestic duties', etc. – which resulted in progressive replacement of females by males (V. Patel 1990: 3; for conflicting evidence see Papola 1993: 51–2). Omvedt, in another contribution to the same seminar, restated the marginalization thesis by pointing out that the main problem of women's work is that it has remained so highly invisible in census reports and other official statistics:

> We should conclude that in agriculture and in almost all of the unorganized sector, women work harder than men - particularly when all forms of 'subsistence production' are included - whether or not this is reflected in the census data. Above all, we cannot at this point accept *any* generalizations regarding women's 'declining participation' as a result of overall economic trends. (Omvedt 1990: 63)

Like Omvedt and many other researchers, I am inclined to argue that households living in poverty operate on the assumption that they can only survive by selling the labour power of female members unconditionally, i.e. to the extent possible and for prices which are generally much lower than paid to men. Because of the readiness of women to do any kind of work to maintain the survival level of the family, they constitute in Omvedt's terminology 'the ultimate reserve army of labour' (Omvedt 1990: 70).

The informal sector in the urban economy is terrain which is hostile to family life. Even those who have been in town or city for many years usually do not earn sufficient to allow their spouse and offspring to join them. The fact that dependent members of the household remain behind in the home village means that a large part of the mass of workers in the informal sector do not live with their families for long periods. It is separation which exacerbates the miserable life at this level of material deprivation. The prohibitively high cost of setting up a household in relation to income, keeps the circulation going. Moreover, these workers so far from home are only required to take part temporarily in the labour process at the place of arrival. This lasts no longer than the moment when their physical ability and mental resistance become subject to permanent wastage. The horde of workers needed to keep 250,000 or more powerlooms in Surat alone in operation are so fagged out after ten or fifteen years that they have to make way for fresh blood, brought in over long distances from various parts of the hinterland. The rejected workers have no choice but to return to their home village. Longitudinal research into the cycle of these working lives would throw more light on the costs and benefits for the victims who are exposed to such nomadism.

During the past thirty years, the economy of south Gujarat has undergone rapid growth, reflected in steady expansion of urban population. However, only a small proportion of new residents originate in the countryside of the state. This also applies to the inflow into the informal sector with which such a large part of the total economic space in cities is filled. As remarked, the landless or semi-landless milieu is the principal supplier of this mass of workers. In my fieldwork area these are predominantly members of the de-tribalized castes, listed by government as 'scheduled tribes'. In 1961, they represented 50 per cent of the total population of Surat and Valsad districts, but no more that 14.5 per cent of the urban inhabitants. On that occasion Halpatis were counted separately as a sub-category. Numerically, they included 11 per cent of the district's population, but only 6 per cent of the urban population. Between 1961 and 1971, the urban contingent among Halpatis grew only marginally, from 12.6 to 13.2 per cent. These caste-wise data (more recent ones are not available) agree with the results of my fieldwork in Gandevigam and Chikhligam. Dhodhiyas and Halpatis from these two villages who have settled in one of the urban centres of south Gujarat during the last thirty years, are few in number. The majority of Halpatis whom I encountered in the course of my research in Surat, Navsari, Bilimora and Valsad, all situated along the north–south railway line in the western part of the plain, proved to have lived in the towns from a young age or even to have been born there. Does this mean that rural landless have stayed away from the urban employment arena? Such a conclusion would be incorrect. I have pointed out that many unskilled workers from villages commute daily to and from the towns. In addition to those who have found more or less permanent employment for an indefinite period in factories, workshops, shops, etc., these commuters also include daily paid workers from the intermediate zone between town and countryside. In the bazaar they hire themselves out early in the morning to any employer who needs their services immediately and usually for a short period varying from a few hours to a week. Finally, there are the seasonal migrants who leave home under the command of jobbers. They journey to diverse destinations, including workplaces nearby or in cities, where they stay for months. On a number of occasions I have visited Halpatis and Dhodhiyas from Chikhligam in Bombay or Surat where they were employed in brickworks. Even those who made this journey for many years consecutively did not succeed in escaping to other and more permanent kinds of urban employment. They continued to be sojourners, forced to come and to depart again. The work rhythm during the annual cycle expresses the fact that, even outside agriculture, significant activity of economic life takes place in the open air and is marked by interchange of heat and cold, rain and drought. On the other hand, this does not necessarily mean that work in closed spaces is carried out by labour that is specialized and which works on a basis of continuity. Men and women who literally have a roof over their heads while working, e.g. in factories and other walled-in locations, are by no means always more protected in their conditions of employment than are those who work under the open sky.

Circulation of unskilled labour in particular, I would conclude, applies not only to the change from one branch of industry to another. The fluidity that this continual movement of one of the major factors of production gives to the economic system as a whole is further augmented by the spatial mobility with which it is accompanied. In the debate on the concept, the 'informal sector' is taken to mean the unregulated segment of the urban economy. I have pointed out in earlier publications that it is impossible to distinguish in terms of employment between the rural and urban economy. Based on research reported upon in the preceding chapters, there is good reason to reconsider the frequently made distinction between urban and rural labour markets. As regards the mass of workers who have been the subject of my attention, there is no reason why they should be divided into two more or less closed circuits, urban and rural. On the contrary, I am much more inclined to emphasize the linkage between them in terms of labour circulation. The horizontal mobility which dominates the rural-urban market for unskilled labour is connected to a mode of production that is minimally capital-intensive and which does not put a premium on establishing a stable work climate. Considered according to standards of efficiency, the continual trek of massive armies of temporary workers over long distances seems to be an enormous waste of time and money. It should be remembered, however, that the costs of that movement, i.e. the long journey time and the outlay needed to reach the worksite or the home village, are passed on to the migrants themselves. This overhead charge is included in the price of labour in such a manner that the employers benefit, while on the other hand the already scant resources of the workers are further depleted. The rationality of taking circulators away from their own habitat and employing them in an inferior capacity in distant enclaves, detached from the households to which they belong and deprived of all facilities that form part of a minimally acceptable social life, is connected above all to the disinclination to treat these people in any other way than as a commodity. That commoditization is accompanied by the refusal to contribute to the costs that are consequential to the reproduction of this underclass. Urban slum habitats do not enhance the social status of people who have managed to escape from the rural hinterland. Living in conditions of squalor and misery reflects negatively on the dignity of migrants who have come to seek refuge in informal sector employment which is more easily available here than in their village of origin. Gender bias in access to jobs is a main reason for females of rural households to stay back even if male members have secured a foothold in the city. More is at stake than just differential economic opportunities. On the one hand there is the urge to live jointly and earn collectively, but on the other hand the risk of tainting the reputation of the whole household remains an overriding concern. A strict code of conduct is required, as one slum dweller in Surat explains:

Living physically so close to each other and having sexual infringements is not very unusual. What we do is to marry off our girls fairly young or send them off to the village and find a boy there. A girl who gets spoiled is also bundled off to the village. (Lobo 1993: 100)

I consider the strongly increased size of the footloose proletariat, transported to regions that have their own surplus labour, to be an expression of economic dynamics along capitalist lines. Labour circulation connects various sectors and locations of the economy. To differentiate them in terms of capitalist and non-capitalist, as McGee suggests for example (1982: 56; see also Armstrong and McGee 1985), in my opinion would be to introduce artificial dividing lines. Such a segmentation does not acknowledge that the economy is integrated and controlled by rules and regulations that destroy the contrast between town and countryside.

Control and escape

The various compartments into which the unregulated part of the economy is dispersed are filled with segments of workers whose social identity is highly diverse. This segmentation along lines of regional origins and caste membership emphasizes the heterogeneous composition of the labouring landscape that I have mapped out above. Brickwork owners in Bombay, for example, prefer to use Surthi gangs, with which they roughly mean to indicate the home area of Halpatis. The cane-cutters who harvest the fields in south Gujarat are mostly Khandeshis from the similarly-named region of western Maharashtra. Throughout Gujarat road workers are primarily tribals from the hills of Panch Mahals. It so happens that the tyre repair workshops along the highway of south Gujarat are all manned by young males from Kerala. Kathiawadis have an unrivalled reputation as navvies. Finally, large construction projects seem to be manned mostly by Rajasthanis. The manner of recruitment provides an obvious explanation for this segmentation according to branch of industry. In most of these cases it concerns seasonal workers recruited by contractors who have the same background as members of their gangs. Without thus being rooted in the milieu of origin, jobbers would have no chance of securing the workforce for which the employer has a temporary need. Primordial ties also play a role in employment for an indefinite period. Diamond cutters and textile workers are taken on through the mediation of their kinsmen, caste mates or co-villagers already employed in the ateliers and workshops. I have earlier referred to the presence in industrial enterprises of a small core of permanent workers surrounded by a reserve labour force of fluctuating size. In this configuration the former act as agents of their employers and are responsible for bringing in *badlis*, the temporary workers. Those who have secured a more or less protected position are under pressure from family and caste members and people from the same village or district to open the way to the bridgeheads that they occupy in this arena of employment as early arrivals.

Entrepreneurs in different branches of industry have no problem in admitting that their labour originates in particular regions, belong to specific castes, or have some other collective characteristic. The way in which they explain this fact gives little if any significance to recruitment mechanisms. Their reasons are that Halpatis have a special skill in brick-making, Khandeshis are particularly suitable for the harvesting of sugarcane, Rajasthanis are the best construction workers, etc. These words of praise are supported with statements suggesting that present practices are based on long-standing tradition. Even at first sight, such explanations carry little conviction. These stereotyped opinions, which gain a certain social validity through constant repetition, are often accompanied by denigration of local labour which is abundantly available for the same work. Acute need sometimes compels employers to radically change their recruitment strategies, as threatened for a time at the end of 1992 in Surat. After the destruction of the *Babri masjid* in Ayodhya on 6 December 1992, a pogrom broke out in the city during which some hundreds of Muslims lost their lives (see Breman 1993a). The spiralling terror and counter-terror also involved migrant workers, as both hunters and hunted, who reacted by leaving the city wholesale. The departure of some hundreds of thousands, principally single males, took place within one or two days. The harrowing events that they had witnessed or of which they had been victim caused many to swear that they would never return to Surat. The escalation of violence resulted in enormous economic damage. Production was brought to a halt and the textile magnates in particular feared that in future they would have to manage without migrant workers from Orissa, Uttar Pradesh, Andhra Pradesh and other far distant places. While the pogrom was still in progress, the organization of textile employers turned to the District Development Officer to ask that a plan be drawn up for the large-scale recruitment of young males from lower castes in the nearby countryside. From one day to the next, these men thus lost the stigma of being 'unsuitable material'. What had always been said to be impossible, i.e. a paid three-month apprenticeship, overnight gained approbation among employers. The energetic pioneers of this operation were not able to put it into effect, however. Within two months of the nightmarish events, the majority of those who had fled had returned to their looms, undoubtedly forced to do so by sheer economic necessity. Business as usual, was how the industrialists waved away my queries about the future. Nevertheless, the presence of a labour reservoir in the immediate vicinity is reassuring, a few of them were prepared to admit.

In my analyses I have indicated the exercise of control through primordial connections as the most important motive for providing access to employment on the basis of regional or social segmentation. Halpatis, who until the middle of this century cut sugarcane in south Gujarat as bonded farm servants, are now disqualified as seasonal harvesters by the agro-industry. According to present employers in the area of my research, Halpatis are too lazy even to earn the meagre wage that is paid to agricultural workers. That exclusion apparently contradicts the refusal by brickwork owners in Bombay to change from 'alien' to local workers, when requested to do so by a government committee. They made it known that replacement of the Surthi gangs would be injurious to industrial interest since everyone knew that the migrants, i.e. Halpatis, worked much harder than people from nearby. The general preference for outsiders is usually explained with the aid of such qualifications as diligence, reliability, amenability and other virtues which workers from their own region seem systematically to lack. However, the procedure followed in recruitment of industrial workers shows that positive group labels are tested on the personal characteristics of the candidates in question. The persistent preference shown by textile mill owners in Surat for workers from Orissa is connected by one author with the specific characteristics that are attributed to this category as a whole: 'Oriya labourers are by nature hardworking, docile, sincere and submissive' (Barik 1987: 177). According to another source on the same type of employment, however, the status of 'alien' in itself is not a sufficient recommendation for admission. The employer tries to sift out undesirable elements in advance by making enquiries.

It is reported that the workers who show some militancy at the workplace or express their desire to form unions are blacklisted and scrupulously kept out of the selection process. Such a caution is exercised by the contractors also. They too insist on recruiting docile, submissive and abiding teams of workers. (*Working and Living Conditions* 1984: 65)

When the embroidery market faced the downward trend, the traders carefully weeded out the 'new' or 'militant' workers. They discontinued the former and punished the latter for their upright and 'defiant' nature. (S. P. Punalekar 1988: 126)

While casual workers, who form part of the reserve workforce of every enterprise, regularly change their employers, a transfer to another branch of industry is less common. The circular migrants are entrapped in corridors running from their homes to the workplace and back again. Movements sideways are hindered by the same primordial ties that helped the newcomers in finding 'their' destination: the bringing-in of fellows and rejection of outsiders. In my fieldwork I have rarely come across a case of a textile worker who has become a diamond cutter, or *vice versa*. Even more than other circular migrants, seasonal workers are entering circuits that are intended to remain closed. They are tethered both by the provision of a cash advance and by months-long deferment of wage payment. The annually recurring mobilization of these armies of men, women and often children in conditions of immobility would be inconceivable without the mediation of jobbers. These agents in the large-scale 'hire and fire' operations ensure not only that necessary numbers of workers reach their destination but that they also leave it when the time for departure has come.

The protected trajectories that have been drawn across the labouring landscape differ from one another in the rapidity with which migrants are supplied and taken away again, varying from a few weeks to an entire season to many years. Variation is large and so too is the difference in wage levels. Among these diverse categories, all concerned with employment in the unregulated sector of the economy, the return to labour differs enormously. These wage differences in themselves are a sign of the friability of the structure of the labour market. They concern reservoirs of labour at a short distance from one another and which may be reached from my fieldwork villages immediately or within a few hours. Non-qualified outsiders are well acquainted with the existence of various circuits of better-paid employment, realize that they could double their current wage if they were allowed to join, but even in their own opinion do not meet the criteria necessary to get access. This attitude does not necessarily imply internalization of the group opinions maintained in social exchange, but arises from a pragmatic view of the trouble, expressed in time and money, that it would cost to venture into unknown territory in combination with the factual incapability to attune economic behaviour to a long-term strategy. Landless workers and marginal peasants, whose life is already made vulnerable by under-payment of their labour, can seldom permit themselves the luxury of leaving niches of employment into which they have been confined more or less by accident.

The existence of dividing walls between branches of industry should not cause one to think that a completely homogeneous labour force exists behind those walls. The majority of employers prove to be well aware of the risks involved in any one-sided selection from one particular region or caste. The co-operative sugar factories of south Gujarat, which originally brought in their fieldworkers for the campaign exclusively from Khandesh, have changed to recruiting part of the annually increasing army of cane-cutters from tribal regions in their own state. I attribute this trend to diversification to management's fear that labour unrest would be more difficult to manage if the inflowing horde of migrants had the same origins (Breman 1990: 558-9). I have observed the same phenomenon on a smaller scale in brickworks, whose owners prefer to do business with more than one *mukadam* in different parts of Gujarat. In this way they limit the damage if brick-making gangs do not turn up at the start of the season, while, in their opinion, the mixed composition of gangs also lessens the chance of labour unrest. This seems to be a successful strategy. Migrants feel themselves not only to be strangers in the region to which they are brought, but behave as such towards one another.

When I asked the Halpatis from Chikhligam who offered me hospitality for a few days in such a seasonal workplace near Navsari about the other workers, I did not become much wiser. They had no contact with other brick-making gangs, neither with the donkey drivers from north Gujarat nor the coal sifters from the Dangs, although for some months now they had worked at a distance of 10 or 20 metres from one another. 'We don't know those people and have nothing to say to them or to ask. The work takes all our energy. Why should we interfere with others when we hardly have the opportunity to sit down with our own kin?' (Fieldwork notes)

I have remarked above that informal sector employers, notwithstanding assertions to the contrary, are not interested in establishing stable labour relations. Workers who are brought in from elsewhere and who, after intensive and exhaustive use, are replaced by fresh blood, have only superficial contacts with the social milieu in which they are branded as outsiders. And that has to remain so. The reticent behaviour that is expected and even demanded of them as 'aliens' impairs their scant scope for manoeuvre. I have personally ascertained that the majority of Oriya textile workers, even those who have been in Surat for several years, speak only a few words of Gujarati. To attribute their few contacts with local people entirely to their obvious lack of interest in getting to feel 'at home' in their employment milieu is to ignore the fact that their employers have no wish for their isolation to be discontinued. In fact, this is why employers prefer to employ alien workers, even when an abundant reservoir of local labour is available. The migrant workers in Surat's textile industry have no bargaining power whatsoever.

There is no paid holiday, sick leave or leave of any type – except forced unpaid weekly holidays due to power cuts – bonus, P.F., gratuity, first aid, ESJ, safety measures, accident benefit and workmen's compensation. Ninety per cent of the Oriya workers have no appointment letter, identity card or pay slip. Medical help is a luxury. The seriously injured is sometimes paid a few hundred rupees. At least 15 per cent of the workers are forced to do extra unpaid labour at some or other times. Potential recalcitrant workers are often forced to sign blank papers, scolded and even assaulted and retrenched without any notice or compensation. Many units maintain paid musclemen to 'discipline' the workers. (Pathy 1993: 12–13)

The possibility to retreat into a social space of their own at least at the end of the workday and to create a sphere of privacy, which negates the power of the bosses, explains why so many sources of informal sector employment in the city are declared to be out of bounds for Halpatis and other segments of the proletariat in the countryside of south Gujarat.

I have argued that in the landscape of my research a wide variety of wage labour modalities dominate. There is a strong tendency to define informal sector work in terms of self-employment. This label is taken to mean that the initiative rests with a huge but diffuse body of workers acting on their own account and at their own risk in their struggle for subsistence. According to this point of view, the unregulated sector of the economy is populated by a mass of small manufacturers, home workers, service producers and other petty entrepreneurs who ingeniously, though with varying degrees of success, keep their heads above water by operating more or less independently. However, one should not overlook the fact that in most cases this concerns employment of the last resort to which men and women, adults and children take refuge by sheer necessity, because of non-availability of wage labour. The essence of self-employment is, moreover, strongly determined by the predominant practice of paying labour not according to time but for a standardized quantum (number, weight, or any other measure rates). Such piece-work, combined with sub-contracting of work, arouses the suggestion that self-employment is the common modality for earning a livelihood. This interpretation negates the fact, however, that in daily practice wages are paid to workers who have no means of production of their own and are paid merely for their own labour power pure and simple. What is called self-employment is nothing other than a method of payment which forces the wage-dependent worker towards self-exploitation and subjects him in the work process to the dictate laid down by the employer or his agent. Under-payment inherent in this form of employment compels the workers, e.g. the operators of powerlooms, to work an exceptionally long day. Frequently, however, as in road construction, brickworks or sugarcane harvesting, under-payment is a way of forcing the involvement of women and children in team operation. In such cases, self-exploitation is not of an individual character but is extended to other members of the working household, usually via the family head.

Contract labour on an individual or gang basis puts a premium on the income of those who are capable of maximum effort. Such an employment pattern almost automatically leads to the exclusion as full-time workers of men and women of less than 15 years old or older than 40 years. My fieldwork findings are comparable to those of Kapadia who reports on her research among female agricultural labourers in a South Indian locality:

I had asked if women preferred to recruit their own kin. She replied, 'No, we don't. What's important is that the woman should be a good worker – she must be fast, because if she's slow she'll delay us all. So we don't take anyone who's old – because the old women have become slow – and we don't allow anyone very young because they don't know how to do it.' . . . Another factor, proximate residence, is of great importance as well. Rajalakshmi explained why: 'You've got to rush off for work early in the morning and can't spend time going to houses further away. So you call the other women for work very discreetly. If you wake the others they'll want to come too and when you refuse them they'll get angry and abuse you. So we take close neighbours: we wake them quickly and go off, with no fuss.' The discretion required in calling others for work is important, and for this reason, the recruiter usually keeps the job secret, telling only those women whom she wants on her team. (Kapadia 1995: 227)

This does not mean that those who fall below or above these limits are freed from taking part in the labour process. However, they do not yet, or no longer, meet the heavy demands made on physical strength and stamina, and therefore are not the first to be considered for work on a contract basis. The wastage that is an inevitable part of the work process causes people to be transferred to the less able-bodied part of the army of wage hunters and gatherers. Apart from older men and women who have literally been used up in the labour process, these include single women with small children and those who, even while still young, suffer from ailments or chronic diseases that invalidate them for full-time work. As a result of the little open visibility of such desperate cases, who keep a low profile also in the home milieu of the landless, not only the intense misery but also the numerical size of this category is not sufficiently known.

The contractualization of labour relations has created a harsh climate of competition in the milieu of the working poor. Incompetent, slow, feeble, handicapped and other sorts of inferior workers tend to remain excluded from participation in joint-work arrangements. The members of a self-constituted gang, for example, have a shared interest in not only recruiting the most qualified but also as small a number as possible in order to maximize their income. Emergent practices of exclusionary labour arrangements are not only noticeable in south Gujarat but have also been observed in south India (Athreya, Djurfeldt and Lindberg 1990: 145; Kapadia 1995: 226) and on Java in Indonesia (Hart 1986: 681–96; Breman 1995a: 27–9).

A permanent job such that makes working life more bearable and dignified, i.e. gaining access to the formal sector of the economy, is a far distant ideal for the great majority of the workers who find themselves at the broad floor of the labour hierarchy. However, lack of regularity which characterizes their daily rhythm does not only have disadvantages. The term casual labour, *chhuta majuri*, also connotes an existence that is not conditioned by attachment to and dependency on a permanent employer. Wage hunters and gatherers are free. To be sure, they are free in the first place of the means of production and of other capital (skills, money with which to buy a secure job) needed to reach the higher zones of labour. Secondly, however, they are also free of the subjugation to a master that was formerly the fate of a farm servant. The landless proletariat try as far as possible to avoid modes of employment that infringe upon their gained freedom. That is possible only to a certain degree. The need to accept a cash advance on wages entails the obligation to subject oneself to the orders of an employer for the direct future. Back payment has a similar binding effect. The loss of independence that adheres to such a labour contract explains why it is only entered into through lack of a better alternative. That so many nevertheless have recourse to this last resort of employment indicates the enormous pressure on sources of livelihood in the bottom echelons of the economy. Even that disenfranchisement is subjected to restrictions of durability, range and intensity. The work agreement is not entered into and continued for an indefinite time, as was the case with the *hali* of former times. The neo-bondage is further strongly economic in nature and restricts the imposition of the employer's will and his claims of superiority *per se*. The behaviour of wage hunters and gatherers not only expresses their longing for material improvement, but also manifests their basic unwillingness to seek security in bondage. Theirs is a type of social consciousness that might be expected from the proletarian class.

The footloose proletariat reacts to the control over them exercised by employers by attempts to escape it. This is done in various ways. In my fieldwork villages Halpatis show little interest in entering into permanent employment with a landowner belonging to the dominant Anavil Brahmin caste. The status of bondage that is still associated with farm servants has an avoidance effect on the younger members of this landless caste in particular. They choose the more risky but freer life of a day worker. The new generation of Halpatis seems to grasp every opportunity to escape the agrarian regime. Away from the village and from agriculture they earn a few extra rupees, mostly countered by greater effort besides the longer journey and work times. Their motivation for migrating is the anonymity which accompanies them in the outside world:

Hired for the day as loader-unloader, these young men and women stand in the back of the truck and together with their mates enjoy a freedom that is denied them when working in the fields. For them, that is also the attraction of the urban casual labour markets. They are certainly treated there as commodities, but at least they are not immediately identified and stigmatized as *sala Dubra*. (Fieldwork notes)

Their economic behaviour displays great flexibility in the sense that they work in and out of the village and combine agricultural labour with many other jobs, usually of short durability. Their strategy to constantly search for alternative sources of income is oriented towards preventing an employer securing their labour for a price that is far below the current daily rate for casual work. In addition to helping them to keep their heads above water in difficult circumstances, their occupational multiplicity is also a form of resistance to the pressure brought to bear on them to shut themselves into a more permanent dependency relationship. That they do not object to steady work is shown by the eagerness with which day workers seize the opportunity to hire themselves out to an employer who is prepared to take them on for an indefinite period at a reasonable wage. The scarcity of such jobs forces landless men and women to enter into contract with a *mukadam* with whom many of them will leave the village at the end of the monsoon. This is undoubtedly accompanied for the length of their absence with loss of autonomy. However, that restriction on their freedom of movement lasts no longer than a few months and is over when they return to the village.

In the effort to increase their manoeuvrability and independence, casual workers not only do not object but have a definite preference for piece-work. I have earlier called such modes of sub-contracting self-exploitation, and I have no reason to rescind that view. This does not alter the fact that to work for one's own account and risk has another and more emancipatory aspect. Piece-work enables men and women in the prime of their working lives to free themselves of a direct tie to an employer which is felt as galling. The tendency to explain self-employment as a regrettable example of *petit bourgeois* behaviour ignores the possibility that employment on the basis of such contracts might benefit the dignity of labour.

When there is need for their labour power, payment based on piece-rates and sub-contracting of work in general offer the young and able-bodied in particular the chance to increase their earnings, often to more than the current day-rate for unskilled or semi-skilled labour. Lack of regularity, however, is a noticeable characteristic of the disorderly lives of wage hunters and gatherers. Periods of top demand are interchanged, often unexpectedly, with days or weeks of little activity. Peaks and slacks are not restricted to agriculture and other sources of open-air employment, but also occur in the urban-industrial sector of the economy. This can be illustrated by the under-utilization of labour power of textile workers and diamond cutters amounting to 25 per cent or even more of their availability on an annual basis. The cycle of production and stagnation also follows a fickle course in the informal sector, entirely consistent with the hunting and gathering reality.

Employers individually and collectively blame labourers for their lack of discipline. What do they mean by that? Pre-capitalist work regimes are considered to know of no haste or punctuality and do not accept the idea that time is money. All this changes, as Thompson has explained, in the transition to industrial capitalism which calls for a new type of labour discipline marked by the clock. 'Time is now currency: it is not passed but spent' (Thompson 1993: 359). He adds that the new valuation of time came about gradually and even in the heartland of the industrial world irregular labour rhythms were perpetuated right into the present century. The compulsion of clock-time took much longer to get established in the peripheral zones of capitalism, such as the Bombay cotton mills in India, resulting in a factory proletariat only partially and temporarily 'committed' to the industrial way of life (Thompson 1993: 398).

As observed in chapter 5, landowners in Gandevigam and Chikhligam are of the opinion that the landpoor and landless fall short of the self-discipline which is a precondition for getting access to steady employment outside the village and agriculture. Nowadays, however, labour-thrift is not merely claimed for urban-industrial work but has also become a trait required of labour engaged in the rural economy. A workday of eight hours is the yardstick chosen by the government for the fixation of minimum wages in agriculture. By way of excuse for non-payment of this legal rate farmers insist that labourers report for duty much later than 8 a.m., do not keep working until noon, take a meal break which is longer than two hours and leave the fields again much earlier than six in the evening. *Kam chor – dam chor*, thiefs of work and (therefore) thiefs of our money, is the bitter complaint directed against local labour in general and the Halpatis in particular. In an effort to check this sort of evasive, non-committal behaviour agrarian employers feel that they have to exercise tight and constant surveillance. The rigorous discipline which they demand is, however, in striking contrast with the highly insecure terms offered by them: casual instead of regular employment and wage payment not based on time but on piece-rate. By switching to piece-rate payment modalities employers seem to have found an adequate response to their increasing lack of control over the quality and quantity of labour time about which they never stop complaining. Giving out work on contract is certainly of major importance in the internalization of self-discipline among a reluctant labour force (see also Kapadia 1995: 232).

In comparison with the agrarian cycle of the past the workload has definitely increased. Indeed, labourers then had to work from dawn to dusk or even after nightfall. The bonded farm servants of south Gujarat were at the beck and call of their master and other members of his household at all hours of the day and night. However, their service conditions used to be less contractual and labour-intensive. These *halis* received a daily allowance for which they had to work but at a lower intensity than nowadays or, in the slack season, were tolerated to just hang around without doing much (Breman 1974). Such pre-capitalist work styles are not condoned anymore. The *mukadam* and other agents who assist informal sector employers in patrolling the worksites can be recognized by paraphernalia needed to measure output and adequate performance, such as a notebook and pencil in their breast-pocket together with a wrist-watch. In the landscape of my contemporary research a clear demarcation between 'work' and 'life', which Thompson points out is a hallmark of mature industrial societies, continues to remain absent. It is therefore anything but surprising that the new schedule of capitalist employment that has emerged, characterized by less control over labour's person but more rigorous control over labour time, although thoroughly commoditized, is still not regulated by the clock. I want to emphasize, however, that clock-time is not what informal sector employers have in mind when they talk about workers' lack of discipline. Their blame concerns first and foremost the 'irrational' refusal of a massive army, which is periodically redundant and chronically vulnerable, to surrender unconditionally; i.e. the reluctance or even outright unwillingness of both males and females to make themselves available for the lowest possible price and to the maximal extent whenever or wherever required. To the immense chagrin of the owners of both agrarian and non-agrarian capital that dictate for unrestrained extraction is flatly rejected.

There can be no doubt that employers' endless complaints about the thriftlessness of the workforce form a little convincing exoneration for their refusal to pay a reasonable price for labour. Rather than interpreting the defects of which they accuse their subordinates as expressions of economic irrationality, I have pointed out that those subordinates often have no choice but to stay away. That absence may be due to the necessity now and again to work somewhere else in order to repay a loan by providing labour, or to the need to allow one's body to recover at least minimally from the overuse to which it has been subjected. However, indiscipline is a correct term insofar as the described laziness, irregularity and lack of responsibility, result directly from the refusal of the workers to submit themselves completely to the yoke laid on them by the employer. Lethargy, intractability and fickleness hide an attitude of resistance caused by the longing to keep the adversary at arm's length, even when self-interest is apparently not served or may even be impaired by such deeds of open or hidden sabotage. After all, why should men and women who are under-utilized and underpaid purposely renounce an income which, in view of their poverty, they cannot really do without? Simply because uninhibited continuation of the effort does not provide such a wage that it is possible to escape the chronic state of poverty. In this respect I would remind the reader that a number of budget enquiries in the milieu of unskilled labour to which I have devoted my attention, i.e. agricultural labourers, brick-makers, cane-cutters, etc., have shown that they have to spend around 70–80 per cent of their income on food. This high percentage notwithstanding, many of them suffer from malnutrition. The idea that continual work would enable them to improve their lot substantially is completely implausible. In my opinion, it is essential to consider their 'fugitive behaviour' against this background, not as a sign of economic irrationality but as a demonstration of protest.

Subsistence needs demand that landless enter into commitments that will restrict their freedom of movement for some time. This takes the form of accepting cash advances in exchange for making one's labour power available if and when the employer has need of it. But those who receive such an advance show little scruple in withdrawing from the obligation to adapt to the wishes of the sponsor. Halpatis from Chikhligam who had deserted from brickworks grinned as they told me how the jobber who had contracted them made fruitless attempts to catch them. They clearly did not think of returning the earnest money they had received from him. It had long been expended on necessities. Accusations of bad faith would leave them cold. Their only worry seemed to be that on the following occasion it might be difficult to find someone willing to give them an advance in exchange for the pledge to work. Without their intending it, something always happened that hindered them from complying with the contract in full and on time. Such a reflection indicates concern for the future but no remorse at having infringed a code of conduct that had been imposed upon them. Members of the rural proletariat would certainly not hesitate to grasp any opportunity that might occur to evade their existing bonds.

In the strategy followed by the massive workforce that stems from the rural underclass, marginal landowners have an advantage over their landless fellows. Other than the Halpatis, increasing numbers of Dhodhiya households have succeeded during the last two decades in withdrawing from the annual trek to the brickworks. This is due to the small piece of cultivable land that they own, even though its yield is not sufficient to ensure a livelihood. Work for a wage elsewhere is unavoidable, but the possibility of supplementing those earnings with food crops harvested on their own plot of land, however small, has given these mini-farmers a better starting point than that of the completely landless Halpatis. Dhodhiyas have always preferred to leave their wives at home, both to look after a bullock or cow and to enable the children to go to school, and perhaps also to spare the women the heavy labour in the brickworks. Landowning Dhodhiyas are able to take a ration of grain with them when they leave their homes at the end of the rainy season; this means they require less money during their stay outside the village for daily needs and are thus able to take more with them when they return home at the end of the season. Investing these savings in the farm by digging a well or buying an oil-pump and in education for children, Dhodhiya males ultimately managed to avoid the brickworks (see also Veen 1979: 51–2). The little that they owned was sufficient at first to distinguish them from landless households in the village, and later to increase their distance from those who were economically more vulnerable.

The state of affairs in Chikhligam has shown me how misleading it is to suggest that a small plot of land is like a millstone around the neck of its owner. According to this spurious argument, the pseudo-farmer is worse off than the true proletarian who, it is assumed, can go and stand where he will in an expanding economy. This notion also played a role in the idea of excluding landless workers from the policy of redistribution of agrarian resources that was half-heartedly implemented during the first few decades after Independence. The example of Dhodhiyas in my fieldwork village and of other tribal castes of marginal landowners in south Gujarat shows that if Halpatis had each been given a small plot of land this would have strengthened their resistance in a development process in which the demand for labour has increased less slowly than its supply. This is also Bharadwaj's conclusion in her study of India's rural labour market:

the access to land appears to be a very important need for gaining livelihood in the rural areas and the dependency relations in exchange which the poorer land-operating and landless households are compelled into, arise due to the essential insecurity of this access. Since the perverse effects of exchange involvements act through such dependency relations the social power structure and the hegemony of the strong over the weaker party's livelihood derives from the same insecurity. Land and tenurial reforms could work as a first step in breaking this hegemony. (Bharadwaj 1990: 72)

Still, the social advance that the almost landless might have over the landless should not be exaggerated. The limited autonomy enjoyed by marginal landowners among the Dhodhiyas even in the past has been consolidated by using part of the yield of that land to gain access to resources away from agriculture and the village. In view of the continual increase of population, this strategy seems to have provided no more than a breathing space. It is almost impossible to sub-divide family land any further, and the simultaneous growth of the literate part of the population entails that an ever-increasing level of education is needed to buy a protected position in the non-agricultural labour hierarchy that has emerged. Nevertheless, younger Dhodhiyas have a better chance of escaping a threatened existence than do the new generation of Halpatis who have to seek their way upwards from a situation of total landlessness and thus greater dependency.

Social struggle

The footloose proletariat is made up of an enormous mass of men and women, adults and children, who possess little if any means of production of their own and who lead a circulatory existence in the lowest regions of the labour system. It is a conglomerate of diverse categories distinct from the social class of employees in formal employment, who usually carry out skilled and better paid work, and whose conditions of employment have gained recognition and protection through the organized promotion of their interests. In fact, lack of collectively organized resistance is the principal reason why working life in the echelons of economy that I have researched continues to be so unbearably heavy and miserable. The meagre countervailing power of labour vis-à-vis capital is surprising in view of the greater volume of the former as against the latter factor of production. There are numerous reasons that prevent or hinder the creation of mutual solidarity that must precede any common efforts to improve the lot of workers.

The initial and most important obstacle is undoubtedly that by far the majority of economic sectors, almost all year round, experience such an overwhelming supply of unskilled labour that employers have little difficulty in satisfying their demand for it. Structural overcrowding creates an imbalance which has a crippling effect on attempts to achieve social progress at the bottom of society. There are quite alarming reports that the expansion rate of total employment hardly keeps pace with the growth of the working population (Report NCRL, vol.1, 1991: 33–4). Intense competition for the limited work available creates a lot of tension among those who desperately seek ways to ensure their own immediate livelihood. The dissension which this can cause among workers is illustrated by the state of affairs in the urban casual labour markets:

Some labourers in Vadodara casual labour markets told us that if they do not get work continuously for 2–3 days they become restless and impatient. They try desperately to avail of the first opportunity to secure job, whatever the terms of work and wages. This infuriates others who witness the sliding down of the wage rates in such circumstances. Arguments and counter-arguments ensue, and occasionally it bursts out in open scuffles and physical fights. The contractors and *mukadams* keep their cool and watch the scene discreetly without much of an intervention. Of course, the labourers would not like to admit that such a thing happens. Most of them (83 per cent) said that there was never any quarrel, or cut-throat competition among them. (Punalekar and Patel 1990: 120)

Another obstacle is created by the transience, multiplicity and unspecified nature of the jobs available. Working experience is undirected and contacts with employers are much too brief to provide the initial impetus to a collective stand. Moreover, modes of payment within the same enterprise and even for an identical job can lead to considerable differences in income. The bringing-in of women and children by means of male workers also has an obfuscating effect. These forms of indirect employment contribute to a multi-layered subjugation to exploitative regimes and are coupled with interest conflicts that can extend into the household sphere. Circulation along various sectors and sites of employment is given a further accent by the inclination employers demonstrate to give preference not to local but to imported labour. Migrants who have little if any contact with the social milieu at the place of arrival are forced as 'aliens' to keep a low profile. The vulnerability of their position prevents them from taking a militant attitude. On the other hand, temporary employment and an alien background may help to strengthen bargaining power. Outsiders often show an indifference and

absence of collective struggle

even impertinence which local workers would not dare to manifest. Recruitment of workers along lines of primary group identities also hinders the development of solidarity in a wider circle. The feelings of loyalty that accompany this segmentation are of a different kind to those that are rooted in class contradictions. The immobilizing effect caused by horizontal division is increased by the pressure emanating from the need to invest in vertical dependency relationships. To rise in the labour hierarchy is only possible to a certain degree, but favoured treatment such as change from casual to permanent employment requires obediency towards the employer and the agents who surround him. Conversely, attachment of labour by means of cash advance or post-payment hinders the development of organized counter-action. Fixing in bondage is sometimes direct but also occurs with the aid of intermediaries such as jobbers and labour contractors. A summing-up of the many obstacles that explain the absence of any collective struggle to improve the workers' lot has as common denominator the enormous social heterogeneity of the army of workers, the unregulated rhythm of employment in large parts of the rural and urban economy, and the strongly fragmented nature of the market for unskilled labour. Thus these three aspects have to be understood in their mutual interrelationships.

Markedly different is the more institutionalized promotion of interests by the much smaller force of wage workers who have managed to gain a permanent footing in the regulated, formalized and protected sector of the economy. The greater bargaining power in the higher zones of the labour regime is given shape in the presence of trade unions, among other things. Leadership of these social movements in which the self-organizing capacity of better educated labour in permanent employment shows itself, exhibits little or no interest in the army of casual workers who roam around in the foothills of the economy. Would it not be attractive for the established trade unions to extend their mandate and care for the interests of this unorganized mass of workers? Apparently not, because one of the few common characteristics of the type of industries that I have researched is the lack of any trade union activities. This is due in the first place to disinclination of employers to countenance intervention of third parties in their supreme control over their workforce. It is a form of hegemony that is concealed behind the assertion, which I have frequently had to listen to, that unsolicited intervention of outsiders only disrupts the direct and cordial relationship between owner and worker. According to this line of thought, trade union activists are nothing but killjoys in the peaceful coexistence that has traditionally existed between capital and labour. It is a doctrine of harmony which has been propagated far over the state borders as a hallmark of economic and social life in Gujarat. The following statement, taken from a study of industrial entrepreneurship in the city of Surat, is a fine example of this wishful thinking:

Surat has remained since long, a city inhabited by people with a cosmopolitan outlook. Peace loving people of different castes, creeds and communities like Hindus, Parsis, Jains, Muslims etc. have lived together peacefully in Surat. People of this area are generous, broad-minded, and peace loving and easy going. They have broad humanitarian outlook, mutual fellow-feeling and love, dislike towards frictions and disputes, which have favourably influenced the climate of employer-employee relationship in the industries of Surat comparatively. Surat has therefore enjoyed comparatively a very peaceful environment in its industrial life. (Bhatt 1979: 37)

After having set the tone in this manner, the author then reports on his research among a wide sample of entrepreneurs in various branches of industrial production. Trade unions were largely inactive and were entirely lacking in 87 per cent of the industries examined. Summarizing the extremely negative opinions of trade unions held by his informants, the author concludes in a measured tone that: 'entrepreneurs generally did not like trade union activity and they did not hesitate to express their views' (Bhatt 1979: 172). Such opinions are easily recognizable for anyone who is to some degree familiar with the social Darwinistic mentality of the new middle class of employers. Their preference for a non-formalized style of management is connected above all to their refusal to comply with labour legislation and to their attempts to prevent employees from joining in a closed front. It is important to remember in this connection that the construct of the informal sector as an unorganized branch of industry does not apply as far as employers are concerned. Owners of saltpans and brickworks, quarry manufacturers and diamond shop owners, have all set up their own associations to promote their professional interests. High on their list of priorities is to make sure, in concerted action, that their workforce does not achieve any organized countervailing power.

Moreover, government also shows little inclination to promote self-organization of the economic down-and-outs. This is evidenced by the irresolute labour legislation and even more by its extremely defective implementation. While official pronouncements emphasize the role of government as neutral arbiter above the two parties in the social conflict, in reality the interests of state and capital are interwoven. In day-to-day practice, their collective orientation easily causes a common front against the fragmented and defenceless proletariat. The editors of a recent national report on the deplorable situation of rural labour commissioned by the government, state that they would already be well satisfied with only a mild opposition by the powerful coalition of state and capital to the slowly advancing process of social emancipation:

Whenever the rural labour organizations are started, first comes the resistance from the vested interests and the Govt. machinery. The rural workers will gain strength if the resistance is not harsh and strong. (Report NCRL, vol. 1, 1991: 242)

That class-based alignment is clearly noticeable and helps to explain why trade unions are unable to get a foot on the ground in zones outside the formal sector of the economy. In addition to all the obstacles mentioned, this is the principal argument with which labour leaders try to explain their absence in the lower echelons of employment. Although defensively formulated, it is a plausible explanation of the limits encountered by organized action on the part of labour. But this is not the whole story. The attitude of established trade unionism towards the class of casual labour and unprotected workers amounts to a combination of indifference rising almost to enmity. Trade union leaders are in fact convinced that the mass of workers at the bottom is too numerous to be accommodated within the formal sector system. They fear that pressure from below would lead to gradual erosion of the rights gained during a long struggle by protected labour. In this opinion, trade union leadership is assured of the support of the majority of its members. It is almost impossible to persuade the rank-and-file to show solidarity with workers who are less favoured in all respects. This is the classical statement going back to Marx, maintaining that the interests of formal and informal sector workers are antithetical.

It was in the interests of the formal workers to restrict the entry of informal workers to the labour market, which could lower their wages; and conversely, informal workers saw their chances of joining the formal labour market restricted by the high wages that organized formal sector workers managed to extract from their employers. The employers, Marx argued, would opt for labour-saving production processes as a result of such higher wages. (Sanyal 1991: 49–50)

By suggesting a dichotomy in the world of labour, consisting of a fairly small top and a broad basis, and reaching the conclusion that the two are separated from one another by an almost unbridgeable rift, it is made easier for the privileged to keep their distance from those who are deprived of their rights. However, this construction fails to appreciate that the zones of employment are indeed fluid and merge into one another to some extent. To see the heterogeneous horde of circular migrants at the bottom of the ladder merely as a reserve labour force that is ready to be brought in when the time demands and to be dismissed afterwards, is to show too mechanical an interpretation of the dynamics that characterize the labour system. These are undoubtedly tendencies that indicate a process of informalization of formal sector industry. The social forces underlying these dynamics cannot simply be reduced to the replacement of protected by unprotected labour, but are also connected to a reorganization of capital. This can be illustrated by the dismantling of textile factories in Bombay and Ahmedabad and the simultaneous installation of mechanical looms in small-scale workshops in Surat which operate in a work climate controlled by little more than the law of the jungle. A trade union strategy which is content to do little more than attempt to prevent the deformalization of enclave production and which does not bother itself about the fate of the many more men and women who work in the 'unregulated' part of the economy, is doomed to failure before it even starts.

Industrial unions can not be organized when factories cease to exist; proletarian mobilization becomes more difficult when the formal proletariat represents a shrinking component of the labor force and its remaining members fear for their privileges; employers can not be easily confronted when they remain well-concealed under multiple layers of subcontracting. (Portes, Castells and Benton 1989: 258)

In opposition to this trend much could be learned from experiences in Kerala during the last twenty to thirty years. In this southern state of India, informal sector workers in many branches of industry have been able to consolidate their bargaining position built up over many years of social struggle by organizing themselves into trade unions (Kannan 1988, 1990, 1992). However, the policy line currently favoured in India is to rectify such 'distortions' in the labour market as part of a more comprehensive process of structural readjustment. Actively promoted by national and international economic agencies the trend is to do away with provisions and institutions regulating conditions of employment and job security and to neutralize trade union pressure identified as both cause and effect of legally protected labour statuses.

Does it follow from the above that there is no form of collective struggle in the absence of trade unions? Not at all. In various branches of industry informal workers have now and again been involved in forms of agitation whose purpose was to improve their situation. It is actually remarkable that all cases with which I became familiar in the course of my research are concerned with seasonal migrants, a category that has the name of being the last to undertake acts of resistance. The labour unrest during the mid-1940s in the saltpans along the coast near Bombay in fact confirms that opinion. The initiative was taken by labour rooted in the locality. Only in the second instance, and even then only marginally, did the Kharwas from south Gujarat become involved.

Practically all the local labour is organized, but there are many obstacles in organizing the imported workers. The Kharwas are very illiterate and ignorant and are rarely aware of their rights or interests. Moreover, the Kharwas move from centre to centre for employment practically every season and consequently the same set of workers are not often found with the same employer or at the same centre every year. This comparatively high labour turnover renders organization very difficult. It was also reported that employers prefer not to recruit Kharwas who happen to be active Union workers. The Kharwas thus are mostly inactive and efforts at organizing them have of necessity to be through the Khatedars. (Report Salt Pan Industry, 1950: 29)

Khatedars are the gang bosses who accompany the migrants to saltpans for the duration of the season. The strikes called by the local unions ended in the formalization of employment in this industry. By only registering the gang bosses as members of trade unions, however, the spoils that materialized have been monopolized by them. The initiative for action in agro-industry in south Gujarat was taken by an urban trade union by whom the semi-permanent factory hands of the co-operative sugar enterprises were called out on strike for improvement of their working conditions, first in 1973 and again in 1981 (Breman 1978: 1358; 1985b: 431). On the first occasion an appeal was made to cane-cutters in the fields to down their *koytas* in a show of solidarity, but their appalling working conditions did not even come up for discussion. In 1981 the set of demands did include an increase of cane-cutting rates and employers were thus faced by a closed front of factory and fieldworkers. The first of these were employed on formal terms and the latter on informal conditions. However, negotiations were concerned exclusively with concessions to the factory hands, while the much larger force of fieldworkers were ignored. That marginalization did not remain unchallenged, however. On the last pay day at the end of the season some thousands of harvest workers gathered in the factory grounds to protest about the low price paid per tonne of cane. The disorders that arose ended with the arrest of some of the agitators, while factory management arranged for the harvesters to be immediately transported back to their place of origin. In 1989 unrest was again stirred by social activists who were concerned with the fate of the cane-cutters. They forced government to intervene and managed to persuade a number of harvest gangs to demand a better wage, but in vain, because managements of the co-operative sugar factories gave short shrift to those who had dared to stick their necks out. An important factor is that both trade unions and social activists directed their action strategy towards the gang bosses while, on the other hand, employers exerted themselves to defuse the commotion by ensuring themselves of the loyalty of these key figures. In an earlier publication I described the pressure from above to which the latter were subjected:

managements convened a meeting to which all *mukadams* were summoned and said that they would not concede to the demands, attributed to irresponsible agitators. The labour contractors were then made to sign a blank sheet of paper, thereby enrolling themselves as members of a fake *mukadam* trade union, used as a legal fence by factory managements to cover up their shady labour practices. Gang bosses who refused to sign or who had a record showing that they did not put allegiance to the industry above all else, were told that they need not return for the next campaign. (Breman 1990: 593)

The history of the labour movement shows that the role of labour contractors and gang bosses is highly ambivalent. In situations with which I am familiar they usually act as agents of the employers. But that the loyalty of these professional middlemen can take another direction is shown by the fact that they belonged to the vanguard of trade unions which came up early in the present century, for example in Bombay's textile industry. The changes in methods of management which preceded that movement and by which the gang bosses in their advanced position felt themselves to be threatened, do not fall within the scope of this study.

The last example of collective action to which seasonal migrants sometimes resort concerns labourers in brickworks near Vadodara. In 1983, at the initiative of social activists, a trade union was set up which pressed employers and government to comply with existing labour legislation. That the gang bosses managed to retain their key position is shown by the strike demand that these *thekedars* should be given a commission of 20 per cent on the total wages of their gang members. In this case too, employers tried to break the collective protest with the use of force (Randeria and Yagnik 1990: 85). The course taken by the protest has been discussed in the preceding chapter. Ultimately, thanks primarily to the attention given to the affair by the local press, a compromise was reached, but one which individual brickworks owners did not heed. The season after all was coming to an end. As was customary every year, the owners cut off the water supply and removed the corrugated iron sheets with which the migrants had built their temporary shelters. These brick-makers had no alternative but to undertake the journey back to Uttar Pradesh and accept the amount of money to which they still had a right, according to the patron who settled the final accounts. Had this disappointing outcome brought a definite halt to the willingness of this vulnerable labour force to take action? Not in the least. When I visited Ahmedabad in January 1993, work in the brickyards was once again at a standstill.

Between Ahmedabad and Gandhinagar lie the worksites of numerous brickyards which adjoin one another in this open plain. This proximity makes it easier for workers to adopt a common stand and to ensure that everyone adheres to it. Their demands are considerable. Firstly, cash advances paid during the monsoon must not be deducted from earnings during the season. Second, deductions from the rate per 1,000 bricks for breakages, supply of firewood, etc., must immediately be abolished. Third, the introduction of a new standard brick larger than the former *deshi* type means more work and should therefore be accompanied by an increase in the piece-rate. The owners show little haste to put an end to the strike. Production has now been in progress for some months and they will not be prepared to make any concessions until the piled-up stocks have been sold. So far, they have continued to pay the weekly allowances, indicating that they do not intend to force the conflict. Today (25 January 1993), the strike leaders are meeting to discuss the state of affairs. Their meeting place is in an open field somewhere along the main road between Ahmedabad and Gandhinagar. About 20 men are present and talking together. After about an hour the decision is unanimous: continue. They disappear again in various directions over the open plain. (Fieldwork notes)

In none of these cases has militancy by the workforce been crowned with any success. There has been no actual improvement to their situation, let alone achieving the higher goal of formalization of their employment. The value of their actions has been primarily in bringing pressure to bear on bureaucrats and politicians to put their paper promises into effect. Even after the outburst of such agitations, however, these third parties are reluctant to do so. The trouble involved in shifting the balance even an iota in favour of the underdogs is sufficiently illustrative of their weak bargaining power and the lack of outside support. The scale enlargement that has come about in the market for unskilled labour makes it possible for employers immediately to replace their workers by new ones, whether or not by tapping new sources of recruitment.

It has been possible to describe these labour conflicts in the branches of industry in which I am particularly interested, thanks to the availability of documents, statements by informers, and other source material. This does not mean that the social struggle which is waged has been restricted to those industries. Similar forms of collective action involving no more than some tens or hundreds of men and women are frequent occurrences, without even becoming widely known. This can be illustrated by considering the manner in which agricultural labourers' wages are increased in the villages. Although this concerns a working class that is the largest in the land, we are poorly informed about the course of events that precede such wage increases. In general, there is no case of any formal negotiations. I have found no evidence, however, for the suggestion made by Rudra that wage rises in agriculture are invariably the result of unilateral action taken by the employers (Rudra 1984: 260–1). Representatives of landowners and landless ultimately reach agreement on the introduction of new rates after a lengthy and loosely structured dialogue. This can be coupled with separate meetings among themselves involving varying numbers of farmers or labourers respectively. I further disagree with Drèze and Mukherjee who argue that no wage bargaining ensues when labourers are 'called to work', a colloquial expression often used. As they themselves have pointed out in their U.P. based fieldwork report, both farmers and labourers agreed that a wage hike had to be extracted from the employers. Both parties

show a fair degree of agreement on the circumstances when the wage standard changes: it increases when a farmer cannot find labourers at the going wage and is desperate to complete an urgent task. (Drèze and Mukherjee 1989: 260; see also Kapadia 1995: 223)

The two parties are well acquainted with the other's spokesmen, and leave them to come to an arrangement. Sometimes the wage increase is introduced immediately for all, but on other occasions some of the landowners stick to the old rate for some time before accepting the new arrangement. In negotiations for a new round existing differences in payment are not necessarily standardized in a common tariff.

Outsiders find such a course of events ambiguous. Even with hindsight it is not easy to ascertain who has taken the initiative, who has taken part in the negotiations, and what reactions were shown by the two sides. This changes, however, if agreement is not reached and the parties see themselves forced to find more emphatic support for their point of view within their own milieu. While local agricultural labourers show signs of unwillingness to work, the landowners check whether replacements are available in the near vicinity or let it be known that they will make do with the labour power of their own households. The escalation can increase into a frontal stand, led by the hard nucleus on each side. If it comes to strike action, this is mostly taken by the agricultural workers at the start of harvesting. Such action seems to signal the existence of a kind of proto-union (Athreya, Djurfeldt and Lindberg 1990: 158).

Such labour conflicts, which also occur in other sectors of rural employment, have three elements in common: spontaneity, local containment, and brevity. The first of these has already been discussed. The strike may be preceded by a long process of 'negotiations' but leadership is informal and the decision to strike can be taken on the spur of the moment. Lack of organization is further shown by the limited reach of the action. Only exceptionally does this extend beyond the village where the workers live. Finally, a strike seldom lasts longer than a week. Landless households simply do not have the reserves available to allow them to manage for more than a few days without income. Rudra has made the following comment on the highly localized character of the negotiating process:

The labourers belonging to the same village do share some kind of community feeling; they do move as a group with the local employers. It is this group behaviour that explains the uniform wage rate of casual labourers within the same village. (Rudra 1990: 499)

The strategy followed by both parties in promoting their own interests has entered a new phase as a result of the temporary inflow of migrant labour into the countryside of south Gujarat on the one hand, and the easier access to employment away from agriculture and the village for the local landless, on the other hand. In that respect, my views differ from that of Rudra according to whom the social consciousness of the landless class does not extend beyond the borders of the village. Nor do I agree with him that, within the village, landowners and agricultural workers are linked as in the past by vertical solidarity (Rudra 1990: 499–500). Rudra's model of village-wide complementarity and consensus, overriding contradictions based on caste as well as class, is ill-conceived. To express their relationship purely in the terminology of patronage would be to ignore the change that has occurred in south Gujarat and, one would guess, not only there. I further disagree with Dasgupta who, following up on Rudra's argumentation, not only overstates the immobility of labour between villages but also assumes that the wage for casual labour is uniform within one and the same village (Dasgupta 1993: 235). Different terms of employment are actually a major source of conflict between landowners and agricultural workers giving rise to strikes, lock-outs and other industrial disputes at the local level. The willingness to resort to action in order to enforce wage demands has undoubtedly increased, but this does not signify that the landless proletariat manages to transform its growing militancy into supra-local solidarity. This precondition for the effective improvement of their situation is not satisfied. Commenting on the segmentation of labour, Kapadia noticed in her village of fieldwork in Tamilnadu a very strong mutuality between workers of the same caste-street but a much weaker mutuality between same-caste workers in different villages (Kapadia 1995: 236). Her conclusions are similar to my findings in rural south Gujarat.

Men and women who try to sell their labour power on the urban casual labour markets with varying degrees of success, know all too well that open access to this arena seriously weakens their negotiating position versus employers. In the realization of their own isolation against the far greater social reach of the opposition, who would dare openly stick his or her neck out? Employers are able to collect and disseminate information on the workers with sometimes dreaded results.

Their [i.e. contractors'] contacts are wider. Their influence is greater. They are capable of spreading the news that such and such person is mobilising the workers against the contractors; and thus stall any further move on our part . . . said one female worker from Surat casual labour market. (Punalekar and Patel 1990: 168)

In view of the risk involved it is understandable that resistance usually takes on a more veiled form. At a casual labour market in Bharuch, a regular attender who remained anonymous, had written with chalk on the wall of a building: Labourers wanted: men Rs 25, women Rs 15. This advertising of the going wage rate was apparently an effort on the part of the workforce to close ranks. The researcher who reported this incident also noted the following complaint voiced by one of the women:

'Too many labourers in the market and lack of unity among them defeats our purpose of any collective action against the contractors and *mukadams*. They are few and we are many. They have the choice to pick and choose, while we have to silently agree to their terms of employment. They can dictate terms to us, and we are helpless. Some control over the entry of "new" labourers will exercise check over these tendencies', one labourer said in an agitated voice. (Punalekar and Patel 1990: 157)

Their ambition, it appears from discussions with workers, is that work be allocated through a registration system. New workers would then only be added to the list when vacancies arise. In fact, this would be similar to the rules regarding porters at railway stations and to that introduced many years ago by the government of Maharashtra for various categories of casual workers.

Inclusion and exclusion: widening circles of identification

In the present economic and general social climate, clear limitations are set on collective action initiated from below. To conclude from this that the rural proletariat has little choice but to submit itself passively to the labour regime imposed from above would not do justice to numerous other individualized forms of protest to which this vulnerable army of workers resorts. For the sake of brevity, I refer to Scott (1985) for a discussion of the arsenal of 'weapons of the weak', while noting that his micro-level report on the course of the anonymous everyday encounter between landowning and landless classes in the Asian countryside no longer occurs solely or even principally within the sphere of agriculture and the arena of the village.

As we have seen, employers prefer to bypass local labour, among other reasons for their lack of 'discipline'. However, the asserted adaptability and amenability of the aliens are largely a mirage, a type of behaviour caused by their lack of roots in the milieu to which they have come. Rotation of wage hunters and gatherers along various sites of employment is due not only to sectoral and seasonal fluctuations in the demand for labour, but also to the unconcealed disinclination of members of this footloose proletariat to enter into a labour contract considered by them as oppressive. That rejection can be expressed by refusing to set out with a gang boss who has the reputation of intimidating and disfranchising members of his gang, and more generally by tending to withdraw from any employment that infringes their freedom of movement. I consider the avoidance of vertical dependency and of subordinate behaviour with which that is linked, as the manifestation of a proletarian consciousness. In that sense, the circulation of labour must in my opinion also be explained as a deed of protest. Evasive behaviour certainly, but caused by the desire to keep one's own dignity intact. Put in rather different words, this was the essence of what workers told me in several ways during the course of my fieldwork. That escape from pressure exercised by superiors is indeed a frequent reason for leaving home, or returning to it, is shown by the report on the investigation among workers in Surat's textile industry.

Whenever conditions at workplace become unbearable, the popular response of the workers is to seek jobs in other factory units. This is the mode of response that involves no confrontation with the immediate supervisors or contractors or factory owners. The dissatisfied workers quietly leave that factory, and join some other factory. We found that as many as 583 workers (36 per cent) left a factory unit at least once due to some dissatisfaction with their working conditions. (*Working and Living Conditions* 1984: 71-2)

If they find the behaviour of the contractor objectionable, they change their employer. They very much resent the arbitrary role of the contractors and *mukadams*. They dislike if they are scolded for slight delay in reaching the workplace or if they are not provided tea at the work sites or if they are abused in foul language. They do not accept such insults meekly. (Punalekar and Patel 1990: 176-7)

For the same reason, gangs of seasonal labourers who search for work in the countryside during harvesting, will sometimes abscond in the middle of the night without finishing their work, to the rage of the farmer by whom they were employed. Landowners then speak of desertion, blaming the 'impulsiveness' of the alien workers. They never admit that it could be due to their own improper behaviour: a combination of too many curses, too long working hours, too low wages and late or non-payment.

The vulnerability of unskilled labour at the bottom of the economy does not mean that this mass of workers shows restrained or even submissive behaviour. Their ability for active and prolonged struggle is limited, but that does not mean that they accept the yoke laid upon them as unresisting victims. As employment becomes less regular and wages lower, the intrepidity of the underdog seems to increase. 'Even dogs have a better life', one cane-cutter stated before a committee set up by the High Court of Gujarat (Breman 1990: 582). In the open field, before this company of notables, the man made this unvarnished statement, not at all deterred by the presence of the manager of the factory for which he worked. What had he to lose? Nevertheless, such outbursts are rare expressions of anger which has to be kept pent up. That this weapon usually has little effect when used by the weak is shown by the story of a Halpati woman who works as a domestic servant in Surat.

Very often I ask the family where I serve to increase my wages. But my request falls on deaf ears. Sometimes, I disclose my protest by absenting from work or reaching their place late, and sometimes making a sullen and gloomy face. But nothing of this works. When I see the same family spending money freely on cloth, ornaments and Sunday parties, my heart burns with indignation. They have no money to increase my wage, but they have money to spend in ice-cream parlour. My children, Sunita and Balwant who sometimes accompany me to help me in my work often ask me unsettling questions. What answer should I give them?' (D. S. Punalekar 1992: 246)

Reservedness, lack of communicativeness, apparent docility and other risk-avoiding behaviour certainly form an element of the working climate that I encountered in various branches of industry. But to describe such behaviour would be incomplete without emphasizing characteristics that suggest the exact opposite: bouts of open anger and flashes of defiance, a crude showing of bitterness and resentment. The inability to give free rein to this gamut of feelings *vis-à-vis* the opposite party causes the silenced protest to be turned inwards or to be vented against those who are even more vulnerable, particularly women and children. According to information received from women attending the urban morning markets for casual labour, more than a quarter of them are occasionally beaten by men of the household (Punalekar and Patel 1990: 142). Based on my own findings gained in this milieu, cases of child abuse are probably even more frequent. Moreover, it is a regular occurrence that local workers use extra-economic methods, i.e. violence, to oppose the ingress of 'aliens' into their arena of employment. What begins as ordinary fisticuffs frequently results in destruction of property, theft, rape and even murder. It will be clear that the discharge of frustration and aggression on others victimized by the same regime detracts from any feelings of solidarity among fellow-sufferers and gives rise to a 'domination within domination' (Scott 1990: 26).

Early discussions of informal sector workers living in urban slums implied that, once roused to political consciousness, these people would foment radical movements and eventually join hands with the rural poor in a frontal attack on the established social order (Sanyal 1991: 43). I have found no evidence to back up such a scenario. The closed-shop character of most sources of employment in the segments of the rural and urban economy which were the focus of my research prevents proletarian consciousness from being transformed into class solidarity and its manifestation in class struggle.

In various recent publications it has been argued that neighbourhood bonds more than class action give meaning and direction to individual choices as well as social action in the informal sector. In seeking openings in the labour market there is no doubt evidence of change from a more vertical to a more horizontal orientation. For the time being, that change in direction is accompanied by an investment in primordial loyalties along lines of caste, religion, regional origin, etc. The Halpatis in the villages of my research do have a common identity articulated in a lifestyle which, in their eyes and those of others, emphasizes their communality and reproduces it for the next generation. To suggest that the social culture inherent to it is an expression of false consciousness does not do justice to the protection and security which is sought and partly found in such particularistic collectivities.

In south Gujarat the village quarters, segregated according to caste, are the bases to which work migrants return at the end of the day, after a few weeks or an entire season, or for an occasional visit. Within that familiar domain the wage hunters and gatherers find the opportunity to exchange their experiences and discuss the contacts that they have made 'outside'. What should not be overlooked is that caste consciousness can undergo scale enlargement in such a way that it approaches class consciousness: recognizing members of other sub-castes as fellow sufferers and feeling solidarity with them. To describe the mass mobilization of men and women, whether individually or in families, for far distant destinations as indicating a high degree of subjugation of labour to capital, is to ignore the tenaciousness with which the army of workers at least temporarily withdraws into its own sphere of privacy. However fragmented and heterogeneous their 'home' arenas may be, the forming of such *cordons sanitaires* restricts the reach of their work bosses. To the latter, their incomplete grip on the almost inexhaustible supply remains a source of immeasurable irritation. It also augments their inclination to depict this lack of control as a defect on the part of labour.

The great majority of Halpatis lead a segregated existence. In the countryside members of this bottom caste are housed in neighbourhoods that have been built for them during the last two to three decades. In towns and cities too, the proletariat prefers to live in caste concentrations, although more intermingling does occur with other categories of similar social-economic status. When such living quarters are built at the initiative of Congress politicians, they usually carry names that refer to patrons from the Nehru-Gandhi dynasty: Indira *Vasahat*, Jawahar Lines, Rajiv Colony, Sanjay *Nagar*, etc. Almost always they are slums which nevertheless provide their inhabitants with a clearly marked territory of their own. The cohesive quality of such localities is made manifest when ranks have to be closed against outside attacks. Time and again 'mobs' tend to resist municipal authorities when they try to demolish slums and deport their inhabitants. Other official agencies such as police, representative of and mainly catering to formal sector interests, similarly meet in this milieu with a united stand based on physical proximity. However, slum habitats only become arenas of solidarity in order to deal with hostile forces from outside. Internal divisions create strong tensions and fears of unsocial elements from within are quite acute. Illustrative for that other side of the story is Lobo's narrative about a Surat slum:

Madhubhai even though residing in central part of the slum says that he sleeps just at the entrance of his hut with his family inside. Till about 12 at night the door is kept open as it is very warm inside. However, he is alert even if a cat or dog were to enter. If someone passes by he or she is asked to declare his or her name. If the name is familiar the person is allowed to pass. Many neighbours pass by humming a tune and from it people know who they are. The reasons for suspecting robbers from inside is mainly because they know who is at home and who is not at a particular time. One way of coping with the threat of robbery is to remain at home and find some means of earning while watching one's hut. 'My work of preparing boxes is done in the house itself', said a man. 'When we go to our native place or out for longer time we always ask someone to sleep in our house or to look after our huts. Thus we protect each other's huts in our mutual absence.' (Lobo 1993: 11–12)

A portrait in those terms may be linked to the idea that slum dwellers together with other marginalized categories, contrary to having revolutionary sympathies, are prone to support authoritarian regimes which ensure political stability (Sanyal 1991: 44; Kruyt 1994: 11). According to the same line of thinking the informal sector is a non- or even an anti-democratic environment from which reactionary politicians find it easy to recruit the lumpen elements they need to gain or remain in power. What happened during the communal riots which affected Surat in December 1991–January 1992 seems to provide solid evidence for this point of view. Both diamond cutters and powerloom workers took part in a pogrom targeted on the Muslim minority:

Our information indicates that certain Oriya small traders having links with the B.J.P. encouraged a section [note: of Oriya workers] to retaliate the initial looting and burning of some Hindu shops. The possibility of securing housing plots at cheap rate and issuance of ration cards were promised. Some cronies of a couple of industrial houses roused them to take revenge for damaging Shantinath dyeing mill by some Muslim miscreants. Incidently a large number of Oriya workers were working in that mill. A few bootleggers, slumlords, underworld gangs with whom a few Oriya workers were acquainted assured them of all protection. (Pathy 1993: 5).

In Panchsheel slum one informant reported on the same wave of violence and looting:

Our own slum people have done the following things to us. We know that some Dublas [Halpatis] and Malias [Oriyas] have done this. They have broken this shop and have taken away things that were there; they got in Abdulbhai's house through the window and have taken away all the things, especially those new dresses and other things bought for his daughter's wedding. (Lobo 1994: 142)

My research findings suggest that the localities in which the rural and urban poor reside are neither cradles of revolution nor quarters accommodating a vast mass of lumpen elements will-lessly manipulated by outside agents. There are other observers who argue that the large majority of informal sector workers are inclined to assess each and every event on its own merits, with a shrewd eye to protecting and furthering their own interests. It is a political ideology motivated by flexibility and pragmatism (Sanyal 1991: 44). Is the conclusion then that such behaviour is opportunistic? This label, substantiated by pointing out that informal sector workers are in fierce competition with each other, would seem to find favour with the protagonists of 'market forces' who in similar fashion oppose the claims of 'moral economists' in explaining the ethos of petty producers in agriculture. The rational peasant to be found in Asian paddy fields, shrewdly adjusting to the market economy in a satisfactorily self-interested and normless manner (Thompson 1993: 342), becomes a meta-phor which is logically extended to a proletarianized code of conduct associated with both rural and urban slum dwellers. I disagree also with that third and last type of analysis.

The informal sector is not without social fabric, a mere jungle where each and everybody fights for his or her own survival.

Group identity helps to live in slum conditions. It gives some sort of security. 'I know that my group members will stand by me whenever some crisis comes around. For instance, when someone falls sick we look after him, take him to the doctor, give him food and company and be with him so that he does not feel alone. When someone leaves for native place we look after his hut and belongings and protect it. Whenever there is a fight we come together,' said some respondents. (Lobo 1994: 99)

Collective identities are constantly asserted and reproduced by kinship, neighbourhood and other primordial attachments. Over and over again, anthropological research confirms that Halpatis continue to seek marriage partners in their own caste and at close distance, usually within the same sub-district (Vyas 1979: 158–9; D. S. Punalekar 1992: 320). Should such behaviour be understood to express the stubborn tenacity of tradition? Certainly not. Of course, caste (*jati*) bonds established and maintained since long ago help in handling all sorts of day-to-day and lifetime crises. But in an alien setting *jati* loyalties are not adequate any longer for directing social interaction and confrontation. The circle of identification gets widened and tends to include people with the same regional, religious or language background. In a Surat slum Khandeshis who generally belong to Dalit castes are known, and also acknowledge each other, as *khanara-peenara*, those who eat and drink anything. However, in closer contact such region-based formations fall apart again in different categories. One researcher of a Surat slum observes:

it looked as though there were only regional groups such as Khandeshis, U.P. Bhayias, Oriyas and Gujaratis. But later I realized that there are sub-groups among them. Among Khandeshis there are Hindus and Muslims. Hindu Khandeshis are sub-grouped on basis of kinship and location in the slum. Among Muslims the group affinities are along kinship, e.g., Khans and Sheikhs. Among Bhaiyas there are caste groups. Oriya men though less in number consider relatives and villagers residing in one room or adjoining rooms as a group. The residents of Gujarat region do not appear as a group in their activities. Yet they interact locationally among themselves. I identified sixteen groups over a period of time. (d'Souza 1993: 12)

In accordance with the bifurcation of economy in a formal and an informal sector a similar dichotomy is applied to society. This parallel duality is supposed to rest on two separate legal systems, each with its own logic and its own sanctions: the civil order and the social justice of the formal sector, *vis-à-vis* the tacit anarchy which is the destiny of the larger part of mankind coping with life in the backstreet (Kruyt 1994: 5–9). In earlier critical appraisals of the informal sector concept I have consistently challenged the notion that the complexities of economy and society can be reduced to two distinct segments (Breman 1976). For basically the same reasons I want to express strong reservations about the new inclusion–exclusion contrast, that has in recent years rapidly gained popularity. Splitting up work and life in south Gujarat, the arena of my empirical research for more than three decades, in a simple two-part division of which the segmented halves stand in hard and fast opposition to each other would do insufficient justice to a much more intricate reality. The inclusion-exclusion terms can be quite useful, but as dynamic instead of static mechanisms. Moreover, as all dual concepts they require contextualization in specified temporal as well as situational settings and should not necessarily be understood in total and closed separation from each other.

As for the widening circle of identification, Shah has recently written several interesting essays (1993, 1994), essentially arguing that traditional *jati* sentiments have been transcended to more encompassing bonds among a broader social spectre for which *qaum* (in Gujarati pronounced as 'kom') – still understood as caste or cluster of castes – has become the operative word. His point of departure is the wave of communalism reflecting the changing social fabric and, thus, politics of Gujarat.

Politicians whose primary support base is the *qaum* and who endorse communal politics as a legitimate form for mobilization, invoke or articulate the identity of the members, emphasizing their common interests and the need for unity and organization. For them, the *qaum* is a basic category for social division. It is argued that internal differences – if they exist – within the *qaum* are artificial, false and the result of the degeneration of the social system. The *qaum* leaders – traditional as well as modern – repeatedly induce this ideology with periodic emotional and sentimental reminders of the need to preserve *abru* i.e. prestige and status, and/or *dharma* of the *qaum* for development. These idioms are not alien to the members as they are inculcated in them from childhood. And their day-to-day experiences to a large extent confirm what is told to them by the ideologues of the *qaum*. Jobs or information about new opportunities are often obtained through linkages of caste and kinship. The members of the *jati* provide them security and help during small and big crises. And they realize that if a person from their *qaum* is in government office, it is easier to get their work done. Feelings of 'we' and 'they' are therefore reinforced. At another level, the notion of *qaum* gets extended to include all those who claim to be followers of the same religion. Though religious beliefs and value systems vary, the perceived commonality of symbols, rituals and beliefs tends to persuade the followers to believe in the 'we'. (Shah: 1993: 36–7)

Qaum is an advance towards vagueness, an imagined community between on the one hand the *jati*, the group consisting of 'real' caste mates to whom lines of kinship can be traced, and on the other hand the amorphous body of believers to which in principle all practitioners of the same religion belong. In this highly fluid field of various and variable social clusters people move around, aligning themselves in terms of inclusion versus exclusion according to the need to assert their identity in a specific context or at a particular moment. Underlying the search for affinity and solidarity in loosely structured, caste-like collectivities is a must for the floating mass of urban and rural slum dwellers to maximize their security. Discussing the *modus operandi* of the labour nomads employed in Surat's main industry, Pathy has this to say:

In an alien place, hard, stressful and insecure working and living environment, recurrent problems of health and language of communication, day to day humiliation in and around, and the fear of indiscriminate police implications in petty crimes, it is not surprising that the Oriya migrant workers tend to revalidate and consolidate their sense of community, caste, language, region and religion. (Pathy 1993: 15–16)

It would be wrong to conclude that informal sector workers only invest in communal bonds stretching on a diffuse continuum from *jati* to religion in order to safeguard their material interests. *Qaum* has also become an agent for articulating aspirations of emancipation in concerted action. Stigmatized social categories increasingly tend to seek redemption from a status of inferiority and dependency which are major features of the adverse circumstances under which they are compelled to live and work. New claims for dignity can be heard in the localities where the downtrodden reside. In Chikhligam it became a major reason for Dhodhiya men to leave their women and children at home when they depart on the arduous trek to the brick-kilns each year at the end of the monsoon. Earlier I have explained the absence of regular family life among the migrant population of urban slums by referring to bad and costly housing conditions. However, it should be added now that many migrants also try to avoid exposing other members of their household, whom they consider to be particularly vulnerable, as long as possible to the multiform sources of pollution and denigration associated with these habitats. On the inhabitants of such a locality in Surat Lobo reports:

The future of their children and insecurity of their women and girls constantly worry the slum dwellers. Many of them don't bring their wives and children to the slum but leave them at their native villages. Because they have to put up with dirt, bad behaviour and they will get spoilt in the slum. They will be brought later when they grow up for jobs. One of the U.P. wallas said, 'We are staying in the slum because of our *majburi* (helplessness). Given a chance we would like to quit this slum and stay in a room in a dignified manner.' (Lobo 1994: 93)

It is an aim difficult to realize in daily practice. Still, in a fundamental way the ideology of inequality, presumably the hallmark of Hindu civilization, to a large extent seems to have lost social legitimacy. I consider this observation to be the most significant recapitulation of my research findings over a period of more than thirty years in south Gujarat. As noted earlier, there is a definite shift from a more vertical towards a more horizontal orientation in the principles of social organization. Of course, if need be people are willing to openly acknowledge their dependency on patrons who are in a position to distribute favours and benefits, but the blatant sycophancy which used to mark their private and public behaviour as clients is a thing of the past. *Qaum* consciousness is rooted in communal and not hierarchical sentiments. At least at the ideological level the emphasis is on shared instead of differentially ranked identities of all included in the same walk of life. Outsiders are defined as the excluded who supposedly have their own *sanskar* (culture) on which to base their fraternity. To the extent that these categories are better off and have more political power, their elevated status does not give them the ingrained right to social hegemony. Claims for domination and superiority from above are not easily conceded nowadays and may even be actively resisted by those at the bottom of society.

In my scheme of analysis duality is not a key concept. Social life and economic activity are multi-layered and not segmented in only two circuits of formality and informality, separating people in just two broad categories: insiders or outsiders. Although rejecting the existence in theory and practice of a comprehensive and consistent bifurcation, it cannot be denied that wilful neglect of the misery imposed on the proletarianized rural and urban masses, floating around in a state of flux, cannot continue for much longer without creating the conditions for such a dialectical opposition. Segregation coming close to a system of apartheid is the ultimate result of the policy to make 'the informal sector' a no-go zone for policy-makers. However, a planned and constructed duality is ultimately also bound to end in failure. A state which only accepts the market as a regulatory mechanism for dictating the terms under which labour has to work and live is not able to maintain a regime of law and order restricted to privileged citizens in their formal sector enclaves. The explosion of violence which Surat witnessed at the end of 1991 and beginning of 1992, or for that matter, the so-called plague which broke out in August 1994, should be read as signals that the informal sector outcasts cannot be kept in isolation and in a state of exclusion.

I shall make no attempts to generalize. Let me just reiterate, by way of conclusion, that the description and analysis presented focus on a region in India which has shown rapid and sustained economic growth. During the last thirty years these dynamics have provided great benefit to owners of capital but without fundamentally reducing the degree of exploitation of labour. In the total production costs, the proportion of wages paid has declined rather than risen during this period. The force with which the process of social transformation is continuing manifests a brutal and predatory type of capitalism. Does it mean that this mode of production is still in a formative stage in India? I am inclined to disagree with authors representing that school of thought. What has been going on in south Gujarat during the last half-century suggests a pattern of capitalist development that in terms of industrial relations is not characterized by gradual but progressive expansion of formalized employment conditions.

On the contrary, after having been made mobile the workforce at the massive bottom of the economy is kept in circulation, does not become stabilized but finds itself entrapped in an on-going state of casualization, is not fully free in labour market negotiations but remains neo-bonded in some critical aspects, and is paid not constant (time) but flexible (piece) wage rates.

The trajectory of capitalist development which has come to dominate the South Asian landscape seems to be significantly different, on the one hand, from the earlier factorized production characteristic for the process of industrialization and urbanization during the nineteenth century in the North Atlantic part of the world and, on the other hand, from the brand of industrial capitalism that has emerged more recently and so forcefully in parts of East Asia (Taiwan, South Korea). More comparative work is required to trace the linkages between these various patterns of development at the global level and to analyse their separate but also their joint dynamics in a historical perspective. That comparison in both time and space is beyond the scope of this monograph. The case study presented remains confined to south Gujarat economy and society during the last few decades of the twentieth century. The findings reported will have to be contextualized in a wider national and international setting. This book has been written to throw light on the mechanisms of exclusion from life and from work in dignity of poor people in a region of high economic growth. Their plight, subsistence not far above the level of survival, is shared by a considerable part of mankind.

Bibliography

GOVERNMENT PUBLICATIONS

Census of India 1931, vol. XIX, pt. 1, Baroda, Bombay 1932.
Census of India 1961. Gujarat, District Census Handbook no.16, Surat District, Ahmedabad 1964.
Census of India 1981, 1983. Series 5 Gujarat, pt. II-B. General Population Tables – Primary Census Abstract. Delhi 1983.
Census of India 1991. Series 7 Gujarat. Provisional Population Totals. Paper-1. Ahmedabad 1991.
Gazetteer of the Bombay Presidency, vol. 11, Gujarat: Surat and Broach. Bombay 1877.
Gazetteer of India. Gujarat State, Surat District. Ahmedabad 1962.
Report of the Committee on Fair Wages, 1948. Government of India. New Delhi 1948.
Report of the Salt Pan Industry in Bombay Province for the Year 1947–48. Government Central Press, Bombay 1950.
Report of the Saurashtra Salt Works Labour Enquiry Committee 1952. Saurasthra Government, Bhavnagar 1955.
Report of the Minimum Wages Advisory Committee for Employment in Agriculture, 1966. Government of Gujarat, Education and Labour Department, Ahmedabad 1966.
Report of the Minimum Wages Committee for Employment in Bricks or Roof Tiles Manufactory in the State of Maharashtra, 1969. Government of Maharashtra, Bombay 1969.
Report of the National Commission on Labour. Government of India, Ministry of Labour, Employment and Rehabilitation, Delhi 1969.
Report of the Committee on Unprotected and Unorganized Labour. Government of Gujarat, Education and Labour Department, Gandhinagar 1972.
Report of the Advisory Committee Appointed for Fixing Minimum Wages in Stone Breaking and Stone Crushing Industry. Office of the Labour Commissioner. Government of Gujarat, Education and Labour Department, manuscript 50 pp., Ahmedabad 1974.
Report of the Minimum Wages Advisory Committee appointed for Salt Producing Industries. Office of the Labour Commissioner, Gujarat State, Department of Education and Labour, manuscript 65 pp., Ahmedabad 1974.
Report of the Advisory Committee appointed by the Government of Gujarat

under Section 5 (1)(A) of the Minimum Wages Act, 1948, Concerning the Improvement in the Minimum Wages Being Paid to Workers Employed in Road Construction or Maintenance and Building Operations. Office of the Labour Commissioner. Government of Gujarat, Education and Labour Department, manuscript 103 pp., Ahmedabad 1975.

Report of the Advisory Committee Appointed by the Government of Gujarat under Section 5 (1)(A) of the Minimum Wages Act of 1948 in Order to Determine the Rates of Minimum Wages for the Workers Engaged in the Brick Manufacturing Industry. Office of the Labour Commissioner, Gujarat State, Department of Education and Labour, manuscript 78 pp., Ahmedabad 1975.

Report of the Minimum Wages (Revision) Committee for Employment in Bricks or Roof Tiles (Terra Cotta or Earthen) Manufactory. Government of Maharashtra, manuscript 33 pp., Bombay 1976.

Report of the Minimum Wages Committee for Employment in the Salt Pan Industry in the State of Maharashtra 1974. Government of Maharashtra, Bombay 1976.

Report of the National Commission on Rural Labour, 2 vols. (Reports of Study Groups). Government of India, Ministry of Labour, New Delhi 1991.

ARTICLES AND BOOKS

Armstrong, W. and McGee, T. G. (eds.) 1985 *Theatres of Accumulation: Studies in Asian and Latin American Urbanization*. Methuen, London.

Athreya, V., Djurfeldt, G. & Lindberg, S. 1990 *Barriers Broken: Production Relations and Agrarian Change in Tamil Nadu*. Sage, New Delhi/London.

Awachat, A. 1988 'The Warp and the Weft – 1 & 11', *Economic and Political Weekly*, 23: 1732–6 and 1786–90.

Barik, B.C. 1987 'Unorganized Migrant Labour in the Textile Industry of Surat', in V. Joshi (ed), *Migrant Labour and Related Issues* 165–78 .

Basant, R. 1993 'Diversification of Economic Activities in Rural Gujarat: Key Results of a Primary Survey', *The Indian Journal of Labour Economics*, 36: 361–86.

Basu, K. (ed.) 1994 *Agrarian Questions*. Oxford University Press, Delhi.

Brass, T. 1990 'Class Struggle and the Deproletarianisation of Agricultural Labour in Haryana (India)', *The Journal of Peasant Studies*, 18, (1): 36–67.

1993 'Some Observations on Unfree Labour, Capitalist Restructuring, and Deproletarianization', in: T. Brass, M. Van der Linden and J. Lucassen, *Free and Unfree Labour*, 31–50.

1995 'Unfree Labour and Agrarian Change - A Different View', *Economic and Political Weekly*, vol.30: 697–9.

Brass, T., Van der Linden, M. and Lucassen, J. 1994 *Free and Unfree Labour*. International Institute for Social History, Amsterdam.

Breman, J. 1974 *Patronage and Exploitation; Changing Agrarian Relations in South Gujarat, India*. University of California Press, Berkeley 1974/ Manohar, Delhi 1979.

1976 'A Dualistic Labour System? a Critique of the "Informal Sector" Concept', *Economic and Political Weekly*, 11: 1870–6; 1905–8; and 1939–43.

1977 'Labour Relations in the "Formal" and "Informal" Sectors: Report of a

Case Study in South Gujarat', *The Journal of Peasant Studies*, April and July, 4: 171–205 and 337–59.

1978/79 'Seasonal Migration and Cooperative Capitalism: The Crushing of Cane and of Labour by the Sugar Factories of Bardoli, South Gujarat', *The Journal of Peasant Studies*, pt. 1, 6: 41–70 and pt. 2, 6: 168–202; also published in *Economic and Political Weekly*, Special Number 13: 1317–60.

1980 *The Informal Sector in Research: Theory and Practice*. Comparative Asian Studies Programme no 3. Erasmus University, Rotterdam.

1983 'The Bottom of the Urban Order in Asia: Impressions of Calcutta', *Development and Change*, 14: 153–83.

1985a '"I am the Government Labour Officer . . ."': State Protection for Rural Proletariat of South Gujarat', *Economic and Political Weekly*, 20: 1043–55.

1985b *Of Peasants, Migrants and Paupers: Rural Labour Circulation and Capitalist Production In West India*. Oxford University Press, Delhi/Clarendon Press, Oxford.

1990 '"Even Dogs Are Better Off": The Ongoing Battle Between Capital and Labour in the Cane Fields of Gujarat', *The Journal of Peasant Studies*, 17: 546–608.

1991 'From Cane Fields to Court Rooms: Legal Action for and against Rural Labour in Gujarat, India', in G. Shah (ed.) *Capitalist Development: Critical Essays* 270–88.

1993a 'The Anti-Muslim Pogrom in Surat', *Economic and Political Weekly*, 28: 737–41.

1993b *Beyond Patronage and Exploitation*. Oxford University Press, Delhi.

1994 *Wage Hunters and Gatherers* (Collection of essays including several articles mentioned above and published in 1977, 1978/79, 1980, 1985a, 1990, 1991). Oxford University Press, Delhi.

1995a 'Work and Life of the Rural Proletariat in Java's Coastal Plain', *Modern Asian Studies*, 29, (1): 1–44.

1995b 'Labour Get Lost: A Late-Capitalist Manifesto', *Economic and Political Weekly*, 30: 2294–2300.

Chadha, G. K. 1993 'Non-Farm Employment for Rural Households in India: Evidence and Prognosis', *The Indian Journal of Labour Economics*, 36: 296–327.

Chakrabarty, D. 1989 *Rethinking Working Class History; Bengal 1890–1940*. Princeton University Press, Princeton/Oxford University Press, Delhi.

Chakravarty, S. (ed.) 1989 *The Balance Between Industry and Agriculture in Economic Development*. vol. 111, Macmillan, London.

Chambers, R., Longhurst, R. and Pacey, A. (eds.) 1981 *Seasonal Dimensions to Rural Poverty*. Francis Pinter, London.

Chopra, S. 1985 'Bondage in a Green Revolution Area: A Study of Brick Kiln Workers in Muzzafarnagar District', in: U. Patnaik and M. Dingwaney (eds), *Chains of Servitude: Bondage and Slavery in India*: 162–86.

Connell, J., Dasgupta, B., Laishley, R., and Lipton, M. 1975 *Migration from Rural Areas: The Evidence from Village Studies*. Report to the International Labour Organisation, Geneva.

Dasgupta, P. 1993 *An Inquiry into Well-Being and Destitution*. Clarendon Press, Oxford.

Desai, A. R. (ed.) 1990 *Repression and Resistance in India: Violation of Democratic*

Rights of the Working Class, Rural Poor, Adivasis and Dalits. Popular Prakashan, Bombay.

Desai, M., Rudolph, S. and Rudra, A. (eds.) 1984 *Agrarian Power and Agricultural Productivity in South Asia.* Oxford University Press, Delhi.

Desai, R. and Tiwari, R.S. 1985 'Jari Industry of Surat; A Study of Characteristics of Household Sector', *The Indian Journal of Labour Economics,* 27: 275–91.

Devi, M. 1981 'Contract Labour or Bonded Labour?', *Economic and Political Weekly,* 14: 1010–13.

Drèze, J. and Mukherjee, A. 1989 'Labour Contracts in Rural India: Theories and Evidence', in S. Chakravarty (ed.), *The Balance Between Industry and Agriculture in Economic Development.*

Engineer, I. 1994 'Backward Communities and Migrant Workers in Surat', *Economic and Political Weekly,* 29: 1348–60.

Gordon, D. M. 1972 *Theories of Poverty and Underemployment: Orthodox, Radical and Dual Labour Market Perspectives.* Lexington, Mass.

Gulati, L. 1979 'Female Labour in the Unorganised Sector: Profile of a Brick Worker', *Economic and Political Weekly,* 14: 744–55.

Hart, G. 1986 'Exclusionary Labour Arrangements: Interpreting Evidence on Employment Trends in Rural Java', *Journal of Development Studies,* 22: 681–96.

Hart, K. 1973 'Informal Income Opportunities and Urban Employment in Ghana', *Journal of Modern African Studies,* 11: 61–89.

Holmström, M. 1984 *Industry and Equality: The Social Anthropology of Indian Labour.* Cambridge University Press, Cambridge.

Jaganathan, N. V. 1987 *Informal Markets in Developing Countries.* Oxford University Press, New York/Oxford.

Jodhka, S. S. 1994 'Agrarian Changes and Attached Labour; Emerging Patterns in Haryana Agriculture', *Economic and Political Weekly,* 29, Review of Agriculture: A102–6.

1995 'Agrarian Changes, Unfreedom and Attached Labour', *Economic and Political Weekly,* 30: 2011–13.

Jose, A.V. 1988 'Agricultural Wages in India', in: *Economic and Political Weekly,* 23, Review of Agriculture: A46–68.

Joshi, V. (ed.) 1987 *Migrant Labour and Related Issues.* Gandhi Labour Institute, Ahmedabad. Oxford and IBH Publishing Co, New Delhi.

Joyce, P. 1980 *Work, Society, and Politics: The Culture of the Factory in Later Victorian England.* Rutgers University Press, New Brunswick/Harvester Press, Brighton.

Kalathil, M. 1978 'Industrial Relations in a Small Scale Industry', in E.A. Ramaswamy (ed.), *Industrial Relations in India: A Sociological Perspective:* 89–107.

Kannan, K.P. 1988 *Of Rural Proletarian Struggles: Mobilization and Organization of Rural Workers in Southwest India.* Oxford University Press, Delhi.

1990 *State and Union Intervention in Rural Labour: A Study of Kerala.* ARTEP Working Papers, New Delhi.

1992 'Labour Institutions and the Development Process in India', in T. S. Papola and G. Rodgers (eds.) *Labour Institutions and Economic Devlopment in India:* 49–85.

Kapadia, K. 1995 *Siva and Her Sisters: Gender, Caste, and Class in Rural South India*. Studies in Ethnographic Imagination. Westview Press, Boulder, Colorado/ Oxford.

Kruyt, D. 1994 *Informal Sector Economy and Informal Society: Poverty and Social Change in Latin America*. Reprint Series Development Cooperation no 13. The Hague, Directorate General Ministry of Foreign Affairs.

Kulkarni, A. P. 1993 'Employment in Informal Sector: Some Issues', *The Indian Journal of Labour Economics*, 36: 654–9.

Lal, R. B. 1982 'From Farm to Factory', *Adivasi Gujarat*, 4: 24–93.

Marla, S. 1981. *Bonded Labour in India*. National Survey on the Incidence of Bonded Labour, Final Report. Sponsored by the Gandhi Peace Foundation and the Academy of Gandhian Studies, New Delhi.

McGee, T. G. 1982. 'Labour Mobility in Fragmented Labour Markets: The Role of Circulatory Migration in Rural-Urban Relations in Asia', in H. I. Safa (ed.), *Towards a Political Economy of Urbanization in Third World Countries*: 17–66.

Mehta, P. C. & Gandhi, R. S. n.d. *Man-Made Textile Industry of Surat*. Mantra, Surat.

Miles, R. 1987 *Capitalism and Unfree Labour: Anomaly or Necessity?* Tavistock Publications, London/New York.

Mukhtyar, G. C. 1930 *Life and Labour in a South Gujarat Village*. Longmans, Green & Co. Ltd., Calcutta.

Naidu, K. M. 1993 'Unemployment and Employment in India: An Overview', *The Indian Journal of Labour Economics*, 36: 8–29.

Nathan, D. 1987 'Structure of Working Class in India', *Economic and Political Weekly*, 22: 799–809.

Papola, T. S. 1992 'Labour Institutions and Economic Development: The Case of Indian Industrialization', in T. S. Papola and G. Rodgers (eds.), *Labour Institutions and Economic Development In India*: 17–47.

   1993 'Employment of Women in South Asian Countries', *The Indian Journal of Labour Economics*, 36: 48–56.

Papola, T. S. and Rodgers, G. (eds.) 1992 *Labour Institutions and Economic Development in India*. Research Series no. 97. International Institute of Labour Studies, Geneva.

Patel, B. B. 1987 'Seasonal Rural Migration Pattern and Some Alternatives for Effective Protection of Legal Rights of Migrant Labour', in V. Joshi (ed.), *Migrant Labour and Related Issues*: 143–51.

   1988 *Workers of Closed Textile Mills: Patterns and Problems of Absorption in a Metropolitan Labour Market*. Gandhi Labour Institute, Ahmedabad. Oxford and IBH Publishing Co., New Delhi.

Patel, B. B. (ed.) 1993 *Social Security for Unorganised Labour*. Gandhi Labour Institute, Ahmedabad. Oxford and IBH Publishing Co., New Delhi.

Pathak, H.N. 1993 'Case of the Diamond Cutting and Polishing Industry', in B. B. Patel (ed.), *Social Security for Unorganised Labour*: 249–57.

Patnaik, U. (ed.) 1990 *Agrarian Relations and Accumulation: The Mode of Production Debate in India*. Oxford University Press, Delhi.

Patnaik, U. and Dingwaney, M. (eds.) 1985 *Chains of Servitude: Bondage and Slavery in India*. Sangam Books, Madras.

Peattie, L. 1987 'An Idea in Good Currency and How It Grew: The Informal Sector', *World Development*, 15: 851–60.

Pillai, S. D. and Baks, C. (eds.) 1979 *Winners and Losers: Styles of Development and Change in an Indian Region*. Popular Prakashan, Bombay.

Portes, A., Castells, M. and Benton, L.A. 1989 *The Informal Economy: Studies in Advanced and Less Developed Countries*. Johns Hopkins University Press, Baltimore.

Ramaswamy, E. A. (ed.) 1978 *Industrial Relations in India: A Sociological Perspective*. Macmillan, Delhi.

Randeria, S. and Yagnik, A. 1990 'Holiday from Labour Laws', in A. R. Desai (ed.), *Repression and Resistance in India: Violation of Democratic Rights of the Working Class, Rural Poor, Adivasis and Dalits*: 82–8.

Rempel, H. 1981 'Seasonal Out-Migration and Rural Poverty', in R. Chambers, R. Longhurst and A. Pacey (eds.), *Seasonal Dimensions to Rural Poverty*: 210–14.

Rudra, A. 1984 'Local Power and Farm Level Decision-Making', in M. Desai, S. Rudolph and A. Rudra (eds.), *Agrarian Power and Agricultural Productivity in South Asia*: 250–80.

1987 'Labour Relations in Agriculture: A Study in Contrasts', *Economic and Political Weekly*, 22: 757–60.

1990a 'Emerging Class Structure in India', in T. N. Srinavasan and P. K. Bardhan (eds.), *Rural Poverty in South Asia*: 483–500.

1990b 'Class Relations in Indian Agriculture', in U. Patnaik (ed.), *Agrarian Relations and Accumulation: The Mode of Production Debate in India*: 251–67.

1994 'Unfree Labour and Indian Agriculture', in K. Basu (ed.), *Agrarian Questions*: 75–91.

Rutten, M. A. F. 1994 *Farms and Factories: Social Profile of Large Farmers and Rural Industrialists in West India*. Oxford University Press, Delhi.

Safa, H. I. (ed.) 1982 *Towards a Political Economy of Urbanization in Third World Countries*. Oxford University Press, Delhi.

Sanyal, B. 1991 'Organizing the Self-Employed', *International Labour Review*, 130: 39–56.

Scott, J. C. 1985 *Weapons of the Weak: Everyday Forms of Peasant Resistance*. Yale University Press, New Haven.

1990 *Domination and the Arts of Resistance: Hidden Transcripts*. Yale University Press, New Haven.

Shah, G. 1991 'Tenth Lok Sabha Elections: BJP's Victory in Gujarat', *Economic and Political Weekly*, 26: 2921–4.

1993 'Surat 1993', *Seminar* 411: 34–7.

1994 'Identity, Communal Consciousness and Politics', *Economic and Political Weekly*, 29: 1133–40.

Shah, G. (ed.) 1991 *Capitalist Development: Critical Essays*. Felicitation volume in Honour of Prof. A. R. Desai. Popular Prakashan, Bombay.

Shah, P. G. 1958 *The Dublas of Gujarat*. Bharatiya Adimjati Sevak Sangh, Delhi.

Sheth, K. A. 1987 'Legal and Administrative Aspects of the Implementation of the Inter-State Migrant Workmen (Regs) Act – 1979 in Gujarat State', in V. Joshi (ed.), *Migrant Labour and Related Issues*: 237–55.

Singh, M. and Iyer, K. G. 1985 'Migrant Labourers in Rural Punjab', in U. Patnaik and M. Dingwaney (eds.), *Chains of Servitude: Bondage and Slavery in India*: 218–57.

Srinavasan, T. N. and Bardhan, P. K. (eds.) 1990 *Rural Poverty in South Asia*. Oxford University Press, Delhi (2nd impression).

Srivastava, A. K. 1987a 'Labour Relations in Agriculture', *Economic and Political Weekly*, 21: 1974.

1987b 'Identifying Bonded Labour, A Knotty Problem!', *Yojana*, 31: 13–17.

Streefkerk, H. 1985 *Industrial Transition in Rural India: Artisans, Traders and Tribals in South Gujarat*. Popular Prakashan, Bombay.

Thompson, E. P. 1993 *Customs in Common*. Penguin Books, Harmondsworth. (Included in this volume: 'Time, Work-Discipline and Industrial Capitalism', an essay originally published in *Past and Present*, 38, December 1967.)

Tokman, V. 1992 *Beyond Regulation: The Informal Economy in Latin America*. Lynne Rienner, Boulder/London.

Veen, K. W. van der 1979 'Urbanization, Migration and Primordial Attachments', in S. D. Pillai and C. Baks (eds.), *Winners and Losers: Styles of Development and Change in an Indian Region*: 43–80.

Working and Living Conditions 1984 *Working and Living Conditions of the Surat Textile Workers: A Survey*. Submitted to the Honourable Chief Justice of Gujarat High Court (17 December 1984). South Gujarat University, Surat.

World Development Report 1995 *Workers in an Integrating World*. Published for the World Bank. Oxford University Press, New York.

UNPUBLISHED MANUSCRIPTS AND DOCUMENTS

Agrawal, S. 1992 *Women, Work and Industry: A Case Study of Surat Art Silk Industry*. Ph.D. thesis. South Gujarat University, Surat.

Barik, B. C. 1981 *Migration of Agricultural Labourers: A Study of Oriya Labourers in Surat*. M.Phil. thesis. South Gujarat University, Surat.

1985 'Industrial Development and Migrant Labour: A Study of Unorganised Sector Labour in Textile Industries of Surat'. Seminar on *Industrial Workers and Social Change*. Centre for Social Studies, Surat.

Bharadwaj, K. 1990 'On the Formation of the Labour Market in Rural Asia'. Centre for Economic Studies and Planning, School of Social Sciences. Jawaharlal Nehru University, New Delhi.

Bhatt, P. K. 1979 *Growth of Entrepreneurship in South Gujarat*. Ph.D. thesis. South Gujarat University, Surat.

Brass, T. 1994 'Reply to Utsa Patnaik: If the Cap Fits'. Written but unpublished comment.

Das, B. 1990 *Migrant Labour in Urban Areas*. Report commissioned by the Study Group on Migrant Labour on behalf of the National Commission on Rural Labour, Government of India. Centre for Social Studies, Surat.

1993 *Migrant Labour in Quarries and Brick-Kilns; An Overview*. Occasional Paper. Centre for Social Studies, Surat.

1994 *Socio-Economic Study of Slums in Surat City*. Centre for Social Studies, Surat.

272   Bibliography

Das, B. (ed.) 1993 'Urban Poor in India: Some Issues'. Seminar on *Urban Poor in India*. Centre for Social Studies, Surat.

Desai, I. P. 1966 *The Patterns of Migration and Occupation in a South Gujarat Village*. Deccan College, Poona.

Desai, J. L. 1981 *Art Silk Processing Industry in Surat City*. M.Phil. thesis. South Gujarat University, Surat.

Desai, K. M. 1985 'Artisans of Diamond Industry'. Seminar on *Industrial Workers and Social Change*. Centre for Social Studies, Surat.

Desai, N. 1990 *Women's Work and Family Strategies in a Rural Community in South Gujarat*. manuscript, 145 pp. Indian Council of Social Science Research, New Delhi.

Joshi, M. A. 1985 'Closure of Textile Mills in Ahmedabad Through Workers' Eyes'. Seminar on *Industrial Workers and Social Change*. Centre for Social Studies, Surat.

Joshi, S. 1993 'Organizing and Managing a Large Scale Survey Research in the Slum Localities of Surat'. Seminar on *Urban Poor in India*. Centre for Social Studies, Surat.

Kannan, K. P. 1994 'Labour Institutions and Economic Development in India: Some Exploratory Hypotheses'. Keynote Paper 35th Annual Conference of the Indian Society of Labour Economics. 21–23 Jan., Ahmedabad. (Revised version: 'Levelling Up or Levelling Down?', *Economic and Political Weekly*, 29, 1994: 1936–47.

Kapadia, K. 1995 *Women Workers in Bonded Labour in Rural Industry*. Paper. Wageningen.

Kashyap, S. P. and Tiwari, R. S. 1982 *Shaping of Diamonds in Surat: An Enquiry into Some of its Passas (Facets)*, 203pp. Sardar Patel Institute of Economic and Social Research, Ahmedabad.

Koelen, J. H. 1985 *Stenen: arbeidsmobiliteit in Zuid Gujarat. Een onderzoek naar de werkgelegenheid van de tribale bevolking in diamantslijperijen en een steengroeve*. M.A. thesis. Anthropological-Sociological Centre, Dept. South- and Southeast Asia, University of Amsterdam.

Lobo, L. 1993 'Problems and Coping Mechanisms of People in a Surat Slum'. Seminar on *Urban Poor in India*. Centre for Social Studies, Surat.

1994 *Urbanism Encountered*. Centre for Social Studies, Surat.

Mehta, B. V. & Pathak, P. G. 1975 *The Art Silk Industry of Surat*. Centre for Regional Development Studies, Surat.

Mishra, L. 1984 'Report of Inquiry into the Alleged Existence of Bonded Labour in the Stone Quarries and Stone Crushers of Faridabad District and Implementation of the Provisions of the Minimum Wages Act, Contract Labour (Regulation and Abolition) Act and Interstate Migrant Workmen's (Regulation of Employment and Condition of Service) Act'. manuscript, 49 pp. Delhi.

Omvedt, G. 1990 'The "Unorganized Sector" and Women Workers'. Seminar on *Women and Work*. Centre for Social Studies, Surat.

Pandya, V. 1993a 'Development Challenges Facing Urban Politics'. Seminar on *Urban Poor in India*. Centre for Social Studies, Surat.

1993b 'A Case Report on "Naka Workers" in Bombay'. Seminar on *Urban Poor in India*. Centre for Social Studies, Surat.

Papola, T. S. 1994 'Structural Adjustment, Labour Market Flexibility and Employment'. Presidential Address 35th Annual Conference of the Indian Society of Labour Economics. 21–23 Jan., Ahmedabad.

Parikh, G. O. 1985 *Economic and Social Survey of Agricultural Labourers in Gujarat State*. Sardar Patel Institute of Economic and Social Research, Ahmedabad.

Patel, V. 1990 'Perspective on Women's Work and Status'. Seminar on *Women and Work*. Centre for Social Studies, Surat.

Pathak, H. N. 1984 'Diamond Cutting and Polishing Industry of Gujarat'. Indian Institute of Management, 296 pp. Ahmedabad.

Pathy, J. 1993 'The Dreary December and the Oriya Textile Workers in Surat'. Paper. Surat.

Patnaik, U. 1994 'On Capitalism and Agrestic Unfreedom'. (Written in reaction to Brass 1994).

Punalekar, D. S. 1992 *Urbanization and Social Change: A Case Study of a Fringe Village*. Ph.D. thesis. Sardar Patel University, Vallabh Vidyanagar.

Punalekar, S. P. 1988 *Informalization and Dependency: A Study of Jari and Embroidery Workers in South Gujarat*. Centre for Social Studies, Surat.

1993 *Seeds of Marginalization and Instability: A Study of Street Children in Gujarat Cities*. Centre for Social Studies, Surat.

Punalekar, S. P. and Patel, A. 1990 *Survival Struggles of Female Casual Labourers in Gujarat: A Study of Female Workers of Casual Labour Markets (Chakla Bazars) in South and Central Gujarat Cities*. Centre for Social Studies, Surat.

Sahoo, U. C. 1981 *A Sociological Study of Child Labour*. M.Phil thesis. South Gujarat University, Surat.

1985 'Child Labour in Industrial Set Up: A Case Study of Surat'. Seminar on *Industrial Workers and Social Change*. Centre for Social Studies, Surat.

Shah, G., Kumar Bose, P., Hargopal, G. and Kannan, K. P. 1990. *Migrant Labour in India*. Report commissioned by the National Commission on Rural Labour, Government of India, Centre for Social Studies, Surat.

Soni, J. 1990 'Jari Industry and Women Workers'. Seminar on *Women and Work*. Centre for Social Studies, Surat.

d'Souza, P. 1993 'Coping with Problems of Investigating Conditions of Slum Dwellers'. Seminar on *Urban Poor in India*. Centre for Social Studies, Surat.

Subrahmanya, R. K. A. 1985 'Policy and Administrative Aspects of Labour Migration'. Paper contributed to *National Seminar on Migrant Labour and Related Issues*. Gandhi Labour Institute, Ahmedabad, 10–12 Oct. Manuscript, 9 pp.

Vyas, K. I. 1979 *Tribals in a Non-Tribal Setting; A Sociological Study of Tribals in an Urban Community*. Ph.D. thesis. South Gujarat University, Surat.

Index

Printed in the United Kingdom
by Lightning Source UK Ltd.
9657600001B/101-110